Trauma-Informed Pedagogies

"Carello and Thompson have created a much-needed reference describing trauma-informed care for everyone working in higher education. I teach graduate students as well as undergraduates and never stop being shocked at the extent to which these young people have already experienced their own trauma and adversity or have witnessed firsthand the traumatic experiences of loved ones. Anyone who serves as faculty, administrators, or staff in academic settings must understand what this means for the ways in which they teach and interact with their students."

—Sandra L. Bloom, *Associate Professor, Health Management and Policy, Drexel University, USA*

"This book is nothing short of a miracle for higher education professionals who are eager to answer the call for trauma-informed change in a tumultuous world. It provides thoughtful, evidence-based approaches to light the path ahead, addressing the seismic shift in college student demographics, the knowledge gained from two decades of scientific studies into adversity and brain development, and the urgent need for inclusion and equity in higher education. Each chapter includes innumerable insights into the challenges higher education faces today. As a whole, this book is simply indispensable."

—Karen Oehme, *Director, Student Resilience Project, Florida State University, USA, and Chairperson, Academic Resilience Consortium (ARC)*

"This is the book that every teacher needs right now. Thompson and Carello have crafted a masterful guide to the changing landscape of student stress and anxiety that is written by leading practitioners in trauma-aware pedagogies. Full of compelling stories and engaging reflections, this guide is an essential roadmap for the future of teaching."

—Leah K. Matthews, *Executive Director, Distance Education Accrediting Commission, USA*

"This book is a must read for educators as we embrace the 'new normal' in education. As Carello and Thomson point out, the classroom shouldn't be only about the information that we provide to students, but about providing a safe space for students to grow and to transform. Without this safe space, students may treat their experiences as burdens that hold them back rather than as opportunities for growth."

—Dr. Phyllis Okrepkie, *President, International Accreditation Council for Business Education, USA*

Phyllis Thompson · Janice Carello
Editors

Trauma-Informed Pedagogies

A Guide for Responding to Crisis and Inequality in
Higher Education

Editors
Phyllis Thompson
Women's, Gender, and Sexuality Studies
East Tennessee State University
Johnson City, TN, USA

Janice Carello
Department of Social Work
Edinboro University
Edinboro, PA, USA

ISBN 978-3-030-92704-2   ISBN 978-3-030-92705-9   (eBook)
https://doi.org/10.1007/978-3-030-92705-9

Cover credit: estudio Calamar

This Palgrave Macmillan imprint is published by the registered company Springer Nature Switzerland AG
The registered company address is: Gewerbestrasse 11, 6330 Cham, Switzerland

For Momma, Daddy, Barbara, Robin, and David
—Phyllis Thompson

For Eric, Tuesday, Milo, Winter, and Bird, and in memory of Janet and Brad
—Janice Carello

FOREWORD

I try to take my vacation every year during the second week in August, the week of my birthday. It is my designated time to take a break and reconnect with nature and my family. I strive to make it the one week a year where I unplug. This year was significant because it was the first birthday without my mom. My mom passed away on June 16, 2021, quite unexpectedly. I pushed through the months of June and July, busier than planned with speaking engagements, facilitation sessions, and trainings. I coped with her loss through avoidance and by immersing myself in my work; holding space for others felt healing, while I also recognized that it was a way for me to dissociate. But when August 8th came and we were scheduled to leave the familiar surroundings of our home and venture out to big skies, wide plains, and the ocean, I had to prepare for the grief work that was inevitably coming and for the healing that the ocean brings every time I touch the sand. My mom's passing reminded me that trauma and the grief that accompanies it hit us in unpredictable waves. The sounds, smells, sights, and felt spiritual energies surprise us with their appearance. This time around I let it. I did not reach for a tissue when the waves of grief hit me in the middle of the drive, or when my tears matched the heavy rain that fell the morning of my birthday August 9th, and I did not stop calling her name as I sat under the stars and felt her presence in the night sky. My children saw and felt my loss and that, too, was ok. I accepted their hugs and held onto them tighter and longer than usual.

August 9th was also the day I received an email from the co-editors of this book asking me to write this foreword. The email was a beautiful invitation to share space with so many incredible authors and educators who also are working to disrupt the traditional space of trauma work, all of us using ourselves, our platforms, and our research to highlight the need for equity-centered trauma-informed approaches. In addition to the invitation, the email was flooded with words sharing the impact that my work on incorporating diversity and inclusion into trauma-informed practice and leadership and my recent book *Incorporating Diversity and Inclusion in Trauma-Informed Social Work* has had on others in and outside of the trauma field and across disciplines. I interpreted this invitation as a gift, a gift that validated my higher order purpose to positively disrupt and build a practice that is centered on belonging, a practice that moves the focus from individual deficit to the impact systems of oppression have on the individual, a practice that shares stories and collective experiences of intergenerational trauma and how that trauma has laid heavy on generations, often times impacting mental health.

My mom lived a life of intergenerational trauma and was also a healer. I learned, in the weeks after her passing, of all the work she had done with communities of color, specifically youth. I also learned more about the impact she had on young women educators in the K-12 space. And so, in addition to the intergenerational traumas of my family, I also carry on the legacy of what it means to be a healer. I have thought deeply about what I have inherited and what I chose to hold on to and what I must let go of in order to live in my essence and do the work that I am here to do. I did this through my own personal work and also through connection and community. I talk about the importance of the practice principle of use of self in trauma-informed work, that is, sharing personal experiences from the place of intention and with the mindfulness of building a community of healers who are courageous enough to disrupt systems and spaces of oppression and exclusion in everyday practice.

This book is a gift to all of us who strive to create communities of belonging where trauma is normalized, named, and understood in the larger context of systems of oppression. I encourage you to write in the margins of this book, sit in quiet spaces of accountability, build a collective of healers, challenge yourself to be courageous, spend time in gratitude and continue to cultivate beauty.

August 2021   Laura Quiros, Ph.D., LMSW
                                                              Martha's Vineyard
                                                              Garden City, USA

Laura Quiros, Ph.D., LMSW (she/her) is an Associate Professor of Social Work at Adelphi University. Her research and scholarly interests focus on trauma-informed practice and leadership from a social justice lens. The common thread in her consulting, teaching, and scholarship is elevating complexity and furthering the mission of social justice, including diversity, equity, and inclusion. Using her lens as an educator, researcher, author, practitioner, trauma survivor, mother, and woman of color from a multiracial and multiethnic background, Laura identified a deficiency and an interconnectedness in the fields of trauma, diversity and inclusion and social work education and leadership. Her practice is one of liberation, love, and generosity.

ACKNOWLEDGMENTS

We would like to acknowledge the traditional lands on which we work and express our gratitude and appreciation for the past and present Indigenous caretakers of these lands. We would also like to thank the many educators who submitted chapter proposals that we did not have space to include. We look forward to seeing their ideas about trauma-informed teaching in print elsewhere. We would also like to recognize the resilience and struggles of all educators, especially during the COVID-19 pandemic. You make a difference. Hopefully you will gather many takeaways from this collection. And hopefully one of the main takeaways will be that whatever your role in education—faculty, staff, student, administrator, community partner, policy maker—the work you do, the relationships you foster, the words you speak, your physical and virtual presence, these all make a difference.

Contents

NOTES ON CONTRIBUTORS

Andrea Alexander, MSN (she/her) has served as an Assistant Professor of Nursing at Simpson University in Redding, CA and George Fox University in Newberg, OR since 2017. Her main areas of expertise include mental health nursing, medical-surgical nursing, and nutrition. She has held a number of nursing positions, including as a family nurse practitioner and as a registered nurse in various specialties. Andrea earned her MSN with a concentration as a family nurse practitioner from Sonoma State University in 2014. She earned her BSN from Rush University in 2007. Prior to that, she earned two BAs in Interpersonal Communication and World Arts and Cultures from UCLA in 2002. Andrea's research interests include trauma-informed educational practices with nursing students, barriers to mental health care, and preventive mental health and nutrition.

Hans Bernier, MPA, LSCW (he/him/his) as an education/social service professional that has dedicated over 15 years to social justice practices, I am aiming to continue this commitment by drawing on my MPA, from The Metropolitan College of NY, and LCSW, from the Silberman Social Work at Hunter. Given my years coordinating school and community-based programming I have acquired the skills needed to collaborate with the range of stakeholders supporting social work. I am currently working at the Columbia School of Social Work as an Associate Director of Field. I have also provided direct clinical support through a number of NYC-based community organizations, DOE schools and my private practice.

Jay A. Breneman, MSSA (he/him) joined the US Army after 9/11, serving two enlistments, and three tours overseas, including two deployments to Iraq. He was honorably discharged at the rank of Staff Sergeant (E-6) in 2009. Since then, he has earned his bachelor's and master's in social work specializing in macro practice, and is currently pursuing his doctorate, focused on racism and housing inequality. Jay served in elected office for four years on Erie County

Council where he created the county's Department of Veterans Affairs, having also served as veterans program manager at two area universities. Jay teaches social work, political science, and policy courses, and he lives in Erie with his wife and their three children.

L. Lauren Brown, Ph.D., LCSW (she/her) is the Director of Behavioral Health & Research at Nashville CARES and an Adjunct Assistant Professor of Medicine and Adjunct Assistant Professor of Human and Organizational Development both at Vanderbilt. As an educator, clinician, macro practitioner, and community-based investigator, she provides a strong link between medical and community-based HIV care that helps bridge research-to-practice gaps. A major focus of her work has been on the implementation of trauma-informed care (TIC) in HIV care settings.

Elodie Button (she/elle/ella) is a non-Indigenous facilitator and educator who has been working at the intersections of social justice and education for two decades. Her work is grounded in her relationships with beloved Elders and community members. Having spent thousands of hours in the classroom and on the land with Indigenous youth and adult learners, Elodie is passionate about supporting non-Indigenous educators in decolonizing their pedagogies, hearts, and minds. Elodie completed a Masters of Education in Adult Education and Community Development from the University of Toronto. She lives with her partner and their daughter on unceded lək'ʷəŋən and WSÁNEĆ territories.

Janice Carello, Ph.D., LMSW (she/her) is an Assistant Professor and MSW Program Director at Edinboro University. She received her Ph.D. from the University at Buffalo where she also earned her MSW degree and a Certificate in Trauma Counseling. Her scholarship focuses on retraumatization in educational settings and trauma-informed approaches in higher education. She co-edited *Lessons from the Pandemic: Trauma-Informed Approaches to College, Crisis, Change* and *Trauma and Human Rights: Integrating Approaches to Address Human Rights*. She also publishes trauma-informed teaching and learning resources on her blog: traumainformedteaching.blog.

Kortney Carr, LCSW, LSCSW (she/her) is an Associate Professor of Practice and Ph.D. student at the University of Kansas School of Social Welfare. Within her teaching, she focuses on assisting students build advanced, competent, multi-system skills while infusing DEI, and social justice into every MSW course taught. Her scholarly interests include exploring the impact of social isolation and complex hope on the health and well-being of Black men. Goals of her work and research include engaging Black men in research and working to amplify their voices and experiences within research and the profession.

Andrea D. Clements, Ph.D. (she/her) is a Professor in the Department of Psychology at East Tennessee State University. Her primary areas of research are religiosity, health, and trauma responsiveness, particularly focusing on addiction. She has developed, delivered, and studied trainings for varied audiences around trauma-responsiveness, ACEs science, and resilience-building for the past several years. She has taught psychological measurement and research methods for almost 30 years, and often says, "research is only as good as its measurement tools." She is the Associate Director of Research Design and Implementation in the Strong BRAIN Institute at East Tennessee State University.

Sarah Cole (she/her) is a student in the MSW Program at the University of Kansas, as well as a student assistant to the School of Social Welfare's Diversity, Equity, and Inclusion program. She has also volunteered in Crisis Counseling for the last four years. Though she is a beginning researcher, her research interests include barriers Disabled People face in higher education, as well as the immense resilience and creativity they meet those barriers with.

Lauren Cortez (she/her) has over 10 years experience in GCP quality, compliance, and site performance management of clinical trials and projects in multiple therapeutic areas. In her recent collaboration with the Military and Veteran Caregiver Research Portfolio at UT Health San Antonio, Lauren has extensive familiarity in the academic research arena, pharmaceutical and medical device industries, non-profit organizations, and clinical research organizations. In addition to her broad-based research experience and breadth of roles, she is presently pursuing a doctoral degree in leadership studies. Lauren's research interests include military suicide prevention, post-traumatic stress disorder, traumatic brain injury, and caregiving.

Karen Costa (she/her) is a faculty development facilitator specializing in online pedagogy and trauma-aware higher education. Karen's first book, 99 Tips for Creating Simple and Sustainable Educational Videos, focuses on helping faculty and teachers to make creative use of videos in their classrooms. She lives in Massachusetts with her family. Learn more at her website, www. 100faculty.com.

Dana Crosby, MPH (she/her/her) holds a Master of Public Health from the Oregon Health Science University-Portland State University School of Public Health. Her interests include intersections of education, public health, and equity. She has experience in several educational contexts, including educational consulting in Vietnam, working as a substitute teacher, and mentoring in Portland State University's Studies Department.

Wallace E. Dixon Jr., Ph.D. (he/him) has served as Chair and Professor of Psychology at East Tennessee State University for nearly 20 years. He also serves as Founding Director of the ETSU Ballad Health Strong BRAIN (Building Resilience through ACEs-Informed Networking) Institute. While at ETSU, Dixon established Ph.D. programs in Clinical and Experimental Psychology. He has received funding from the National Institutes of Health and has authored two books and dozens of scientific journal articles. Dixon is well versed in the science of ACEs science and the communication of ACEs messaging.

Óscar Fernández, Ph.D. (He, him, his, *él*) is a faculty member in University Studies and served as its inaugural Diversity, Equity, and Inclusion Coordinator. He specializes in inter-American studies, literary theory, and the intersection of culture, sexuality, and representations of disease in Iberoamerican literature. He earned a Ph.D. in Comparative Literature from The Pennsylvania State University.

Kimberly L. Hardner (she/her/hers) is an Assistant Professor in the Social Work Department at Edinboro University of Pennsylvania. In addition to teaching for the past ten years, her clinical experience of 14 years focuses on work with children and families. Kimberly enjoys qualitative research that: (1) enhances awareness of social justice issues; and, (2) promotes advocacy and policy changes.

Maureen Hickey, Ph.D. (she/her/hers or they/them/theirs) is an instructor in International & Global Studies at Portland State University, with specialties in international development, labor and education migration, and migration policy and advocacy. Her research investigates teacher migration in East and Southeast Asia. She earned her Ph.D. in Geography at the University of Washington.

Mays Imad, Ph.D. is a neuroscientist and an educator whose research focuses on stress, self-awareness, advocacy, and community, and how these relate to cognition, metacognition, and, ultimately, student learning. She received her undergraduate training in philosophy from the University of Michigan and her graduate training in Cellular and clinical neurobiology from Wayne State University-School of Medicine. She has written pieces for *Inside Higher Education* on hope and on trauma-informed pedagogy. She has presented extensively on trauma-informed education focusing on the neuroscience behind it as well as practical strategies to help educators help themselves and their students mitigate the impact of stress and anxiety.

Alexis Jemal, LCSW, LCADC, M.A., JD, Ph.D. (she/her) Assistant Professor at Silberman School of Social Work-Hunter College, is a scholar, writer, artivist, educator, social entrepreneur, and critical social worker whose mission is to recognize and respond to oppressive policies and practices to prevent and eliminate domination, exploitation, and discrimination that pose barriers to life, wellness, liberty, and justice. Dr. Jemal's research integrates participatory action research methods, critical theory, and the creative arts to develop and test multi-level and multi-systemic socio-health practices that incorporate restorative justice frameworks, radical healing, and liberation health models to address structural, community, and interpersonal violence.

Sarah Jen, MSW, Ph.D. (she/her) is an Assistant Professor at the University of Kansas School of Social Welfare. She teaches across Bachelor's, Master's, and doctoral levels in areas of theory, research, and aging-related practice. Her scholarship addresses the intersections of social work, gerontology, and sexuality and aims to improve the health and well-being of sexually diverse and aging populations through the use of critical, qualitative, and creative methods.

Elizabeth Kleinfeld (she/her) is Professor of English and Writing Center Director at Metropolitan State University of Denver. She teaches courses on rhetoric and composition theory and practice. She researches student source use, academic integrity, and ways of teaching and assessing writing that promote inclusivity and social justice. Her pedagogy and research are informed by disability studies, feminism, and social justice theory. She has co-authored a textbook on multimodal and multigenre composition and has published articles on writing center work, digital rhetoric, and student source citation practices.

William J. Koehler, Ph.D., LCSW (he/him/they/them) is Assistant Professor of Social Work at Edinboro University of Pennsylvania. Dr. Koehler's teaching focus is psychopathology, trauma theory and practice, and field practicum. Their areas of research center around bystander intervention in anti-LGBTQ+ bullying and infusing trauma-informed practice in field experience. Dr. Koehler's clinical expertise is engaging in trauma-focused treatment of LGBTQ+ adults and youth as well as those exposed to violence, abuse, and neglect.

Matthea Marquart, MSSW (she/her) is the assistant dean, online education, and a senior adjunct lecturer at Columbia University's School of Social Work (CSSW), where she leads a team responsible for implementing Columbia's online Master's of Science in Social Work program. She is also a CSSW alum. She created and co-facilitates CSSW's intensive Institute on Pedagogy and Technology for Online Courses, an award-winning program that has prepared hundreds of online educators to teach inclusive and engaging online courses. She teaches in CSSW's management program, preparing a new wave of nonprofit and human services leaders.

Heidi Marsh, M.A. (she/her/hers) is executive aide and adjunct faculty in the Women's, Gender, and Sexuality Studies Program at East Tennessee State University where she teaches introductory courses in Women's, Gender, and Sexuality Studies. She has a background in feminist pedagogy and teaching first-year composition and has also served as team-member on several grant-funded initiatives to provide trauma-informed care training to faculty and staff and to provide trauma-informed resources and education regarding gender-based violence on campus.

Diana Morelen, Ph.D. (she/her) is an Assistant Professor in the Department of Psychology at East Tennessee State University and a licensed clinical psychologist with specialization in infant mental health and perinatal mental health. She is a clinical scientist committed to breaking the intergenerational transmission of trauma, adversity, and mental illness through evidence-based prevention and intervention programs. She serves as the Associate Director of Training Dissemination and Implementation for ETSU's Strong BRAIN Institute, a board member for the TN chapter of Postpartum Support International, and a regional lead for her state's infant mental health association (AIMHiTN).

Megan Paceley, MSW, Ph.D. (she/they) is an Associate Professor at the University of Kansas School of Social Welfare. Through their teaching, they aim to promote a critical and trauma-informed lens through which their students view the world and engage in social work practice. Their scholarship attends to the ways in which the social environment (family, school, community) affects the health and well-being of queer and trans youth. They aim to transform systems via improvements in community climate and access to queer and trans resources with the goal of reducing negative health outcomes and promote resilience and well-being.

Joy Patton (she/her) is a licensed master social worker in the state of Texas and Assistant Professor in the Worden School of Social Service. For over a decade, she has been creating and delivering quality online education. She currently is faculty in the online, social work doctoral program at Our Lady of the Lake University. Dr. Patton has worked in community consulting roles including grant writing, community needs assessments, program evaluations, program development, and departmental and organizational strategic planning. Her research interests are with online education, child welfare staff and parent training, children and families, trauma, and domestic violence.

Danielle Peloquin, Ed.D. (she/her) is the Instructional Development Lead for Fusion Education Group. While the majority of her academic and professional background is in adult learning, she relishes the years she spent teaching English and social studies in the 6–12 classroom. She holds two Bachelors of Arts in English and history, a Masters of Science in Library and Information Sciences, and a Doctorate of Education in Curriculum, Teaching, and Learning. Dani has taught at various universities and developed such courses as World History Through the Graphic Novel, Comics as Literature, Social Issues in World Drama and numerous others.

John D. Perkins, DMA (he/him) is an Associate Professor of Music, at Butler University, and a Fulbright Scholar to Malaysia. While teaching at the American University of Sharjah (United Arab Emirates) he shifted away from performativity as a goal of music education. John now focuses on sustaining students' lives and promoting justice through music education. Coursework such as "Peacebuilding through Choral Singing," "Why Music?" and "Musicking Futures in Malaysia" address these values along with research in the *Bulletin of the Council for Research in Music Education*, the *Choral*

Journal, and the *International Choral Bulletin*, book chapters and conference presentations.

Shraddha Prabhu, Ph.D. (she/her) is an Assistant Professor with Edinboro University's Department of Social Work. Her teaching and scholarship focus on issues related to intersectionality, diversity, inequity, and trauma exposure and resilience. Through her clinical work she strives to provide access to anti-oppressive, trauma-specific treatment services for clients from underserved communities. Her advocacy efforts focus on centering the voices and experiences of those who are faced with marginalization and continue to lead the fight for equity.

Megan Quinn, DrPH, M.Sc. (she/her) is an Associate Professor and Interim Chair of the Department of Biostatistics and Epidemiology in the College of Public Health at East Tennessee State University. She is also Coordinator of Global Health Initiatives and the Global Health Certificate and manager of the Tennessee Stroke Registry at ETSU. She is the Associate Director of Extramural Funding and Innovation in the Strong BRAIN Institute at East Tennessee State University.

Dr. Christine M. Rine, Ph.D., MSW (she/her) Associate Professor, Social Work Department, Edinboro University. She received her BSW from Buffalo State College and MSW and Ph.D. from the University at Buffalo. Dr. Rine's practice experience includes HIV/AIDS, youth with mental health concerns, and in program evaluation and administration. Her scholarly endeavors include teaching pedagogy, child welfare, vicarious trauma, end-of-life care, and mapping in social work contexts. Dr. Rine serves as Editor-in-Chief of NASW's Health & Social Work journal and has spoken widely on neighborhoods, palliative end care, technology in teaching pedagogy, and social determinants of health.

Michael Riquino, MSW, Ph.D. (he/him) is an Assistant Professor at the University of Kansas School of Social Welfare. He primarily teaches clinical practice courses at the graduate level. In his pedagogy, he emphasizes critical and contextualized understandings of mental health, and advocates for integrating micro and macro treatment approaches in order to alleviate human suffering. His scholarship focuses on improving interventions and systems for individuals who engage in self-harming behaviors, with a particular focus on centering the perspectives of youth with marginalized identities.

Nykchasia S. Scott, MSSW (she/they) earned her Master's degree in Social Work from Columbia University in May of 2020. Nykchasia studied Social Enterprise Administration with a focus on Health, Mental Health, and Disabilities. She serves the global and local communities through her roles as CEO of TrapTranquility LLC, facilitator for Youth Connect Group with SAC Connect Therapeutic & Wellness Services, and Live Support Specialist for Columbia University's School of Social Work.

Katherine Seibel, MSSW (she/her) is the Director of Public Policy & Advocacy at the National Alliance on Mental Illness Washington and received her MSSW in public policy from Columbia University. Katherine's career has included direct service and specialization in facilitating DBT Mindfulness and trauma-informed yoga groups, multi-state as well as federal policy and advocacy engagement promoting mental health, social-emotional learning, child sexual abuse prevention, and bullying prevention, and she has served as a teaching associate at Columbia University's School of Social Work.

Sam Settelmeyer (he, him, his) is pursuing his Ph.D. in Social Work at Portland State University. Motivated by experiences in alternative education and grassroots community building, Sam aspires to be part of the necessarily incremental and unity-focused process of critical and appreciative educational reform.

Kelly Smith, M.Ed., DSW, MS (she/her/hers) is founder and director of the Institute for Social Work and Ecological Justice and an adjunct professor at Adelphi University and Columbia School of Social Work. She is also a member of the Grand Challenge for Creating Social Responses to a Changing Environment Advisory Council. Kelly earned her doctorate in social work at the University of Southern California, where she was honored with The Order of Arête. Additionally, Kelly holds a master's degree in Gender and Social Policy from the London School of Economics.

Ami Sommariva, Ph.D. (she/her/hers/they/them/theirs) teaches courses on popular culture, American studies, and design justice at Portland State University. Her research examines the public feelings cultivated through television and how they have shaped discourses on racism, gender, and nature. She holds a Ph.D. in Cultural Studies from the University of California, Davis.

Susan K. Steckel, MSSW, LMSW (she/her) is a macro practice social worker, committed to excellence in social work education and advancing the social work profession. Her professional interests include NEAR science (neurophysiology/epigenetics/adverse childhood experiences/resilience), children's mental health policy, trauma-informed care, infant mental health and early childhood development, interagency collaboration and organizational management, and improving systems that serve vulnerable populations. She is an Associate Professor of Practice and Director of Continuing Education with the University of Tennessee, Knoxville College of Social Work.

Lars Stoltzfus (they/them/theirs) is a Lecturer in Communication Studies at Gonzaga University. They are interested in how power and mediated experiences impact and are impacted by identity formation. Lars' most recent work is on queer and/or transgender former Amish, Mennonite, and Brethren individuals navigating cultures, communication, and media. Lars has also written on transgender exclusion in the Women's March movement, Super Bowl advertising, and growing up at queer and trans at the interstices of Amish, Mennonite, and Southern white cultures.

Phyllis Thompson, Ph.D. (she/her) has served as Director of Women's, Gender, and Sexuality Studies at East Tennessee State University since 2012, is currently Interim Chair of Counseling and Human Services, and is Associate Professor. She received her Ph.D. from LSU in eighteenth-century Literature and Gender Studies; publishes on medicinal recipe books, archival studies, and women's contributions to eighteenth-century healthcare; and co-edited *Lessons from the Pandemic: Trauma-Informed Approaches to College, Crisis, Change*. She serves on the Advisory Board for the Office of Equity and Inclusion at ETSU and is a member of the ETSU Strong BRAIN Institute.

Jeanie Tietjen, Ph.D., MFA (she/her) is a faculty of English at MassBay Community College, and founder of the Institute for Trauma, Adversity, and Resilience in Higher Education. She earned her Ph.D. at Brandeis University, and MFA at the University of Massachusetts, Amherst.

Michiel A. van Zyl, Ph.D. (he/him) is Professor and Director of the School of Social Work at the University of South Florida. His work on measurement and training evaluation impacted various fields of practice including child welfare, corrections, education, prevention of behavioral problems in young children, risk reduction, and organizational behavior. He collaborated on studies of STDs, teenage pregnancy prevention, prevention of child abuse and neglect, and other health-risk behaviors. His academic work in child welfare focuses on the prevention of child abuse and neglect, child welfare practice models, and quality improvement in social service delivery.

Hilistis Pauline Waterfall (u'maqs/she) is a Hailhzaqv knowledge keeper from Bella Bella. She and her husband John are proud parents of three children, six grandchildren, and two great-grandchildren. A lifelong educator, Hilistis founded Heiltsuk College, has been an adjunct professor and program advisor, and teaches workshops locally and provincially. She is a recipient of the Order of BC and is a former elected Tribal Councillor. Hilistis continues to work in support of her Nation in numerous capacities, advising traditional and elected leaders on sustainable resource matters, serving on a variety of boards and committees, promoting holistic health and supporting Hailhzaqv language revitalization.

Molly Wolf, LMSW, Ph.D. (she/her) is an Associate Professor and Chair of the Social Work Department at Edinboro University of Pennsylvania. Dr. Wolf's areas of expertise are in trauma, child sexual abuse, traumatic memory, and perpetration of child sexual abuse. As a social worker, she has facilitated parenting groups with at-risk parents, supervised visits with families who had lost custody of their children, and facilitated Seeking Safety groups with female trauma survivors. Dr. Wolf's research has been published and presented internationally.

Nicole Wong, LMSW (she/her) is the Director of Family Support Services at Family Services in Poughkeepsie, New York. Nicole earned her Master's degree in Social Work at Columbia University in Advanced Clinical Practice with a focus on Health, Mental Health, and Disabilities. She has a breadth of experience in non-profit management, trauma and anti-violence, and university administration. In addition to her role at Family Services she is a Clinician at Teamer Counseling and a Live Support Specialist for Columbia University's School of Social Work.

Kelechi Wright (she/her) is a Ph.D. student and Graduate Research and Teaching Assistant at the University of Kansas School of Social Welfare. She has over 14 years as a practitioner and has served various populations. Her research involves the intersection of criminal justice system and social work and ethnic diversity within social work education. Under the leadership of Dr. Becci Akin, she currently serves as a research assistant for a federally funded project conducting implementation science and institutional/policy analysis.

LIST OF FIGURES

CHAPTER 1

Developing a New Default in Higher Education: We Are Not Alone in This Work

Janice Carello and Phyllis Thompson

How does a wound heal when it is repeatedly reopened? How do individual and collective bodies recover when they experience chronic injury?

As part of a paradigmatic shift in our conceptualization of trauma, Sandra Bloom taught us to ask the question, "What's happened to you?" rather than "What's wrong with you?" when working with trauma survivors (Bloom & Sreedhar, 2008). This continues to be a pertinent question, a relevant reframing of trauma as experiences that individuals, families, and communities must cope with and recover from rather than as individual pathology or character flaws that must be cured or fixed. It helps us understand that trauma recovery requires intervention at both the individual and system levels. And it helps us understand that trauma is not the past; it is in the present: "trauma is much more than a story about something that happened long ago. The emotions and physical sensations that were imprinted during the trauma are experienced not as memories but as disruptive physical reactions in the present" (van der Kolk, 2014, p. 206).

J. Carello (✉)
Social Work, Edinboro University, Edinboro, PA, USA
e-mail: jcarello@edinboro.edu

P. Thompson
Women's, Gender, and Sexuality Studies, East Tennessee State University, Johnson City, TN, USA
e-mail: thompsop@etsu.edu

© The Author(s), under exclusive license to Springer Nature Switzerland AG 2022
P. Thompson and J. Carello (eds.), *Trauma-Informed Pedagogies*,
https://doi.org/10.1007/978-3-030-92705-9_1

1

As the field of trauma-informed care develops, some critics, such as Shawn Ginwright (2018), are encouraging us to ask the question, "What's right with you?" in order to emphasize resilience and healing and to remind us that trauma is a political issue as well as a clinical issue. And as scholars and as trauma-informed educators, we—the editors of this book—argue that it is essential to also ask the question, "What is happening to you?" which recognizes that some forms of trauma are ongoing.

WHAT IS HAPPENING TO US?

As we write this introduction, more than 680,000 people in the United States have died from COVID-19 (Centers for Disease Control & Prevention, 2021) and there have been 4.7 million deaths worldwide (World Health Organization, 2021). This is a higher number of deaths than recorded for the Spanish Flu in 1918, which makes COVID-19 stand out as the deadliest disease in American history. A recent *Newsweek* headline reads, "Florida Averaging 11 COVID Deaths Per Hour as Delta Variant, Mask Debates Rage" (Stanton, 2021). Due to rhetoric blaming Asians for spreading the COVID-19 pandemic, the United States has seen a rise in anti-Asian hate crimes (Cabral, 2021).

Shortly after starting work on this book in the spring of 2020, we learned of the killing of George Floyd by Officer Derek Chauvin, and hundreds of Black, Hispanic, and Latino Americans have been killed by U.S. police since, including Breonna Taylor, Daniel Prude, Daunte Wright, Adam Toledo, Ernie Serrano, and Erik Salgado (Chughtai, 2021; Foster-Frau, 2021; Hurd, 2020; Rahman, 2021; Valentine, 2021). In 2021 there has been a rise in fatal violence against transgender or gender non-conforming individuals, including the deaths of Jenna Franks, Thomas Hardin, and Sophie Vásquez (Human Rights Campaign, 2021). Thousands of unmarked graves of Indigenous children have been discovered at the sites of former residential institutions in Canada (Hopkins, 2021) and thousands more are expected to be uncovered in the United States (Hopkins, 2021; U.S. Department of the Interior, 2021).

These are just some of the atrocities that have made the headlines. As someone who has chosen to read this chapter and perhaps this book, you are likely very aware of the magnitude and impact of trauma, adversity, crisis, and inequity in our world. Though the COVID-19 pandemic is a new type of traumatic stressor, it underscores our existing understanding that crisis is always present. College educators routinely work with students and colleagues who are experiencing various forms of trauma and loss, and college educators experience such events themselves: life-threatening injury or illness, death of a loved one, fire, hurricane, interpersonal violence, racism, divorce, miscarriage, assault, unemployment, homelessness, food insecurity.

Our experiences are not just anecdotal. It is well documented that exposure to traumatic and adverse events is common among college students (Bachrach & Read, 2012; Bernat et al., 1998; Frazier, et al., 2009; Read, et al., 2011; Smyth, et al., 2008; Williams et al., 2021). Studies show that 66% to 85% of youth report lifetime traumatic event exposure (and many report multiple exposures) by the time they reach college (Frazier et al., 2009; Read et al., 2011; Smyth, et al., 2008) and that as many as 50% of students are exposed to a potentially traumatic event in their first year of college (Galatzer-Levy et al., 2012). Research indicates that students with cumulative trauma histories are more likely to have difficulty adjusting to college (Banyard & Cantor, 2004), get lower grades (DeBerard, et al., 2004), and drop out (Duncan, 2000). Trauma and other highly stressful life experiences also put college students at greater risk of developing posttraumatic stress, depression, substance use disorders, and other physical and mental health problems (Anders, et al., 2012; Read et al., 2011; Turner & Butler, 2003).

It is no wonder that many college students and educators are experiencing burnout and mental health issues. The World Health Organization (May 25, 2019) recently classified burnout as an "occupational phenomenon," confirming what we have long known: that "burnout is about your workplace, not your people" (Moss, 2019) and those in the helping professions are at the greatest risk (Ben-Zur & Michael, 2007; Maslach & Leiter, 2008). A recent study by the Harris Poll found that 76% of the 1,136 U.S. employees surveyed were experiencing burnout (Spring Health, 2020). A 2020 survey found that the mental health of students and the mental health of faculty and staff were among the top three concerns of college and university presidents (Turk et al., 2020).

How Shall We Respond?

At the heart of trauma is a sense of powerlessness and disconnection. People experience burnout when it seems like nothing they do makes a difference any longer. In their TED Talk, Emily and Amelia Nagoski (2021) provide a layperson's definition of burnout: "that feeling of being overwhelmed and exhausted by everything you have to do, while still worrying that you're not doing enough" (8:40). They also point out that "The cure for burnout is not self-care. It is all of us caring for each other. We can't do it alone. We need each other" (14:43). Though many academics experience burnout, few talk about it, and we are starting to recognize the need not only for individual self-care but also for changes in academic structure and culture (Jaremka et al., 2020).

Being trauma-informed in the context of higher education means recognizing that educators also experience trauma, adversity, crisis, and inequity and that we must implement policies and practices and develop an institutional culture that supports educator well-being. Though research on the prevalence and impact of retraumatization in higher education is still in its infancy, there is some preliminary evidence that experiences of retraumatization are not uncommon among college students, faculty, and staff and that some experiences of retraumatization are related to marginalized identity status (Carello,

2018). Becoming aware of the prevalence and impact of trauma, crisis, adversity, and inequity among students and educators is only the first step in the process of becoming trauma-informed in higher education settings. The next step is to learn how to effectively respond at both the individual and system levels. A transformative pedagogy is one that requires we not only change our pedagogy but also our practice of that pedagogy (hooks, 1994).

LEARNING FROM THE PAST

It is important to keep in mind that trauma-informed care originated in behavioral health systems as an alternative to coercive standard operating procedures that unintentionally retraumatized and revictimized people seeking help and that it was designed to increase retention in treatment services (Harris and Fallot, 2001; Lewis et al., 2016). In their seminal text on trauma-informed care, Harris and Fallot (2001) explicitly caution that "providers need to be aware of the dynamics that characterize abusive relationships and make sure that those same dynamics are not being unwittingly replicated in helping relationships" (p. 9).

It is also helpful to understand that trauma-informed care was conceived as a cultural change process built upon a set of principles (Bowen & Murshid, 2016) and that it is not the same as trauma-specific services such as eye-movement desensitization reprocessing (EMDR; Shapiro, 1995) or Progressive Counting (Greenwald, 2013) which are interventions designed to directly treat trauma-related symptoms and syndromes in individuals. It is possible to be trauma-informed without providing trauma-specific services, to provide trauma-specific services without being trauma-informed, or to both be trauma-informed and provide trauma-specific services (Carello et al., 2019).

In the past two decades, the need for trauma-informed care and trauma-specific services in other systems and settings such as child welfare and K-12 schools has become clear, as evidenced by federal legislation (e.g., the Trauma-Informed Care for Children and Families Act, 2017), by numerous statewide initiatives (e.g., see Prewitt, 2019) and by education and advocacy efforts through organizations such as The Campaign for Trauma-Informed Policy and Practice (ctipp.org), the Strong BRAIN Institute (https://www.etsu.edu/institute/strong-brain), and the PACES Connection network (https://www.pacesconnection.com). The recent COVID-19 pandemic has also highlighted the need to create trauma-informed cultures and to provide trauma-specific services in higher education (Carello & Thompson, 2021).

CONVEYING POSSIBILITY AND HOPE

Just as there is no single path to learning and well-being, there is no one right way to be trauma-informed. Trauma-informed care is one of many anti-oppressive approaches to teaching and learning, and trauma-informed principles are congruent with or embodied in other approaches and best practices (e.g., safe spaces, pedagogy of discomfort, anti-oppressive practices, universal design for learning, growth mindset) that focus on improving access to education, responding to trauma with empathy and support, and promoting social justice to redress policies, practices, and environments that create barriers to learning in the first place. Trauma-informed approaches share a common goal of recognizing and responding to signs of trauma to promote resilience and prevent retraumatization—to help individuals, families, organizations, and communities thrive and not just survive—and many also share a common set of trauma-informed principles (Substance Abuse & Mental Health Services Administration, 2014). Having options for how to operationalize these values and principles in different contexts and communities is essential: without options, we feel trapped. Without options, we cannot create something new; we can only reproduce what already exists. As Audre Lorde (1984) wrote in her now classic essay, "the master's tools will never dismantle the master's house" (p. 112). Without options, trauma-informed approaches become dogma rather than tools for transformation.

Additionally, trauma-informed approaches to teaching and learning in higher education must also convey hope. They shift the classroom from being a place of punishment and penalty to a place of promise and possibility. Our policies and practices must also communicate our belief that teaching and learning are possible—that growth and thriving in the aftermath of suffering are possible —and they must create opportunities that make transformative teaching and learning possible. To realize the possibility of transformation, a trauma-informed approach must also hold space for pain and risk entering the difficult conversations around that pain. Vulnerability lies at the heart of transformation; it is the birthplace of transformation. A trauma-informed approach, then, is one that does not erase the trauma, does not pretend it did not happen, and does not downplay its effects but also does not believe that trauma is our destiny; there is recovery, recuperation, and healing (van der Kolk, 2014). Education, then, is a "location of possibility" from which we can "face reality even as we collectively imagine ways to move beyond boundaries, to transgress. This is education as the practice of freedom" (hooks, 1994, p. 207).

DEVELOPING A NEW DEFAULT

Bruce Perry recognizes that healing is not about understanding and undoing what's happened in the past but about building new associations, new alternatives, "a new default" (Perry & Winfrey, 2021, p. 183). As Perry puts it:

> if you don't recognize the built-in biases in yourself and the structural biases in your systems—biases regarding race, gender, sexual orientation—you can't truly be trauma-informed. Marginalized peoples—excluded, minimized, shamed—are traumatized peoples, because…humans are fundamentally relational creatures.

To be excluded or dehumanized in an organization, community, or society you are part of results in prolonged, uncontrollable stress that is sensitizing...Marginalization is a fundamental trauma. (Perry & Winfrey, 2021, p. 220)

As Laura Quiros (2021) observes, organizations tend to be either trauma-informed or focused on diversity, equity, and inclusion, but not both. Often this is the result of the narrow definitions of trauma which focus on individual trauma and fail to recognize structural trauma. Quiros conceives of trauma-informed practice as a foundation for "positive disruption" in order to avoid retraumatizing those we seek to help. By positive disruptions, she explains, "your focus should be maximizing your ability and effectiveness in opening up a person or system to a different perspective" (p. 109). By contrast, "negative disruption is when the dialogue turns into a debate, when divisions within communities of color are centered instead of unity, or when people who were on the right path and went wrong somewhere along the way are criticized heavily rather than taught and shown their error" (p. 108).

This book aims to create positive disruption and to develop a new default: our goal is to help open up educators and institutions of higher education to more effective means of responding to crisis and inequity in higher education. For us, becoming trauma-informed means interrogating our individual and collective practices as educators and the ways in which we inadvertently perpetuate abuse and oppression. This type of reflection can be challenging and uncomfortable. Rather than claiming expertise, or using it as a tool to criticize others, however, we are developing expertise by sharing what we have learned from our individual and collective experiences and by inviting others to join us in developing a community that embodies equity-based trauma-informed practice.

The Origins and Aims of This Book

Oprah Winfrey reflected that in the thousands of interviews she has conducted, "one common denominator has never changed: All of us want to know that what we do, what we say, and who we are matters" (Perry & Winfrey, 2021, p. 75). As educators, we want our students and our colleagues to know that what they do, what they say, and who they are matters. At the intersection of trauma-informed and anti-oppressive pedagogies are people who are not just surviving trauma, crisis, and inequity but making the turn to thriving. At the intersection of trauma-informed and anti-oppressive policymaking is the possibility of transformed and transformative institutions.

To transform institutions, we must first transform ourselves. And to transform ourselves, we must be willing to take risks.

Phyllis took the first risk. In May 2020, she invited me (Janice) to collaborate on a guide to trauma-informed teaching and learning in the COVID-19 pandemic. I enthusiastically said yes, and the rest of the risks related to publishing this book we have braved together. In July 2020, we circulated a call for proposals. By September 2021, we received over 60 proposals. In March 2021, after going through peer review, we were offered contracts for two books which allowed us to publish more submissions than we originally anticipated. In May 2021, we submitted the final manuscript for our first book, *Lessons from the Pandemic: Trauma-Informed Approaches to College, Crisis, Change*. It is September 2021 as we prepare to submit the final manuscript for this book.

Publishing two books in eighteen months has been an intense process, and also an affirming, restorative, and energizing process. We have also endeavored to make it a trauma-informed process. We have striven to center diversity, equity, and inclusion; to ensure safety; to enhance trust and practice transparency; to support and foster connection; to share power through collaboration and mutuality; to enhance empowerment, voice, and choice; and to foster resilience, growth, and change. These shared values provided a supportive framework as we negotiated priorities and deadlines, navigated new roles and responsibilities, resolved misunderstandings and conflicts, made mistakes, requested revisions without responding like the dreaded "Reviewer Number Two," and advocated for publishing practices that respect and reflect our own and our author's diverse identities, perspectives, and ways of knowing.

Trauma-Informed Pedagogies allows us to follow-up and expand on the conversation that *Lessons from the Pandemic* started by providing a larger, more comprehensive treatment of trauma-informed approaches that centers equity as it navigates crisis and inequity in higher education.

Ways to Use This Book

We designed this book with you in mind.

You may be a student using this book for class. The opening chapters contextualize this approach, provide some background on the framework, and identify the central principles and assumptions of the model to provide a sturdy foundation as you make your way through the remaining chapters, prepare to use the assessments and toolbox in Appendix A, and look forward to further reading and reaching out to others in the field.

You may be an instructor who has more passion than time and needs a few tools to carry into class this afternoon or a suggestion on how to use a specific issue or principle in class. The book's table of contents, overall layout, and toolbox are designed with that *a la carte* approach to using this book in mind.

You may lead a book club. If so, be sure to check out the Questions for Reflection and Discussion in Appendix B, which can be used for developing personal narratives, small group breakout sessions, and large group discussions.

You may be, like us, a trauma-informed educator who is looking for community, to join the conversation, and to learn more. In Appendix C we have listed "for further reading" types of resources as well as the websites of some of the trauma-informed initiatives that have been developed. Resources in Appendix C will also help you get connected with others doing this work at individual universities, at the state level, and nationally.

The descriptions below provide an overview of how the contents of this book have been organized to help you decide how you would like to use this book.

Infusing Trauma-Informed Principles

This section grounds the collection in an equity approach to trauma-informed care that recognizes resilience, embodied knowledge, and relationality as central to the process of healing and the practice of teaching and learning. The first chapter of the section explicates the foundational framework of the book to demonstrate how an equity approach is integral to implementing the principles of trauma-informed care. The other chapters in this section illustrate one or more trauma-informed principles in practice.

Trauma-Informed Teaching Across the Curriculum

Chapters in this section illustrate trauma-informed approaches to teaching in specific disciplines. We open this section by thinking back on the first one that contextualizes trauma-informed practice in critical, liberatory, and feminist pedagogies that seek to dismantle systemic racist and colonializing structures, rupture the status quo, and invite transformative practice. This section demonstrates how to do that work through putting trauma-informed pedagogies into action across several disciplines, including musical travel, nursing education, and social work.

Approaches to Working with Specific Populations

Chapters in this section illustrate trauma-informed approaches to teaching specific populations. Minoritized populations are at higher risk for trauma as well as identity-based and systemic violence and marginalization, particularly linking the current public health crisis to race. This section recognizes how widespread violence adversely affects academic resilience across population groups but also highlights that different population groups do not respond to or heal from trauma in the same way. Do no harm is a mantra in trauma-informed circles. This section takes up that mantra and invites the difficult conversations as we move the dial on health, healing, and resilience through an understanding of working with specific populations in the academy and supporting educators who work with rural Indigenous learners.

(Re)Assessment

Because an equity approach requires consistent and ongoing introspection and reflection, we include a section on (Re)Assessment that provides instruments and strategies for assessment at the institutional, organizational, departmental, class, and employee levels. Antiracist literature reminds us that it is not our intentions that matter but our practice. The (Re)Assessment section offers tools to take stock, collect data, and revise practice.

Trauma-Informed Teaching Toolbox

Appendix A is a collection of thirteen evidence-based and field-tested tools to support college educators on their trauma-informed teaching journey. The toolbox provides readers with the "essentials" they might need to carry on their teaching journey. We think of it as packing for the trip—what do you need for the journey? The tools comprise concrete strategies, tips, policies, practices, assignment prompts, assessments, and activities that readers can use immediately. Some are tools mentioned in other chapters of the book, and some are stand-alone resources.

Questions for Discussion and Reflection

The questions in Appendix B provide readers opportunity to reflect on their own lived experience as they engage with each of the chapters. These questions for discussion and reflection could be used as a guide for writing one's own personal narrative, for classroom use, or for book club discussions. They are an invitation for others to join in the ongoing conversations about using trauma-informed approaches to respond to crisis and inequity in higher education. Every voice in this conversation matters.

Resources

Lastly, Appendix C is a collection of resources that amplifies diverse voices, builds resilience, and supports cross-sector work as we take an equity approach to trauma-informed teaching and learning. These resources also promote community-building and collaboration by providing information about and links to groups currently working on trauma-informed approaches in higher education. We are not alone in this work.

REFERENCES

Anders, S. L., Frazier, P. A., & Shallcross, S. L. (2012). Prevalence and effects of life event exposure among undergraduate and community college students. *Journal of Counseling Psychology, 59*(3), 449–457.

Bachrach, R. L., & Read, J. P. (2012). The role of posttraumatic stress and problem alcohol involvement in university academic performance. *Journal of Clinical Psychology, 68*(7), 843–859.

Banyard, V. L., & Cantor, E. N. (2004). Adjustment to college among trauma survivors: An exploratory study of resilience. *Journal of College Student Development, 45*(2), 207–221.

Ben-Zur, H., & Michael, K. (2007). Burnout, social support, and coping at work among social workers, psychologists, and nurses: The role of challenge/control appraisals. *Social Work in Health Care, 45*, 63–82.

Bernat, J. A., Ronfeldt, H. M., Calhoun, K. S., & Arias, I. (1998). Prevalence of traumatic events and peritraumatic predictors of posttraumatic stress symptoms in a non-clinical sample of college students. *Journal of Traumatic Stress, 11*, 645–664.

Bloom, S. L., & Sreedhar, S. Y. (2008). The Sanctuary Model of trauma-informed organizational change. *Reclaiming Children and Youth, 17*(3), 48–53.

Bowen, E. A., & Murshid, N. S. (2016). Trauma-Informed social policy: A conceptual framework for policy analysis and advocacy. *Perspectives from the Social Sciences, 106*(2), 223–229.

Cabral, S. (2021, May 21). Covid 'hate crimes' against Asian Americans on rise. *BBC News*. https://www.bbc.com/news/world-us-canada-56218684

Carello, J. (2018). *Retraumatization during training: A trauma-informed narrative approach* (Doctoral dissertation). https://ubir.buffalo.edu/xmlui/handle/10477/78089

Carello, J., Butler, L. D., & Critelli, F. M. (2019). Introduction to Trauma and human rights: Context and content. In L. D. Butler, F. M. Critelli, & J. Carello (Eds.), *Trauma and human rights: Integrating approaches to address human suffering.* Palgrave Macmillan.

Carello, J., & Thompson, P. (2021). *Lessons from the pandemic: Trauma-informed approaches to college, crisis, change.* Palgrave Macmillan.

Centers for Disease Control and Prevention. (2021). *COVID data tracker.* https://covid.cdc.gov/covid-data-tracker/#datatracker-home

Chughtai, A. (2021). Know their names: Black people killed by police in the U.S. *Al Jazeera*. https://interactive.aljazeera.com/aje/2020/know-their-names/index.html

DeBerard, M. S., Spielmans, G. I., & Julka, D. L. (2004). Predictors of academic achievement and retention among college freshmen: A longitudinal study. *College Student Journal, 38*(1), 66–80.

Duncan, R. D. (2000). Childhood maltreatment and college drop-out rates: Implications for child abuse researchers. *Journal of Interpersonal Violence, 15*(9), 987–995.

Foster-Frau, S. (2021, June 2). Latinos are disproportionately killed by police but often left out of the debate about brutality, some advocates say. *The Washington Post*. https://www.washingtonpost.com/national/police-killings-latinos/2021/05/31/657bb7be-b4d4-11eb-a980-a60af976ed44_story.html

Frazier, P., Anders, S., Perera, S., Tomich, P., Tennen, H., Park, C., & Tashiro, T. (2009). Traumatic events among undergraduate students: Prevalence and associated symptoms. *Journal of Counseling Psychology, 56*(3), 450–460. https://doi.org/10.1037/a0016412

Galatzer-Levy, I. R., Burton, C. L., & Bonanno, G. A. (2012). Coping flexibility, potentially traumatic life events, and resilience: A prospective study of college student adjustment. *Journal of Social and Clinical Psychology, 31*(6), 542–567.

Ginwright, S. (2018). The future of healing: shifting from trauma informed care to healing centered engagement. *Medium*. https://ginwright.medium.com/the-future-of-healing-shifting-from-trauma-informed-care-to-healing-centered-engagement-634f557ce69c

Greenwald, R. (2013). *Progressive counting within a phase model of trauma-informed treatment*. Routledge.

Harris, M., & Fallot, R. D. (Eds.). (2001). *Using trauma theory to design service systems*. Jossey-Bass.

hooks, b. (1994). *Teaching to transgress: Education as the practice of freedom*. Routledge.

Hopkins, R. (2021, July 14). Unmarked graves at Indian residential schools speak to horrors faced by students. *Teen Vogue*. https://www.teenvogue.com/story/indian-residential-schools-graves

Human Rights Campaign. (2021). *Fatal violence against the transgender and gender non-conforming community in 2021*. https://www.hrc.org/resources/fatal-violence-against-the-transgender-and-gender-non-conforming-community-in-2021

Hurd, C. (2020, June 9). Oakland officials reveal details about shooting death of Erik Salgado. *NBC Bay Area*. https://www.nbcbayarea.com/news/local/east-bay/oakland-officials-reveal-details-about-shooting-death-of-erik-salgado/2306495/

Jaremka, L. M., Ackerman, J. M., Gawronski, B., Rule, N. O., Sweeny, K., Tropp, L. R., Metz, M. A., Molina, L., Ryan, W. S., & Vick, S. B. (2020). Common academic experiences no one talks about: Repeated rejection, impostor syndrome, and burnout. *Perspectives on Psychological Science, 15*(3), 519–543. https://doi.org/10.1177/1745691619898848

Lewis, L. A., Kusmaul, N., Elze, D., & Butler, L. D. (2016). The role of field education in a university–community partnership aimed at curriculum transformation. *Journal of Social Work Education, 52*(2), 186–197.

Lorde, A. (1984). The master's tools will never dismantle the master's house. In N. Y. Trumansburg (Ed.), *Sister outsider: Essays and speeches* (pp. 110–113). The Crossing Press.

Maslach, C., & Leiter, M. P. (2008). Early predictors of job burnout and engagement. *Journal of Applied Psychology, 93*, 498. https://doi.org/10.1037/0021-9010.93.3.498

Moss, J. (2019, December 11). Burnout is about your workplace, not your people. *Harvard Business Review* https://hbr.org/2019/12/burnout-is-about-your-workplace-not-your-people

Nagoski, E., & Nagoski, A. (2021, April). The cure for burnout (hint: it isn't self-care) [Video]. *TED*. https://www.ted.com/talks/emily_nagoski_and_amelia_nagoski_the_cure_for_burnout_hint_it_isn_t_self_care?utm_campaign=tedspread&utm_medium=referral&utm_source=tedcomshare

Perry, B., & Winfrey, O. (2021). *What happened to you? Conversations on trauma, resilience, and healing*. Flatiron Books.

Prewitt, E. (2019, July 25). *State sites on PACEs Connection (PC)*. https://www.pacesconnection.com/g/state-aces-action-group/blog/State-Sites-on-AC

Quiros, L. (2021). *Incorporating diversity and inclusion into trauma-informed social work: Transformational leadership*. Routledge.

Rahman, K. (2021, May 25). Full list of 229 black people killed by police since George Floyd's murder. *Newsweek*. https://www.newsweek.com/full-list-229-black-people-killed-police-since-george-floyds-murder-1594477

Read, J. P., Ouimette, P., White, J., Colder, C., & Farrow, S. (2011). Rates of *DSM-IV-TR* trauma exposure and posttraumatic stress disorder among newly matriculated college students. *Psychological Trauma: Theory, Research, Practice, and Policy, 3*(2), 148–156. https://doi.org/10.1037/a0021260

Shapiro, F. (1995). *Eye movement desensitization and reprocessing: Basic principles, protocols and procedures.* Guilford Press.

Smyth, J. M., Hockemeyer, J. R., Heron, K. E., Wonderlich, S. A., & Pennebaker, J. W. (2008). Prevalence, type, disclosure, and severity of adverse life events in college students. *Journal of American College Health, 57*(1), 69–76. https://doi.org/10.3200/JACH.57.1.69-76

Spring Health. (2020). *Burnout nation: How 2020 has reshaped employees' relationship to work.* https://www.springhealth.com/wp-content/uploads/2020/12/Spring-Health-Burnout-Nation.pdf

Stanton, A. (2021, August 30). Florida averaging 11 covid deaths per hour as delta variant, mask debates rage. *Newsweek.* https://www.newsweek.com/florida-averaging-11-covid-deaths-per-hour-delta-variant-mask-debates-rage-1624388

Substance Abuse and Mental Health Services Administration. (2014). *SAMHSA's concept of trauma and guidance for a trauma-informed approach.* https://store.samhsa.gov/system/files/sma14-4884.pdf

Trauma-Informed Care for Children and Families Act. (2017). H.R. 1757, 115th Congress. https://www.govtrack.us/congress/bills/115/hr1757

Turk, J., Soler, M. C., & Ramos, A. M. (2020, October 8). *College and university presidents respond to COVID-19: 2020 fall term survey.* American Council on Education. https://www.acenet.edu/Research-Insights/Pages/Senior-Leaders/College-and-University-Presidents-Respond-to-COVID-19-2020-Fall-Term.aspx

Turner, H. A., & Butler, M. J. (2003). Direct and indirect effects of childhood adversity on depressive symptoms in young adults. *Journal of Youth and Adolescence, 32*(2), 89–103.

U.S. Department of the Interior. (2021, June 23). *Secretary Haaland announces federal Indian boarding school initiative.* https://www.doi.gov/pressreleases/secretary-haaland-announces-federal-indian-boarding-school-initiative

Valentine, B. (2021). It's time to talk about police violence against Latinos. *AL DÍA.* https://aldianews.com/articles/politics/its-time-talk-about-police-violence-against-latinos/64271

van der Kolk, B. (2014). *The body keeps the score: Brain, mind, and body in the healing of trauma.* Penguin Books.

Williams, T. R., Walker, T. L., & Wyatt, W. N. (2021). Conceptualizing racism through a systemic trauma lens: Impacts on Black college students. *Journal of Psychotherapy Integration.* Advance online publication. https://doi.org/10.1037/int0000206

World Health Organization. (2021). *WHO Coronavirus (COVID-19) Dashboard.* https://covid19.who.int/

PART I

Infusing Trauma-Informed Principles

CHAPTER 2

Centering Equity: Trauma-Informed Principles and Feminist Practice

Phyllis Thompson and Heidi Marsh

Trauma-informed care is an approach developed by The Substance Abuse and Mental Health Services Administration (SAMHSA) that was adapted from Harris and Fallot's (2001) foundational work which highlighted five principles as a frame for practice. Building on this research, SAMHSA added a sixth principle (Cultural, Historical, and Gender Issues), drew on insights from the field, and partnered with survivors to become a model for practice that was traditionally employed in clinical service provision. In recent years, K-12 learning environments, particularly those serving marginalized populations, have taken up this work but diverted from a strict use of the principles to social and emotional learning and Maslow's hierarchy of needs (Venet, 2021). Scholars (Carello & Butler, 2014; Carello & Thompson, 2021; Imad, 2020; Karatekin & Ahluwalea, 2016; Oehme et al., 2019) are now considering how employing a trauma-informed approach, if further adapted for teaching and learning, might serve students, faculty, and staff in higher education.

P. Thompson (✉) · H. Marsh
Women's, Gender, and Sexuality Studies, East Tennessee State University, Johnson City, TN, USA
e-mail: thompsop@etsu.edu

H. Marsh
e-mail: marshh@etsu.edu

P. Thompson and J. Carello (eds.), *Trauma-Informed Pedagogies*, https://doi.org/10.1007/978-3-030-92705-9_2

SHIFTING TOWARD EQUITY

A notable shift in the way trauma-informed care was practiced came when Sandra Bloom changed the question we ask from "what's wrong with you?" to "what happened to you?" and challenged us to focus on systems in addition to individuals (Bloom & Sreedhar, 2008).

Even with that shift, as people who practice feminist and critical pedagogies, we have surfaced gaps in our understanding of the relationship between the six principles this framework employs (Safety; Trustworthiness and Transparency; Peer Support; Collaboration and Mutuality; Empowerment, Voice, and Choice; and Cultural, Historical, and Gender Issues). The gaps become particularly apparent when the intersectional analysis we typically put at the center of our work is neglected. We recognize that the representation afforded by that shift matters, but we also call for a new way to demonstrate the interrelatedness of the principles that reflects the anti-oppressive ethos at the heart of trauma-informed practice.

To better grasp the relationship between the principles, we make a feminist shift from a traditional conceptualization of principles as a hierarchy or list to a reconceptualization as a wheel of practice with Principle Six: Cultural, Historical, and Gender Issues at the center. See how this is illustrated in Fig. 2.1.

SAMHSA (2014) identifies Principle Six as the ways in which

> The organization actively moves past cultural stereotypes and biases (e.g. based on race, ethnicity, sexual orientation, age, religion, gender-identity, geography, etc.); offers access to gender responsive services; leverages the healing value of traditional cultural connections; incorporates policies, protocols, and processes that are responsive to the racial, ethnic and cultural needs of individuals served; and recognizes and addresses historical trauma. (p. 11)

Re-visioning the trauma-informed framework as wheel, we see Principle Six as the mechanism that holds the spokes in place, keeps them true (a bicycle term for in balance), and drives the stability of all the other Principles. Metaphorically, Principle Six becomes the lens through which we process and more thoroughly understand each of the other Principles on the way to the goal, which is a liberatory feminist practice where education becomes transformative and "the practice of freedom" (Freire, 1996; hooks, 1994). This lens is crucial to understanding the Principles as well as how to implement them not just in terms of our good intentions but also in terms of the equity impact of our practices. The feminist shift is significant because in bringing Principle Six to the hub of the wheel, we bring intersections of experience to the center of our practice, a reminder centrally located at the core, not edges, of our work that the path will look quite different according to the intersections of the population groups with whom we are working.

The wheel moves us from a linear representation of the Principles to a more dynamic view of practice, mirroring what we know about trauma response

Fig. 2.1 Trauma-informed principles as wheel of practice

and recovery as a non-linear process and enabling us to better respond to our students' needs as well as our own. Visually reconceptualizing our model helps us make this shift in our practice. Once Cultural, Historical, and Gender Issues become the lens through which we view, analyze, and practice the principles, we effectively shift "margin to center" (hooks, 2015) and begin the work needed to create an equity framework for trauma-informed care.

A STARTING POINT: THREE LESSONS

We come to this work as individuals who sought to investigate trauma-informed care and implement it at our university in myriad ways—from changing the narrative about gender-based violence on campus to transforming our academic programs, office spaces, and classrooms to be more trauma-responsive—but found ourselves dysregulated by it because of the gaps we discovered in the practice. Along the way, we learned first-hand three lessons. First, that our work joining conversations on our campus about trauma-informed care exposed the lack of resources available to faculty and staff about how to identify and respond to trauma and crisis; second, the reality that just because one is well-versed in the theory of trauma-informed approaches does not mean one knows how to apply them; and third, that an intersectional feminist approach is needed to ensure an anti-oppressive, equity model for practice.

Crisis turns "normal" on its head; reminds us in our bones that things are not right. COVID-19 has reinforced that message but is not the end of it. These three lessons inform the goal of this chapter, which is to pause to take a close look at the model at the center of our practice—an equity lens.

A GUIDING THEORETICAL FRAMEWORK

Central to this feminist approach is a recognition of two things: (1) the necessity of seeing the body as not only a site where our experience of trauma lives but also as a site of transformation, and (2) the necessity of attending to privilege, power, and positionality in an equity-centered employment of trauma-informed care.

Bessel van der Kolk (2014) describes the way "traumatized people chronically feel unsafe inside their bodies," experience a "gnawing interior discomfort," and "are constantly bombarded by visceral warning signs" (pp. 98–99). Additionally, trauma lives in the body as "chronic back and neck pain, fibromyalgia, migraines, digestive problems, spastic colon/irritable bowel syndrome, chronic fatigue, and some forms of asthma" (van der Kolk, 2014, p. 100).

The work of trauma expert Bruce Perry (2006) helps us

> better understand the nearly one-third of the adult population who bring to their classroom a history of abuse, neglect, developmental chaos, or violence that influences their capacity to learn, as well as those who, in response to stress-inducing pedagogical methods, have acquired cumulative educational trauma leading to fear conditioning. (p. 21)

Thus, the "traumatized person in a state of alarm (for example thinking about an earlier trauma) is less capable of concentrating, more anxious, and more attentive to nonverbal cues such as tone of voice, body posture and facial expressions—and may, in fact, misinterpret such cues because of anxiety induced hypervigilance" (Perry, 2006, p. 24).

In other words, we must understand what neuroscience demonstrates: toxic levels of adversity in childhood changes forever the developing brain and has a physical impact on the student who is now sitting in our Intro to Women's, Gender, and Sexuality Studies class and the department chair speaking up in the dean's meeting. The more adversity experienced in childhood, the greater the changes in the chemical structures of our brains and the more our brains adapt. That adversity could be racism, homophobia, physical abuse, sexual violence, neglect, an incarcerated parent or guardian, alcoholism (Perry, 2006; van der Kolk, 2014). While ACEs and developmental trauma—including -isms—are one source of toxic stress, adults experience toxic stressors and crises that can impair function as well. The adaptation is the "conditioning" Perry warns about. This "hypervigilance" materializes as living in a low level of fear at all times:

> Even after a stressful or traumatic situation has ended, people can continue to react as if the stress or trauma is continuing. They become self-protective; they spend a lot of energy scanning their environment for threats, their bodies act as if they are in a constant state of alarm; their brains are endlessly vigilant, and they may experience a constant baseline feeling of low-level fear, which leaves less space for curiosity, exploration, and learning. (Davidson, 2017, p. 8)

In the classroom or the conference room, the impacts of trauma may present in a variety of ways: "Difficulty focusing, attending, retaining, and recalling; tendency to miss a lot of classes; challenges with emotional regulation; fear of taking risks; anxiety about deadlines, exams, group work, or public speaking; anger, helplessness, or disassociation when stressed; withdrawal and isolation; and involvement in unhealthy relationships" (Hoch et al., 2015). While we all come to our classes or workplaces with stressors, those who show up with toxic levels of stress may, for instance, hear the professor's revision suggestions or the dean's feedback differently than those who are not navigating toxic levels of stress and may have a response that is not in proportion to the suggestion or feedback. There are times as well when we don't blow things out of proportion and the professor's or dean's comments are racist, abusive, or cruel. Either way, if allowed to remain invisible due to our own misassumptions and lack of awareness, these issues go unaddressed and we inadvertently create barriers to student and faculty success that reinforce social shame and stigma for both but also negatively affect retention and graduation rates of increasingly larger proportions of students (Hallett & Crutchfield, 2017, pp. 7–8, 13–16).

Finding regulation through the processing of trauma and the cultivation of meaningful relationships is a path to healing and resilience, and feminist scholars remind us the space where that work happens can also be a site of resistance (hooks, 1994). As resistance, we foreground Anzaldúa's body of the *mestiza* as a figure for the torn, wounded, ruptured lands between Mexico and the United States, which in *Borderlands* she describes "the historical, social, cultural, and linguistic reasons of this dismemberment and dispossession, proposing, at the same time, a healing process, through the developing of a new consciousness" (qtd. in Vallone, 2014, para. 13). That rupture or wound is crystallized, etched, into the body (Bordo, 1997; Scarry, 1985)—not only the pain but also the journey beyond it—and provides a means for recognizing the cultural, historical, gendered body as "theory in the flesh... where the physical realities of our lives—our skin color, the land or concrete we grew up on, our sexual longings—all fuse to create a politic born out of necessity..." (Moraga, 1983, p. 23). Vallone (2014) explains that for Anzaldúa, Moraga, Bambara, and others writing *This Bridge Called My Back: Writings by Radical Women of Color* (1983), the body is a source of pain and healing and, as Suzanne Bost demonstrates, "pain is not simply material evidence of oppression but is also the rhetoric of political mobilization and resistance" (para. 5). This idea underscores Quiros' (2021) "intentional and positive disruption," which she describes as an "opportunity that moves diversity and inclusion work away from the performative while incorporating a trauma-informed approach" (p. xxvii).

   We see an equity-centered trauma-informed framework as a tool to aid in developing a revolutionary pedagogy of feminist resistance, positive disruption, and liberation. Anti-oppressive education—challenging racism, classism, sexism, heterosexism, ageism, and other forms of oppression in schools— requires an anti-oppressive pedagogy that puts disruption, discomfort, and crisis at the center of the learning process. This pedagogy does not, however, center danger or create dangerous, unsafe spaces. It transforms our classrooms, offices, and institutions into sites where we can recognize the impact of trauma, avoid re-traumatization, and build resilience while moving the needle toward justice.

From Margin to Center: Transforming Principle Six

Cultural, Historic, Gender Issues

As feminists we know that people travel different journeys, carry different baggage with them, and come to the table from different physical, geographic, concrete, social, and emotional locations. An intersectional approach to the Principle of Cultural, Historic, and Gender Issues is necessary to think through and address that difference. It provides a frame to identify how overlapping social identities intersect with structures of oppression to understand how power and privilege are obtained and disadvantage is doled out. Such a frame provides a theoretical foundation for constructing an equity model for the practice of trauma-informed care that builds on the transformative power of an intersectional view which makes apparent that historically marginalized subjects are multidimensional and that intersections of race, gender, sexual orientation, age, class, and ability/disability are neither exclusive nor separable. Theorists like Crenshaw (1989, 1991), Hill Collins (2000), Delgado and Stefancic (2001), and Kendi (2019) have changed the way we think about intersections of experience and given us strategies for recognizing our own blinders, tools for shedding them, and a new lens as we embark on an antiracist journey.

Kendi's (2019) re-framing of racist oppression *from* social construct, ignorance, and hate *to* power, impact, and self-interest re-tools us to re-imagine ourselves and the systems within which we live and work—to engage in self-reflection, evaluate classroom pedagogy, assess organizational operations, and revise policy. This means, for instance, folding back the layers of our own racist ideas and oppressive behaviors by proofreading student assignments for the disenfranchising equity impacts hidden within, taking a universalizing and genealogical position (Beauchamp & D'Harligue, 2012) where we see identities as "historical artifacts rather than static identities" (Drabinski, 2014, p. 140) when teaching, resisting a model of tokenism or a "special guest" approach to inclusion (Malatino, 2015), re-scheduling staff meeting times for greater access, and writing policy that drives change, fosters progressive coalitioning, promotes community building, and shifts the culture in dynamic and innovative ways.

This work is necessary for our setting in higher education, a system that thrives on and nurtures hierarchies and has historically excluded marginalized populations. As actors within and representatives of that institution—each with our own complex personal identities and social locations—we must be willing to interrogate our own positions of power as we employ trauma-informed methods. Locating ourselves in relation to the students we serve, the colleagues we share space with, and the institution we are a part of is a critical first step that can then help us transform the principle of Collaboration and Mutuality into the feminist practice of coalition, for example, or can help us reconceptualize the principle of Safety so that it has breadth to address these issues across multiple sectors and identity groups.

SAMHSA's Principle Six gives us a great place to start—it recognizes that there are stereotypes and biases and calls us to "move past" them, it recognizes that our current systems do not meet the needs of people we want to serve and that historical trauma exists. However, we see that there is a difference between moving beyond stereotypes and working to dismantle systems that create barriers to justice and that is what is at the heart of transforming this toward an equity approach.

Principle Six reminds us of both the "Danger of a Single Story" (Adichie, 2009) or the way that stereotypes flatten experience, dispossess a people, perpetuate bias, and rob us of the reparation stories hold and the way that being unwilling to adapt our practices that recognize the complexity of lived experience simply reinforces paradigms of domination and oppression. It calls us to avoid what Keating (2007) identifies as *"status-quo stories*: worldviews and beliefs that normalize and naturalize the existing social system, values, and norms so entirely that they deny the possibility of change" (p. 23) and instead forge new stories that "enable us to question the status quo and transform our existing situations" (p. 29). These "'new' stories informed by connectionist thinking and infused with the recognition of our interrelatedness" (p. 29) cannot only help us be more responsive to the needs of the people we work with but also help us see the connections between oppressions, launching us toward a practice that is both more intersectional and cognizant of the fact that our oppression is tied to that of others (Lorde, 1983).

As we transform Principle Six, our call is to do more than move past a stereotype, a call requiring us to think critically about why the stereotype exists, how we might be complicit in its propagation, and what responsibility we have to disrupt it. An equity approach to Principle Six calls us toward praxis, toward an intentionally intersectional analysis of our pedagogy, policies, assignments, procedures, and to explicitly include other aspects of identity. It also calls us toward a more connectionist way of thinking and being, to a recognition of the simultaneity of lived experience, and to justice.

Equity-Centered Trauma-Informed Principles

Safety

SAMHSA (2014) describes Safety as "the physical setting is safe and interpersonal interactions promote a sense of safety" (p. 11). We consider Safety as the bedrock, the foundational principle to a trauma-informed approach to teaching and learning.

Trauma-informed expert Bruce Perry (2006) explains it this way: as humans we are explorers, and "Optimal learning depends on... a cycle of curiosity, exploration, discovery, practice, and mastery—which leads to pleasure, satisfaction, and the confidence to once again set out and explore" (p. 25). Victories and successes build interest in exploration and greater curiosity. However, "fear, [anxiety, alarm, lack of safety]... kills curiosity and inhibits exploration;" if "people are fearful, they do not learn" (Perry, 2006, p. 25).

The long-term impact of trauma on adults is that they often function in a state of low-level fear: "The major challenge to the educator working with highly stressed or traumatized adults is to furnish the structure, predictability, and sense of safety that can help them begin to feel *safe enough to learn* [emphasis added]" (Perry, 2006, p. 25). The traumatized person must attempt to learn in a state of low-level fear, not optimal for learning, retrieving, or implementing information. Learning cannot compete with the feeling that danger is on the horizon (Perry, 2006). To address this, educators need to create spaces that are predictable and consistent but not rigid. However, recognizing the fear of danger as a trauma response and employing practices to avoid retraumatizing others (and becoming retraumatized ourselves) does not mean that a safe space is one that shies away from challenges. We are charged with cultivating a certain sense of discomfort for our students—to challenge their own status-quo thinking, to ask them to push themselves toward deeper, more critical thought—and as agents of change in our institutions to challenge practices, policies, and procedures that are barriers to justice, so let us not dismiss either. Let us instead recognize that discomfort and the fear of danger are not the same, that the trauma response of fear shuts us down physiologically and psychologically in a way that intellectual discomfort does not. So, while fear is a paralyzing force, our opportunity is to reinterpret what Safety means in such a way that we can value discomfort as a site of rupture, as transformation, as a generative force that moves us toward envisioning and bringing alive "the classroom [as] the most radical space of possibility" hooks (1994, p. 207) writes about.

To create a space that makes room for discomfort as it values safety, an equity lens invites us to ask questions such as ...
Does this class, my policies, and my decisions

- Perpetuate the status quo or move the dial toward cultural change?
- Require students to hide behind hetero-normative constructions of identity or invite them to celebrate their authentic selves?
- Foster true belonging? Is it a shame-free zone? Or is it full of judgement and pressure to fit in or create the "ideal citizen subject" (Sasaki, p. 33)?
- Reduce uncertainty and promote psychological and physical safety?

Application: When we center equity, "safe enough to learn" means that we

- Create comfort agreements in collaboration with students that not only prioritize safe practices but also put into conversation what safety looks like across population groups.
- Make students and ourselves feel safe enough to take off the armor, to brave vulnerability (Brown, 2012, 2018).
- Put wording in our syllabi about inclusion, resources for all, and symbols that identify the class and its instructor as a safe, inclusive, and welcoming space across populations.
- Honor preferred names, avoid deadnaming, invite pronouns but not require them.

Equity approach: A feminist, equity-centered approach recognizes that Safety looks different across intersections of race, ethnicity, gender identity, sexual orientation, ability/disability, size, age, class—and across institutions of higher education—HBCUs, HSIs, CCes, R1s, teaching institutions as well as across classrooms and offices. It asks us to examine how centering equity changes not only our conceptualization of Safety *and* the questions we ask but also our practice.

Trustworthiness and Transparency

According to SAMHSA (2014), in a trauma-informed approach to Trustworthiness and Transparency, "Organizational operations and decisions are conducted with transparency with the goal of building and maintaining trust among clients, family members, among staff, and others involved in the organization" (p. 11). We agree and also recognize that Trustworthiness and

Transparency builds on the groundwork of Safety, puts connections with people first, practices transparency, and includes the willingness to be accountable, do what we say we are going to do, own our mistakes, apologize, and give grace.

Like the perspective-taking critical to Safety, trust building is relational rather than transactional and must be practiced 365 days a year rather than in response to crisis only. Building trust creates safety nets that people can rely on seven days a week. Brené Brown describes "trust as a slow-building, layered process that happens over time" (Brown, 2012, p. 47), a "stacking and layering of small moments" (Brown, 2018, p. 34). She likens the process to that of a marble jar: "Trust is built one marble at a time" (Brown, 2012, p. 49) and is at the center of meaningful, productive relationships.

Creating meaningful relationships within the academy can be challenging, especially as we take a *person-first* approach in a system that is decidedly *institution-first*. Because as professors, staff, and administrators, we represent the institution, it is our responsibility to do the work of building trust with our students and colleagues by being transparent and consistent, but our positions of authority mean that we may seem less trustworthy to historically marginalized individuals who have been traumatized or abused by other systems of authority. So, a part of an equity model of trust building is giving individuals space to feel doubt, making room for skepticism, and tending to the need for self-protection. Not only can our authority as institutional representatives make us seem potentially less trustworthy but so might the privilege afforded by our own personal social locations as well. A feminist model that moves trust building from a transactional (crisis-first model) to relational (person-first model) process asks us to recognize social, cultural, and historical ways that trust might have been violated, to ask ourselves how we are or might have been complicit in that violation of trust, to share in the vulnerability and risk necessary to grow healing relationships, and to be transparent about the ways we must meet our responsibilities to ourselves and to others.

Just as consistency can help us build Safety, it can also help us build Trust as long as it is paired with Transparency. The best way we can be both consistent and transparent is a commitment to feminist praxis—to put our theory into action, to be vulnerable enough to trust others, value their feedback, admit when we get it wrong, and make changes. This is what scholars (Freire, 1996; hooks, 1994) mean when they say that a liberatory pedagogy requires that we not only change our pedagogy but also our practice of that pedagogy. bell hooks (1994) provides as example progressive faculty members whose curricula resist the status quo but whose pedagogical practices do not. The irony is that while their lectures and readings subvert the dominant paradigm, their practices, including their "body posture, tone, word choice, and so on... perpetuate those very hierarchies and biases they are critiquing" (p. 141). It is not only how we describe our pedagogy that matters, it is how we practice it. According to Paulo Freire (1996), praxis is "the reflection and action which truly transform reality" (p. 81). Being consistent in this commitment to praxis does not mean that we respond to every situation in exactly the same way—we must let go of equality if we want to center equity—but instead it means taking the kind of consistent action that is transparent, accountable, and reliable and that over time builds trust.

To build trust, an equity lens invites us to ask questions such as ...
Does this class, my policies, and my decisions

- Cultivate relationships based on consistency in our ability to be curious and compassionate?
- Establish boundaries as a way to maintain relationships, not restrict them?
- Recognize that everyone has equal value but different gifts and strengths?
- Center feminist praxis as a method for affecting change?

Application: When we center equity in building trust and being transparent, we

- Invite authenticity.
- Admit when we make mistakes which may mean changing deadlines on a syllabus or expectations on a course assignment.
- Are willing to confront the privilege we have when building relationships.
- Openly acknowledge the limits of confidentiality in our setting.

Equity approach: A feminist equity-centered approach to Trustworthiness and Transparency means treating people with dignity and respect and as experts in their own experience. It means recognizing that the trust of others must be earned through transparency, accountability, shared vulnerability, and consistent commitment to equity.

Peer Support

For SAMHSA (2014), Peer Support is a "key vehicle for establishing safety, building trust, enhancing collaboration, and utilizing... stories and lived experiences to promote recovery and healing" (p. 11). We view Peer Support as the vehicle for safety and resilience. Peer Support is a flexible approach to building mutual, healing relationships among equals. For SAMHSA, the term "peer" refers to individuals with lived experiences of trauma. This is in the context of service providers who are working with children and adults, as stated above, "to promote recovery and healing." For higher education, the shift from service provision to teaching and learning informs how we understand Peer Support, where it comes from, and how to navigate it.

While Safety and Trust are described as the foundation for healing and resilience, we understand Peer Support to provide fertile ground where that healing can germinate and grow and resilience take root. Peer Support validates the healing potential of reciprocal relationships, empathy, and care and provides a pliable approach to building relationships among people. Those relationships, based on core values and principles and that are voluntary, nonjudgmental, respectful, and reciprocal, cross sectors and ranks and include both peers and authority figures. In other words, Peer Support can emerge from relationships formed between classmates, between students and their teachers, and between employees and their supervisors. As long as the relationship is empathetic, compassionate, and willing to perspective-take, it can be considered Peer Support.

One of the challenges in creating Peer Support networks hinges on the power differentials inherent in the higher education environment, but we know that to be successful and to cultivate relationships based on care, teaching and learning relationships like any "radical pedagogy must insist that everyone's presence is acknowledged. That insistence cannot be simply stated. It must be demonstrated through pedagogical practices. To begin, the professor must genuinely *value* everyone's presence" (hooks, 1994, p. 8). Paulo Freire (1996) explains it this way: "one does not liberate people by alienating them" (p. 60). If education is the "practice of freedom" (1996, p. 61), it is thus because it is a "pedagogy for all people" (1996, p. 36), not only some, and because teacher and student "become jointly responsible for a process in which all grow" (1996, p. 61). At the same time, we must recognize that "many students, especially students of color, may not feel at all "safe" in what appears to be a neutral setting" (hooks, 1994, p. 39). One way to respond to that feeling of unsafety is to acknowledge it.

It's not impossible to both build a community based on care *and* to recognize that it can contain obstacles. Ropers-Huilman (2009) shares four takeaways about power and caring in the feminist classroom: (1) Learning and teaching are dependent on attention to power and caring; (2) power and care are always intertwined; (3) how we learn is often deeply embedded in hidden assumptions; and (4) we should regularly assess our values around power and care while striving to live in them (p. 54). In short, recognizing the tension between power and care can help us shift toward a focus on shared power—not just power as domination but power as what Shrewsbury (1987) calls "energy, capacity, and potential" (p. 8). It is in this tension that we find fertile ground for Peer Support.

To build peer support, an equity lens invites us to ask questions such as ...
Does this class, my policies, and my decisions

- Make space for peer interactions to happen?
- Encourage mentoring?
- Enhance our ability to care for one another across lines of difference?
- Prioritize belonging and nurture relationships?
- Recognize that support is necessary for community building?

Application: When we center equity in creating peer support, we

- Consider the equity impact of meeting times or social activities offered.
- Ask each other "How can I support you?"
- Provide informal opportunities to build connections.
- Lend a helping hand.
- Listen actively.

Equity approach: A feminist approach to Peer Support recognizes that learning environments can be oppressive and obstruct education as the practice of freedom, that can construct obstacles that get in way of learning, teaching, resilience. By understanding the ways in which power informs good intentions and care mitigates the impact of power, Support not only becomes a vehicle for Safety and Trust but also for rebuilding the "master's house" (Lorde 1984, p. 112) with tools that ensure Support across different groups, environments, spaces, ranks, and population groups.

Collaboration and Mutuality

For SAMHSA (2014), when practicing Collaboration and Mutuality,

> Importance is placed on partnering and the leveling of power differences between staff and clients and among organizational staff...demonstrating that healing happens in relationships and in the meaningful sharing of power and decision-making. The organization recognizes that everyone has a role to play in a trauma-informed approach. (p. 11)

We understand Collaboration and Mutuality are best accomplished through the development of coalition.

Collaboration and the power of shared decision-making is a hallmark of feminist practice, but Collaboration and Mutuality are not inherently feminist, trauma-informed, or antiracist unless we are intentional in our methods. While SAMHSA (2014) tells us in the description of the Collaboration and Mutuality principle that "healing happens in relationships" (p. 10), hooks (1994) also reminds us that as we attempt to build relationships with others, "intimacy and care can coexist with domination" (p. 98); therefore, we must critically examine the relationships we are cultivating with our students and peers to ensure the "meaningful sharing of power and decision-making" (SAMHSA, 2014, p. 10) is equity-centered. One of the biggest threats to this process is misconstruing consensus for Collaboration and Mutuality. A feminist, equity-centered model of this principle calls us to resist the status-quo of consensus and to move beyond Collaboration and Mutuality in favor of feminist coalition by finding "connections across difference rather than sameness" (Sasaki, 2002, 45).

As a long called-for practice in feminist communities and one that emerged out of the work by women-of-color (WOC) feminists in the 1970s, 1980s, and 1990s (Alexander, 2006; Combahee River Collective, 1983; hooks, 1994;

Lorde, 1984; Moraga & Anzaldúa, 1983; Reagon, 1983), coalition asks us to value the differences among us when creating partnerships and to embrace the conflict or discomfort that might emerge in our practice. Opposite of the consensus model we so-often find in higher education, coalition demands that we see "difference is that raw and powerful connection from which our personal power is forged" (Lorde, 1984, p. 112). Coalition emerges as an equity-centered practice because the bedrock of coalition is shared power; its presupposition is that everyone's input makes something good or better, not that something is good because we all (theoretically) agree on it.

Practicing coalition invites us to interrogate consensus as a method that tends to erase people, that tends to view power as something to be consolidated rather than shared, and that is often used as a method for avoiding conflict. Consensus makes us feel good at the end of the day because everyone seems happy; coalition does not: "Most of the time you feel threatened to the core, and if you don't, you're not really doing no coalescing" (Reagon, 1983, p. 356). As Reagon (1983) cautions, "Some people will come to a coalition and they rate the success of the coalition on whether or not they feel good when they get there" (p. 359) but coalition is not the place for comfort. It is the place for positive disruption (Quiros, 2021). Coalition is about relationships, especially those formed at the intersections where differences emerge, and making space for conflict as a method of discovery is key for developing those relationships. If "meaningful sharing of power and decision-making" is based on consensus instead of coalition, we must ask "How meaningful is it and for whom?"

To practice Collaboration and Mutuality with an emphasis on coalition, an equity lens invites us to ask questions such as ...
Does this class, my policies, and my decisions

- Incorporate opportunities for feedback and conversation between myself and my co-workers/class colleagues?
- Make space for disagreement, discomfort, and for "both/and" thinking? Disrupt a power differential?
- Develop new ways of doing things?
- Center shared decision-making where everyone's contribution is invited and valued?

Application: When we center equity in building Collaboration and Mutuality, we

- Cultivate difficult conversations instead of shutting them down.
- Create a built-in mechanism for feedback (with careful consideration and revision when needed).
- Invite co-creation of policies and procedures.

- Partner with seemingly unlikely offices or departments across campus on projects where there are shared goals (albeit different visions).

Equity approach: A feminist, equity-centered approach asks us to examine how centering equity changes not only our conceptualization of Collaboration and Mutuality but also the questions we ask as well as our practice. It recognizes that coalition relies on all of the other trauma-informed principles when viewed through the lens of Principle Six; valuing discomfort as we cultivate Safety, utilizing shared vulnerability and Transparency to build Trust, and recognizing that power and care can coexist are all necessary for building coalition.

Empowerment, Voice, and Choice

For SAMHSA (2014), trauma-informed approaches

> ...foster empowerment for staff and clients alike. Organizations understand the importance of power differentials and ways in which clients, historically, have been diminished in voice and choice and are often recipients of coercive treatment. Clients are supported in shared decision-making, choice, and goal setting ... and cultivating self-advocacy skills. (p. 11)

We identify Empowerment, Voice, and Choice as the best way to help our students, colleagues, and selves transform "silence into language and action" (Lorde, 1984, p. 40).

The principles of Collaboration and Mutuality and Empowerment, Voice, and Choice are interconnected—they rely on one another for success and we cannot foster one without the other. As feminists, we have a responsibility to empower ourselves, and we also have a responsibility to empower others, to leverage our platforms to amplify the voices of others as they develop self-advocacy and agency. Recognizing and reinforcing this connection between individuals in the community (classroom, office, department) creates a more feminist practice and moves toward empowerment, for "empowerment is only possible when there is a sense of mutuality" (Shrewsbury, 1987, p. 10).

In the spirit of that interconnected empowerment, we have an obligation to acknowledge that, as Lorde (1984) says, our silence will not protect us (p. 41). Speaking up and speaking out is hard—we "draw the face of [our] own fear—fear of contempt, of censure, or some judgment, or recognition, of challenge, of annihilation"—but in remaining silent we overlook that the "visibility which makes us most vulnerable is that which also is the source of our greatest strength" (Lorde, 1984, p. 42). More than that, sitting in silence does not transform the shit we're dealing with and certainly doesn't make us less afraid (Lorde, 1984). Cultivating a space wherein everyone feels empowered to push through the "tyrannies of silence" (Lorde, 1984, p. 43) means we can work together better, serve each other better, see each other better. It means we can re-vision the assumptions we have used to create what we believe to be equitable spaces and transform them (e.g. assumptions about what people have access to, whether that is time, energy, bandwidth, resources, and/or support).

That re-visioning requires that we come prepared to do the work—to be vulnerable enough to admit we might have gotten something wrong and that we do not have all the answers—a crucial step in moving toward the self-actualization promoting our own well-being which Brown (2012, 2018) demonstrates is key to *Daring Greatly* and brave work and which hooks (1994) argues is necessary for a pedagogy that empowers students (p. 15). Making space for all voices to be heard and respected means that we get "infinitely more feedback because students do feel free to talk—and talk back" (hooks, p. 42), which is their right as members of a classroom community wherein the goal is to disrupt patterns of forced silence and control through feminist, antiracist methods. Furthermore, validating students' feedback is also a step toward helping them develop the self-advocacy skills prioritized in a trauma-informed framework.

To foster Empowerment, Voice, and Choice, an equity lens invites us to ask questions such as …
Does this class, my policies, and my decisions

- Ensure that the "choices" are not coercive choices? (e.g. invitation to name pronouns; offering public and private opportunities)
- Make a space for write-ins?
- Make assumptions about students' or staff's availability for work?
- Recognize that discussions are best when shared?

Application: When we center equity in fostering Empowerment, Voice, and Choice, we

- Invite students to design a choice or alternative that is comparable to the choices already provided.
- Revisit assignment sheets for access issues and find language that provide avenues for choice.
- Create opportunity for everyone to contribute to the conversation by encouraging individual responses.

Equity approach: A feminist, equity-centered approach recognizes that we can start by giving students as many choices as possible, but we must realize that there are choices students envision that we do not. Most importantly, we need to create spaces where they can use their voices without fear of retaliation, *and* we need to be prepared to be vulnerable and embrace the possibility that we got it wrong because sometimes getting it wrong is an important step on the path to getting it right.

Conclusion

SAMHSA's (2014) four assumptions of a trauma-informed approach guide our practice and charge us to *realize* the impact of trauma, *recognize* signs and symptoms of trauma, *respond* by integrating knowledge, and *resist* retraumatization (p. 8). Re-seeing those assumptions through a feminist framework and equity lens broadens our horizons of care, sharpens our practice, and maps the ways in which oppression complicates trauma. Understanding this helps us unravel, resist, and ultimately recover from its effects. To do that healing work, to foster resilience, to realize transformation, and to leverage real change for our students individually, our classrooms more broadly, and higher education as an institution, we must be willing to take these assumptions to heart and enter uncomfortable conversations, take risks, and recognize that the path is "fraught with danger" (Lorde, 1984, p. 42)—the danger of transgressing structures, of dismantling systems, of demanding that we question our own privilege, oppression, and power; of not-knowing, of getting it wrong, and the shame of either. Navigating these dangers during a pandemic but also during crisis at any time is the bridge that carries us and our students toward resilience and transformation.

References

Adichie, C. N. (2009, July). *The danger of a single story* [Video]. TED Conferences. https://www.ted.com/talks/chimamanda_ngozi_adichie_the_danger_of_a_single_story

Alexander, M. J. (2006). *Pedagogies of crossing: Meditations on feminism, sexual politics, memory and the sacred*. Durham. NC: Duke University Press.

Beauchamp, T., & D'Harlingue, B. (2012). Beyond additions and exceptions: The category of transgender and new pedagogical approaches for women's studies. *Feminist Formations, 24*(2), 25–51.

Bloom, S. L., & Sreedhar, S. Y. (2008). The Sanctuary Model of trauma-informed organizational change. *Reclaiming Children and Youth, 17*(3), 48–53.

Bordo, S. (1997/1993). The body and the reproduction of femininity from *Unbearable weight: Feminism, western culture, and the body*. In K. Conboy, N. Medina, & S. Stanbury (Eds.), *Writing on the body: Female embodiment and feminist theory* (pp. 90–110). Columbia University Press.

Bost, S. (2009). *Encarnacion: Illness and body politics in Chicana feminist literature*. Fordham University Press.

Brown, B. (2012). *Daring greatly: how the courage to be vulnerable transforms the way we live, love, parent, and lead*. Penguin Random House.

Brown, B. (2018). *Dare to lead: Brave work, tough conversations, whole hearts*. Penguin Random House.

Carello, J., & Butler, L. D. (2014). Potentially perilous pedagogies: Teaching trauma is not the same as trauma-informed teaching. *Journal of Trauma & Dissociation, 15*(2), 153–168.

Carello, J., & Thompson, P. (2021). *Lessons from the pandemic: Trauma-informed approaches to college, crisis, change*. Palgrave Macmillan.

Collins, P. H. (2000). *Black feminist thought: Knowledge, consciousness, and the politics of empowerment*. Routledge.

Combahee River Collective. (1983). The Combahee River Collective statement. In B. Smith (Ed.), *Home girls: A black feminist anthology* (pp. 272–282). Kitchen Table: Women of Color Press.

Crenshaw, K. (1989). Demarginalizing the intersection of race and sex: A black feminist critique of antidiscrimination doctrine, feminist theory and antiracist politics. *University of Chicago Legal Forum, 1*(8), 139–167. http://chicagounbound.uch icago.edu/uclf/vol1989/iss1/8

Crenshaw, K. (1991). Mapping the margins: Intersectionality, identity politics, and violence against women of color. *Stanford Law Review, 43*(6), 1241–1299. https://doi.org/10.2307/1229039

Davidson, S. (2017). *Trauma-informed practices for postsecondary education: A guide* (p. 8). Education Northwest.

Delgado, R., & Stefancic, J. (2001). *Critical race theory: An introduction*. New York University Press.

Drabinksi, K. (2014). Identity matters: Teaching transgender in the women's studies classroom. *Radical Teacher, 100*, 139–145.

Freire, P. (1996/1970). *Pedagogy of the oppressed*. Penguin.

Hallett, R. E., & Crutchfield, R. (2017). Homelessness and housing insecurity in higher education: A trauma-informed approach to research, policy, and practice. *ASHE Higher Education Report, 43*(6), 7–8, 13–16.

Harris, M., & Fallot, R. D. (Eds.). (2001). *Using trauma theory to design service systems*. Jossey-Bass.

Hoch, A., Stewart, D., Webb, K., & Wyandt-Hiebert, M.A. (2015). *Trauma-informed care on a college campus. Slides from a presentation at the annual meeting of the American College Health Association*. https://www.acha.org/documents/Pro grams_Services/webhandouts_2015/TH2-322_Hoch.pdf

hooks, b. (1994). *Teaching to transgress: Education as the practice of freedom*. Routledge.

hooks, b. (2015). *Feminist theory: From margin to center*. Routledge.

Imad, M. (2020, June 3). Leveraging the neuroscience of now. *Inside Higher Ed*. https://www.insidehighered.com/advice/2020/06/03/seven-recomm endations-helping-students-thrive-times-trauma

Karatekin, C., & Ahluwalea, R. (2016). Effects of adverse childhood experience, stress, and social support on the health of college students. *Journal of Interpersonal Violence, 1*(23), 1–23.

Keating, A. L. (2007). *Teaching transformation: Transcultural classroom dialogues*. Palgrave Macmillan.

Kendi, I. X. (2019). *How to be an antiracist*. Peguin Random House Publishing Group.

Kumashiro, K. K. (2001). *Troubling intersections of race and sexuality: Queer students of color and anti-oppressive education*. Rowman & Littlefield Publishers.

Lorde, A. (1984). *Sister outsider: Essays and speeches*. Crossing Press.

Lorde, A. (1983). There is no hierarchy of oppressions. *Bulletin: Homophobia and Education*. Council on Interracial Books for Children.

Malatino, H. (2015). Pedagogies of becoming: Trans inclusivity and the crafting of being. *TSQ, 2*(3), 395–410.

Moraga, C. (1983). Entering the lives of others: Theory in the flesh. In *This bridge called my back: Writings by radical women of color* (2nd ed., p. 23). Kitchen Table: Women of Color Press.

Moraga, C., & Anzaldúa, G. E. (Eds.). (1983). *This bridge called my back: Writings by radical women of color* (2nd ed.). Kitchen Table: Women of Color Press.

Oehme, K., Perko, A., Clark, J., Ray, E. C., Arpan, L., & Bradley, L. (2019). A trauma-informed approach to building college students' resilience. *Journal of Evidence Informed Social Work, 16*(1), 93–107.

Perry, B. (2006). Fear and learning: Trauma-related factors in the adult education process. *New Directions for Adult and Continuing Education, 2006*(110), 21–27. https://doi.org/10.1002/ace.215

Quiros, L. (2021). Introduction: Locating myself in purpose. In *Incorporating diversity and inclusion into trauma-informed social work: Transformational leadership* (pp. xvi–xxx). Routledge.

Reagon, B. (1983). Coalition politics: Turning the century. In B. Smith (Ed.), *Home girls: A black feminist anthology* (pp. 356–368). Kitchen Table: Women of Color Press.

Ropers-Huilman, R. (2009). Scholarship on the other side: Power and caring in feminist education. In R. Crabtree, D. Sapp, & A. Licona (Eds.), *Feminist pedagogy: Looking back to move forward* (pp. 40–58). Johns Hopkins University Press.

Sasaki B. (2002). Toward a pedagogy of coalition. In A. A. Macdonald & S. Sánchez-Casal (Eds.), *Twenty-first-century feminist classrooms* (pp. 31–57). Palgrave Macmillan.

Scarry, E. (1985). *The body in pain: The making and unmaking of the world.* Oxford University Press.

Shrewsbury, C. (1987). What is feminist pedagogy? *Women's Studies Quarterly, 15*(3/4), 6–14. http://www.jstor.org/stable/40003432

Substance Abuse and Mental Health Services Administration (SAMHSA). (2014). *SAMHSA's concept of trauma and guidance for a trauma-informed approach.* HHS Publication No. (SMA) 14-4884. Substance Abuse and Mental Health Services Administration.

Vallone, M. (2014). The wound as bridge: The path of *conocimiento* in Gloria Anzaldúa's work. *E-rea. Revue Electronique D'Etudes Sur Le Monde Anglophone, 12*(1). https://doi.org/10.4000/erea.4135

van der Kolk, B. (2014). *The body keeps the score: Brain, mind, and body in the healing of trauma.* Penguin Books.

Venet, A. S. (2021). *Equity-centered trauma-informed education.* W. W. Norton.

CHAPTER 3

Our Brains, Emotions, and Learning: Eight Principles of Trauma-Informed Teaching

Mays Imad

In his book *Descartes Error*, neurologist Antonio Damasio (2008) argues that humans do not make decisions by relying exclusively on the rational or reason-oriented parts of their brain. So how do we make decisions? How does the brain process information? What is the purpose of the brain? And, what do the answers to these questions have to do with student learning?

Our brains are composed of over 86 billion neurons—the building blocks of our nervous system (Lent et al., 2011). When I teach about the brain, I often compare the number of neurons to the stars in the Milky Way (Voytek, 2013) in order to highlight its enormity and potential. Neurons receive, process, and transmit (or communicate) information to other neurons. The site of connections is called the *synapse*, and the number of synapses per neuron varies, with some neurons having around 1,000 synapses while others can form up to 200,000 synapses. The synapse plays a critical role in every thought we conjure, every feeling we experience, and every action we take. Interconnections between neurons form circuits, or neural networks, where cognitive processes—including learning and memory—occur. Learning and memory are biological phenomena arising from physical changes in neural connections (Takeuchi et al., 2013). As teachers, we aspire for our students to learn and retain information to help them apply in the world. Thus, part of being effective teachers necessitates that we understand how we can optimize

M. Imad (✉)
Connecticut College, New London, CT, USA
e-mail: mimad@conncoll.edu

P. Thompson and J. Carello (eds.), *Trauma-Informed Pedagogies*,
https://doi.org/10.1007/978-3-030-92705-9_3

our classroom environment so the neural connection can readily change for learning to happen (Owens & Tanner, 2017).

Understanding how the brain works in the context of education holds the potential for improving our teaching practices and our students' learning. Recent research suggests that certain underlying beliefs about learning are based largely on misconceptions, over-interpretations, and misunderstandings. We are, to quote a recent international report, subject to "neuromyths" about how learning works (Betts et al., 2019). As the report makes clear, the prevalence of online information—and misinformation—means that the need for educators "to ensure that their practice is scientifically grounded and evidence-based" is now more critical than ever (p. 4).

One of the misconceptions about how we learn concerns the role of emotions in our thinking. Emotions are seen as irrational and unruly, something that is connected with being or acting "out of control." From that position comes the idea that by making decisions without emotions, purely rationally, we become more sophisticated thinkers and decision-makers. As a consequence of these misconceptions, we often expect students, and ourselves, to leave emotions outside the classroom. But we know from the work of many neuroscientists that it is impossible to separate emotions from reasoning, on both neurological and even biochemical level. Mary Helen Immordino-Yang (2016), among others, argues for the affective nature of learning, stating that it is "neurobiologically impossible to think about things deeply or to remember things about which you have had no emotion" (3:46). She goes on to say: "Our emotions, our relationships, and our cultural experiences in the social world literally organize and shape the development of brain networks that allow us to learn. ...[E]motional experiences in the learning environment are influencing what we are capable of doing."

Thus, to foster an optimal learning environment, we need to pay attention to emotions and how the learner is feeling, as learning cannot take place in the absence of emotion. The brain chooses which aspects of the outside perceptions to pay attention to, and how to make decisions about them, by assigning emotional importance to them. The teacher's voice, the lesson, the exercises, the homework—all of these are external perceptions that brain has to process, and it will process them according to the emotional state they produce. In other words, Learning can be enhanced or stifled depending on a learner's emotional state (Damasio, 2000; Immordino-Yang & Damasio, 2007). I cannot overstate the central role of emotions in the human experience, especially how emotions affect the learning experience.

MAKING SENSE OF THE WORLD AROUND US

The key to defining any experience lies within the nervous system and how the brain interprets the information it receives. The brain is concerned with our survivability and thus is continually processing sensory information to make sense of our surrounding environment. When sensory information comes into the brain, the brain "asks" the questions: "Is this safe or not? Do I engage or not?" The brain scans the information for potential threats to make predictions related to safety or danger, reward or punishment.

The brain is divided into three distinct regions organized into a hierarchy (Maclean & Kral, 1973; Shanker & Barker, 2017):

- Brainstem = our non-rational brain, concerned with our survival state– Am I safe? Am I breathing?
- Limbic System = our irrational-brain, concerned with our emotional state–Am I loved? Do I matter?
- Neocortex = our rational-brain, concerned with our reflective state–What can I learn from this?

While each of these regions is considered to be responsible for a specific category of brain activities, the brain gives rise to our human experience by integrating information from *all* regions. In other words, each brain region is communicating and integrating information from the other regions. To think optimally, we need to have harmony between our rational, irrational, and non-rational states—or the cortex, limbic system, and brainstem.

Porges (2011) provides helpful explanations of this process: Information about our surroundings is taken in through our senses and sent to the brainstem and limbic system in order first to determine if a situation is safe or unsafe. If the brain perceives danger, regardless of whether it is real or simply perceived, a limbic structure called the hypothalamus triggers the release of hormones which activates the stress response, which is our automatic fight or flight reaction—a ubiquitous instinctive physiological response to a harmful or threatening situation.

Our fight or flight response is mediated by the autonomic nervous system and involves a number of automatic, regulatory functions designed to ready one to resist or to run away. Our autonomic nervous system is divided into the sympathetic nervous system and the parasympathetic nervous system which are activated in times of arousal or recovery, respectively. The sympathetic nervous system acts like a gas pedal to provide the body with the energy it needs to respond to perceived dangers. The parasympathetic nervous system acts like a brake to allow the body to rest and recover or replenish the energy it spent while in the sympathetic-activated fight or flight state. Our fight or flight response is triggered when we feel a strong emotion such as fear or anger or excitement.

TRAUMA AND LEARNING

Emotions are reactions the body has to certain stimuli; for example, when our brains perceive a threat and are afraid, our heart rate increases. Emotional reactions occur automatically and unconsciously and are mediated by the limbic structure—the amygdala. The amygdala receives input before the prefrontal cortex (a structure that deals with reasoning and decision-making) and does a cost-benefit analysis to determine whether it is safe to "engage" the rational state and send information to the prefrontal cortex. If the amygdala senses a threat, it will engage the irrational state, sending information to the brainstem to activate the fight or flight response. Thus, our emotions and how we feel act as a gateway to our thinking and learning by providing "the bridge between rational [prefrontal cortex] and nonrational processes [brainstem and limbic structures]" (Damasio, 2008). For the brain to engage and learn, one must first feel safe, hence the expression, "Maslow before Bloom": Our basic needs come before our ability to learn (Berger, 2020).

Homeostasis is our body's ability to maintain a stable internal environment in the face of changing external conditions (Cooper, 2008). Stress is anything that threatens our homeostasis and requires us to burn energy in order to stay within a physiological range to keep us alive (Shanker, 2017). Stress is an essential part of our physiology. Some stress is useful, for example, the type of stress we experience when we feel aroused and excited, but there is no threat or fear. Good stress allows for productive problem solving as well as motivation. We recover from good stress when the stimulus is gone and resume our resting state. We recover. When stress persists, energy expenditure continues, and recovery or replenishment of energy becomes increasingly difficult. In this case, the stress takes a heavy toll and feels inescapable and overwhelming. As noted by Stuart Shanker in his book *Reframed: Self-Reg for a Just Society* (2020), when such stress reaches a point where we can no longer cope our "limbic brakes" kick in, and the amygdala acts as a "veto center" to silence our prefrontal cortex, preventing our rational thinking. In other words, when the brain senses pressure from a particular situation beyond its capacity to cope this causes a disconnect or disharmony between our rational and irrational states, disrupting the balance between emotions and thinking.

Stress can go from being tolerable to toxic or traumatic. When the brain is under the influence of traumatic stress it releases stress hormones which alter the brain's learning circuitry (Bangasser & Shors, 2010). When the brain experiences toxic or traumatic stress, it is experiencing fear. Our limbic system becomes overactive. In fact, we become stuck in the limbic zone, and in order to engage our prefrontal cortex for learning, we need to get out of that zone. To do so, we need to feel less scared and more relaxed. We cannot merely use reasoning techniques to "snap out" of our limbic zone. This is where the lens of trauma-informed teaching and learning comes in.

The trauma-informed lens is about providing an environment that can help relax the brain to begin to shift back to homeostasis between the prefrontal cortex and the limbic system, a balance between the rational and emotional brains.

Trauma-Informed Teaching and Learning

A philosophy of trauma-informed instruction teaches us that we, as educators, need to be aware of the prevalence and impact of trauma, and that our students' past and present experiences affect their well-being and, therefore, their ability to learn. Additionally, we need to recognize trauma not only in our students but also in ourselves. A calm nervous system is able to calm another nervous system. If we are experiencing trauma and are not aware of it and bring it with us to our classes, our students will pick it up. As one of my Sunday school mentors used to say, "You cannot give what you do not have." In other words, the more able we are to regulate our emotions and calm our nervous system down, the easier it will be to impart self-regulation and sense of calm to our students. We need to respond to our students' trauma or toxic stress by being intentional in promoting safe environments that cultivate connectedness and empowerment.

A trauma-informed pedagogy enables us to recognize that amid a crisis, our students may have a difficult time completing basic tasks they usually would, including keeping track of the slightest changes in our classes, making decisions about their learning, being motivated to study or even to show up, prioritizing assignments, engaging with classmates or the subject, managing their time, or simply not quitting. Before we consider some important basic principles, I want to address a few misconceptions about trauma-informed pedagogy.

First, trauma-informed instruction does not require that the educator has training in social work or clinical psychology. We are not diagnosing or treating our students. Second, trauma-informed pedagogy does not mean that there are no rules, and students can "get away" with anything. On the contrary, we want to give students structures they can follow because the brain likes structure. Third, trauma-informed pedagogy is not synonymous with lowered academic expectations. To the contrary, using the lens of trauma-informed education allows us to challenge students academically to reach their full potential. Fourth, using a trauma-informed lens not only benefits students who experienced trauma and students from under-resourced schools, but also improves the learning of all students. Students who come from a privileged background can and do experience trauma, directly or indirectly. We are social and empathetic beings. Witnessing the trauma of others can trigger trauma in ourselves, especially when we feel helpless. When a privileged student witnesses the suffering of other less privileged students and does not know how or if they can help, that can trigger their own brain to (subconsciously) question if they matter or if they are safe. Teaching through a trauma-informed lens was warranted before the pandemic and will continue to be relevant after the pandemic.

Trauma-Informed Teaching in Practice

The following eight trauma-informed principles, based in part on the Substance Abuse & Mental Health Services Administration (SAMHSA) guidelines (SAMHSA, 2014), evolved from a previous article I published (Imad, 2020a). There are three preconditions for every student to learn and thrive in life: Feeling safe; Making meaningful connections; and Having resources. Each of the following can guide our work as we help our students feel safe and connected so they can learn well. An important component of trauma-informed teaching is getting to know your students as individuals. Therefore, it is crucial that we do not approach these practices as a list of do's and don'ts. Instead, we can apply guiding principles to design a trauma-sensitive classroom—virtual or in-person.

1. Work to ensure your students' emotional, cognitive, physical, and interpersonal safety. To be grounded in and sensitive to your students' experiences of trauma, you have to recognize trauma in yourself and engage in regulating your emotional response and sense of safety. It is vital that you the educator feel safe, empowered, and connected. Remember that you matter—and your work matters for your students and your community (Imad, 2020c). You can begin by asking yourself what makes you feel safe when you are most vulnerable, when you have lost a sense of agency, or when you face uncertainty?

Then, you can ask your students what safety means to them and how you can help them feel safe in your course. Remind your students that they are more than a number and that they each matter to you. Perhaps you can ask for anonymous feedback from your students by asking them: "Is there anything I am doing (or not doing) that is making you or your classmates feel excluded or not welcomed?" Make sure you are ready to read and address the feedback your students will share with you.

2. Foster trustworthiness and transparency through connection and communication among students. A focus on creating and maintaining trust can mitigate the adverse effects of uncertainty and help students find meaning and connections in your class. Being authentic is saying what you mean and meaning what you say, and it is integral to fostering trust. That also means articulating how each assignment relates to the course's objectives and spelling out the steps required to complete each assignment and how it will be evaluated. For more information, see Transparency in Learning and Teaching (TiLT), an approach to teaching that focuses on sharing with students *how* and *why* they learn course content in particular ways (Winkelmes, 2010). TiLT helps students understand the relevance of course materials and assignments and, therefore, promotes student success. When we spell out our whys to our students, it sends two messages: we know what we are doing, and we are not trying to "trick" the students. Students will begin to view our transparency as a reason to trust us, which will reinforce their safety.

Being transparent helps foster trust and increase predictability which, in turn, help mitigate the impact of ongoing uncertainty. Offer a clear roadmap for the short, the medium, and the long term for how to succeed in your course. Consider, sending a weekly email outlining what you will cover this week, this month, and during the semester. The more successful students will be at predicting the structure of the course, the more their brain will feel in control and at ease.

We can help ensure safety by being transparent and intentional in our communication and by reducing uncertainty (see Fig. 3.1).

3. Intentionally facilitate peer support and mutual self-help in your courses. At the heart of trauma is a break in relationships and part of healing from trauma involves fostering healing and meaningful relationships. Facilitate relationship building among your students by encouraging them to check up on each other if they are comfortable doing so. In our virtual classrooms and amid ongoing trauma caused by the pandemic, focusing on peer support is an integral way to foster community. Remind your students that the connections we make not only help others but benefit and help themselves as well. Consider creating group online or in-class activities to encourage peers to complete assignments that share a common goal or purpose. Suggesting smaller low-stakes group assignments might be less stressful than big group projects. Alternatively, allow students to encounter new material, teach, learn, and submit work together that might have been more difficult to accomplish

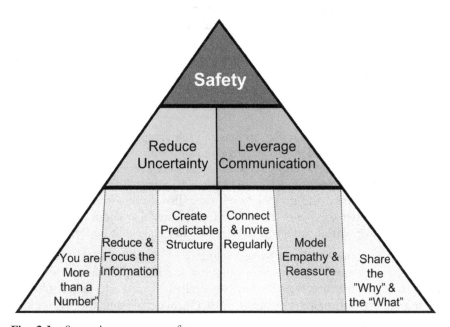

Fig. 3.1 Strategies to ensure safety

alone. Google docs is one of the many technology tools that provide a space where students can collaborate simultaneously in a single document.

4. Promote collaboration and mutuality by sharing power and decision-making with your students. One way to tackle the stress induced by ongoing uncertainty is giving an opposing force—a sense of control. This means that you are intentionally increasing students' perception of control by helping them feel that they are involved in decision-making. Ask your students what matters to them now, what they want to learn, and what interests them. Take notes and incorporate their ideas into your communications and instructions. This practice will send the message to your students that they contribute to the class, that they are part of the learning journey.

In *Teaching Community: A Pedagogy of Hope* bell hooks (2003) argues for us to "make the classroom a place that is life-sustaining and mind-expanding, a place of liberating mutuality where teacher and student together work in partnership" (p. xv). Create a setting conducive to collaboration and the sharing of power between you and your students by, for example, asking them for their opinions or inviting them to co-create assignments. Collect ongoing feedback and incorporate their feedback and ideas into your teaching.

5. Empower voice and choice by identifying and helping build on student strengths. Students who have experienced or are experiencing traumatic stress also experience losing their sense of control or agency. Empower students to have a voice and to advocate for themselves or their classmates. For example, create a short survey and ask your students: "How can I help you feel empowered to learn?" Have students practice advocating for themselves and their needs. Applaud their advocacy by listening and working with students to address what they have communicated. Sometimes, it is easier to listen and we learn by advocating for others. Encourage your students to advocate for their classmates. For example, offer students extra credit at the end of a quiz or an exam where you ask them to advocate for one of their classmates to receive extra credit.

Part of self-advocacy is self-awareness and self-acceptance. We can help validate and normalize students' concerns by talking with them about fear, stress, anxiety, and trauma. You may also want to consider keeping an online journal to document how you handle anxiety when it comes up. This practice will destigmatize anxiety and normalize self-care. Invite your students to keep a diary as an outlet to express how they feel. If they feel comfortable sharing what they have written with your class, offer that space and opportunity.

6. Empower your students to self-regulate by teaching them about the biology of learning. The research on stress and its impact on learning tells us that we can learn to regulate how we deal with stress and hence mitigate its impact on our ability to engage with the materials and learn (Hopkins et al., 2017; McCoy, 2013). After participating in a webinar on how to mitigate stress and anxiety I presented for Pima Community College students in

April 2020, students reached out to me to thank me for helping them understand that the feelings they were experiencing, such as a lack of motivation and energy, were driven by their physiology and that "binge-watching" Netflix was not indicative that they are lazy or do not care about school (Imad, 2020b). They were dealing with traumatic stress and trying to cope. When we help our students understand the relationships between stress, emotions, and cognition, we enable them to have self-compassion when they struggle to connect with the course materials. Consider, for example, inviting your students to keep a learning diary and pay attention to when their learning is interrupted or challenged and what they can do about it.

7. Impart to your students the importance of having a sense of purpose. The brain needs a goal to carry out a planned action. When we experience trauma, it can be challenging to see the big picture; we lose touch with our "why." We want to remind the brain why what we do matters. Intentionally convey to your students your passion for teaching and why you continue to teach even in the midst of a pandemic. Invite your students to identify or reconnect with their own sense of purpose and why being aware of their goals is important to inform and reaffirm their existence. If goals have gone away, invite your students to replace them with short-term achievable goals. Remind them of their longer-term goals by asking them to remember why they are pursuing an education. Foster metacognition by helping students understand how their work contributes to the course and the world outside of the classroom.

8. Pay attention to cultural, historical, and gender issues. Arguably, the most important trauma-informed principle is to ensure that we don't make assumptions about our students but to see them as unique individuals. When we treat our students as if they are all the same, we overlook differences that are integral to their identities—inadvertently erasing some of their singularity. When we marginalize someone's identity, it can be very stressful on the brain. Work to ensure that classroom content reflects the diversity of students in the classroom. For example, provide students opportunities to share a tradition from their family or culture where they draw strength, wisdom, and healing.

Consider how racialized communities may experience trauma more severely due to ongoing oppression, racism, and the impact of intergenerational traumas (Degruy, 2018; Yehuda & Lehrner, 2018). It is crucial that we do not make assumptions about cultures or groups of people, and instead of justifying a mistake, we address its impact and learn from it. Such work also requires a commitment to learning about our own implicit biases and how to ensure that we preemptively mitigate their impact. What are your own default framework and biases related to teaching?

Additionally, commit to learning about and implementing accessible, equitable teaching, and learning strategies. Consider an assessment framework that is less focused on grading and more focused on improving learning (Blum & Kohn, 2020; Inoue, 2015). Alternatively, assessments encourage and celebrate students' creativity (Su, 2020). Finally, go beyond yourself and your classroom. Consider your discipline. What are the practices that have been disregarded or excluded historically in our discipline?

Forging an optimal learning environment necessitates that the learner feels safe and connected which means that we educators must help resolve any uncertainty regarding their belonging in our classes or in the academy. When we make assumption about a student or their background, that can be wounding and stressful on the brain because it sends a message to their brain that we do not see them. We can help build meaningful connections with and among our students by helping them become part of a purposeful community (see Fig. 3.2).

Trauma-informed teaching, while it may be a current buzzword, is not merely a passing trend. It is about wanting to disrupt an educational system that too often prioritizes knowing over caring, competition over collaboration, intervention over prevention, and individuals over community. It is about restoration and healing past injustices at the individual and community levels. It is about revealing our humanity to our students to show them that we are on their side, that we have their back, that we see them and they matter. We build connections with them and empower them to cultivate connections with themselves, their classmates, and the course contents. Trauma-informed education is about centering students' well-being and providing them with the tools to learn, to succeed, and to thrive.

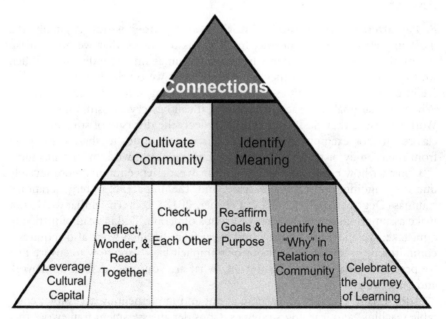

Fig. 3.2 Strategies to build connections

We often think of emotional health as an issue only for counselors or psychologists, but well-being is a higher education issue. It is a societal issue. It is a human rights issue. When practiced consistently, intentionally, and purposively, trauma-informed education benefits everybody, including teachers. Through our collective hope, empathy, love, and brilliance, we can transform higher education to attend to the well-being of the person as a whole.

References

Auerbach, R. P., Mortier, P., Bruffaerts, R., Alonso, J., Benjet, C., Cuijpers, P., Demyttenaere, K., Ebert, D. D., Green, J. G., Hasking, P., Murray, E., Nock, M. K., Pinder-Amaker, S., Sampson, N. A., Stein, D. J., Vilagut, G., Zaslavsky, A. M., & Kessler, R. C. (2018). WHO World Mental Health Surveys International College Student Project: Prevalence and distribution of mental disorders. *Journal of Abnormal Psychology, 127*(7), 623–638. https://doi.org/10.1037/abn0000362

Bangasser, D. A., & Shors, T. J. (2010). Critical brain circuits at the intersection between stress and learning. *Neuroscience & Biobehavioral Reviews, 34*(8), 1223–1233. https://doi.org/10.1016/j.neubiorev.2010.02.002

Berger, T. (2020, September 23). *How to Maslow before Bloom, all day long*. Edutopia. https://www.edutopia.org/article/how-maslow-bloom-all-day-long

Betts, K., Miller, M., Tokuhama-Espinosa, T., Shewokis, P., Anderson, A., Borja, C., & Dekker, S. (2019, September). *International Report: Neuromyths and Evidence-Based Practices in Higher Education*. OLC. https://onlinelearningconsort ium.org/read/international-report-neuromyths-and-evidence-based-practices-in-hig her-education/

Blum, S. D., & Kohn, A. (2020). *Ungrading: Why rating students undermines learning (and what to do instead)*. West Virginia University Press.

Cooper, S. J. (2008). From Claude Bernard to Walter Cannon. Emergence of the concept of homeostasis. *Appetite, 51*(3), 419–427. https://doi.org/10.1016/j. appet.2008.06.005

Damasio, A. (2008). *Descartes' error : Emotion, reason and the human brain*. Random House.

Damasio, A. (2010). *What role do emotions play in consciousness?* [Video]. YouTube. https://www.youtube.com/watch?v=Aw2yaozi0Gg&t=130s

Damasio, A. R. (2000). *The feeling of what happens: Body, emotion and the making of consciousness*. Mariner Books.

Degruy Leary, J. (2018). *Post traumatic slave syndrome: America's legacy of enduring injury and healing*. Joy Degruy Publications Inc.

hooks, b. (2003). *Teaching community: A pedagogy of hope*. Routledge.

Hopkins, S., Shanker, S., & Leslie, R. (2017). Self-regulation, Self-control, and the practice of Shanker Self-Reg®. *Reframed: A Journal of Self-Reg, 1*(1), 58–75. https://doi.org/10.26690/sri20170705

Imad, M. (2020a, June 3). Seven recommendations for helping students thrive in times of trauma. *Inside Higher Ed*. https://www.insidehighered.com/advice/2020/ 06/03/seven-recommendations-helping-students-thrive-times-trauma

Imad, M. (2020b). *How to recognize & mitigate stress & traumatic experiences (for students)* [Video]. YouTube. https://www.youtube.com/watch?v=DiJPj4NbTsw& list=PLC2n3iK0UxHm0TdyzmpRrEijEgvjNLVId&index=3&t=4s

Imad, M. (2020c, November 24). *Dear faculty: "Keep walking."* Insidehighered.com. https://www.insidehighered.com/advice/2020/11/24/advice-how-fac ulty-can-keep-going-and-find-clarity-and-resolve-during-challenging

Immordino-Yang, M. H. (2016). *American Educational Research Association Ed-Talk: Learning with an emotional brain* [Video]. YouTube. https://www.youtube.com/ watch?v=DEeo350WQrs

Immordino-Yang, M. H., & Damasio, A. (2007). We feel, therefore we learn: The relevance of affective and social neuroscience to education. *Mind, Brain, and Education, 1*(1), 3–10. https://doi.org/10.1111/j.1751-228x.2007.00004.x

Inoue, A. B. (2015). *Antiracist writing assessment ecologies: Teaching and assessing writing for a socially just future.* https://wac.colostate.edu/docs/books/inoue/eco logies.pdf

Lent, R., Azevedo, F. A. C., Andrade-Moraes, C. H., & Pinto, A. V. O. (2011). How many neurons do you have? Some dogmas of quantitative neuroscience under revision. *European Journal of Neuroscience, 35*(1), 1–9. https://doi.org/10.1111/ j.1460-9568.2011.07923.x

Maclean, P. D., & Kral, V. A. (1973). *A triune concept of the brain and behaviour.* University Of Toronto Press.

McCoy, D. C. (2013). Early violence exposure and self-regulatory development: A bioecological systems perspective. *Human Development, 56*(4), 254–273. https:// doi.org/10.1159/000353217

Owens, M. T., & Tanner, K. D. (2017). Teaching as brain changing: Exploring connections between neuroscience and innovative teaching. *CBE: Life Sciences Education, 16*(2), fe2. https://doi.org/10.1187/cbe.17-01-0005

Porges, S. W. (2011). *The polyvagal theory: Neurophysiological foundations of emotions, attachment, communication, and self-regulation.* Norton.

Scaer, R., Wilkes, R., & Vartuli, C. (2010). *Trauma interview with Robert Scaer, MD.* https://media.thrivingnow.com/audio/Scaer-Trauma.pdf

Shanker, S. (2017, March 10). Why is my child so mentally lazy? *Psychology Today.* https://www.psychologytoday.com/us/blog/self-reg/201703/why-is-my-child-so-mentally-lazy

Shanker, S. (2020). *Reframed: Self-reg for a just society.* University Of Toronto Press.

Shanker, S., & Barker, T. (2017). *Self-reg: How to help your child (and you) break the stress cycle and successfully engage with life.* Penguin Books.

Su, F. (2020, April 27). *7 Exam questions for a pandemic (or any other time).* https:// www.francissu.com/post/7-exam-questions-for-a-pandemic-or-any-other-time

Substance Abuse and Mental Health Services Administration. SAMHSA's Concept of Trauma and Guidance for a Trauma-Informed Approach. HHS Publication No. (SMA) 14-4884. Substance Abuse and Mental Health Services Administration, 2014. https://ncsacw.samhsa.gov/userfiles/files/SAMHSA_Trauma.pdf

Takeuchi, T., Duszkiewicz, A. J., & Morris, R. G. M. (2013). The synaptic plasticity and memory hypothesis: Encoding, storage and persistence. *Philosophical Transactions of the Royal Society B: Biological Sciences, 369*(1633), 20130288–20130288. https://doi.org/10.1098/rstb.2013.0288

van der Kolk, B. A. (2005). Developmental trauma disorder: Toward a rational diagnosis for children with complex trauma histories. *Psychiatric Annals, 35*(5), 401–408. https://doi.org/10.3928/00485713-20050501-06

van der Kolk, B. A. (2015). *The body keeps the score: Brain, mind, and body in the healing of trauma*. Penguin Books.

Voytek, B. (2013, May 20). Are there really as many neurons in the human brain as stars in the Milky Way? *Scitable, Nature Education*. https://www.nature.com/scitable/blog/brain-metrics/are_there_really_as_many/

Winkelmes, M.-A. (2010). *Transparency in learning and teaching in higher education*. Tilthighered.com. https://tilthighered.com/abouttilt

Yehuda, R., & Lehrner, A. (2018). Intergenerational transmission of trauma effects: Putative role of epigenetic mechanisms. *World Psychiatry, 17*(3), 243–257. https://doi.org/10.1002/wps.20568

Fostering a Spirit of Collaboration by Sharing Power with Students About Course Decisions

Matthea Marquart, Katherine Seibel, Nicole Wong,
and Nykchasia S. Scott

In Spring 2020, Matthea, Nicole, and Katherine jointly taught an online course on Fundraising and Development with the Columbia University School of Social Work's Online Campus. Matthea was the Instructor, Katherine was the Associate (a role that's similar to a teaching assistant and focuses on supporting the academic quality of the course), Nicole was the Live Support Specialist (a role that's similar to a virtual event producer and focuses on supporting the technical quality of the live class sessions), and Nykchasia was a student in the course.

Our spring semester online course began in March 2020, with our first-class session on March 10. The next day, the World Health Organization declared COVID-19 a pandemic (World Health Organization, 2020), and the next week was spring break. Columbia University, which is located in New York City, had already been taking steps to protect student safety, such as moving

M. Marquart (✉) · K. Seibel · N. Wong · N. S. Scott
Columbia University, New York, NY, USA
e-mail: msm2002@columbia.edu

K. Seibel
e-mail: kns2147@columbia.edu

N. Wong
e-mail: nkw2111@columbia.edu

N. S. Scott
e-mail: nss2174@columbia.edu

© The Author(s), under exclusive license to Springer Nature Switzerland AG 2022
P. Thompson and J. Carello (eds.), *Trauma-Informed Pedagogies*,
https://doi.org/10.1007/978-3-030-92705-9_4

49

residential courses online, but our course was already online, with our students located across the United States.

The instructional team implemented trauma-informed teaching strategies in response to the changing circumstances in the world, which were having significant impact on all of us and which had the potential to contribute to increased experiences of trauma (Báez et al., 2020; Báez & Marquart, 2020; Carello, 2019; Carello & Butler, 2015). Trauma-informed teaching recognizes that past and ongoing trauma can impact current student success and employs strategies to foster a supportive environment and reduce barriers to learning (Carello & Butler, 2015). An example is sharing power with students through collaboration and choice about course decisions (Marquart & Verdooner, 2019; Marquart et al., 2019).

Course Origin and Content

Students advocated for this elective offering, which was originally not included in the Spring 2020 online schedule of classes, but was offered on the residential campus. In response to a perceived curricular gap, five online students had appealed for a skills-based, professional development course on fundraising and development specific to the social work sector. They joined forces to advocate for this course based on their individual career aspirations, and the instructional team created an updated fundraising course that aimed to prepare students for those career goals. These updates included weaving themes of social work ethics and power, race, privilege, and oppression into the curriculum, while also modernizing the topics and updating the readings to include a higher percentage of material written by authors of color. The instructional team also shared the course syllabus with students prior to the start of the semester to solicit feedback from the cohort regarding course content, which established a conversation between the instructional team and students about the design of the course.

The creation of this course was noteworthy because of the way students came together as a cohort to support each others' aspirations and also because it would not have been implemented without the physical, emotional, social, and academic respect given by their instructional team. It also built on past Columbia School of Social Work (CSSW) student advocacy and the School's ongoing commitment to address power, race, privilege, and oppression throughout CSSW's curriculum.

This course was a final semester elective for students in the management and leadership track of Columbia's Master of Science in Social Work program, and the course fits into an overall curriculum that includes program planning and evaluation, human resources management, financial management, and macro community practice. The seven-week course entailed weekly synchronous online class sessions in Adobe Connect and assignments in our learning management system, Canvas. The assignments included discussion forums, a student presentation on current issues in fundraising, and a final group project which was organized around weekly themes.

COMMUNITY AGREEMENTS

The instructional team introduced the first week of class and set the foundation for the semester by collaborating with students to create community agreements to foster empowerment, voice, and choice in a trauma-informed approach to the course. At CSSW, online classroom community agreements are established collaboratively with students as a living document that reflects the class's collective ongoing vision for how the community will convene in order to create a supportive and effective learning space. Building community agreements in virtual spaces sets the tone and groundwork for the ways in which we all operate (National Equity Project, 2008). This is a normal part of all online courses at Columbia's School of Social Work. The cohort studying Social Enterprise Administration already had a cohesive rapport which made the conversation about developing community agreements straightforward, intimate, and impactful. While this process can take longer with students who aren't as familiar with each other, as well as in larger groups, the students brought forth concise agreements that honored wellness, educational experience, and personal capacity. It seemed as though the level of intentionality in establishing the community agreements was already built in the framework of the course because of the previous advocacy efforts and cohort experience. As a result, the students' sense of community came before the first live session.

To create the community agreements for this specific course during the first class, the instructional team asked students to share the agreements they wanted for the course by typing into the chat. Next, the instructional team copied and pasted the students' suggested agreements onto a shared virtual note pod, and then discussed and edited together with the students until our community had our agreements. This was a living document that we revisited each week after our guest speakers' presentations, as part of the transition into our regular class time. During one of our early class sessions at the start of the pandemic, the students decided to add the agreement, "Forgive each other; we're all going through a lot right now." Our community agreement process was critical in thinking about a trauma-informed approach to the class.

The following were our class' community agreements, applicable for any other semester, including the final agreement that we added because of the pandemic:

- Be accepting of ideas and allowing them to draw out without judgment
- Be accepting of pace
- Divert from the outlined lecture if needed to delve into a particular area
- Be patient as we're building this collective language around fundraising and development
- Work through audio & connection issues

- Self-care and humility—step away as needed
- Forgive each other; we're all going through a lot right now.

During the first class, the instructional team also talked through the flow of the course with the students in order to structure the course content to create an optimal educational experience and meet the students' learning goals and needs. This level of engagement empowered the students to take an active role in the direction of their learning. This process was an act of sharing power among all participating to promote a harmonious flow of the course.

GUEST SPEAKERS

During weeks two through six, guest speakers had been scheduled to share a breadth of expertise in fundraising from a variety of fields and to provide students opportunities for networking with experienced professionals. After the pandemic began, prior to the second class session in a weekly prep meeting, the instructional team discussed together whether to cancel the speakers in order to simplify the course, but ultimately decided to keep the guest speakers given the tight timeline of the course; we felt that learning from multiple speakers would help our students retain the information long-term despite the stress, and we thought that the career benefits of networking might be even more important for students graduating during a pandemic. The eight speakers included nonprofit leaders, fundraising professionals, a marketing expert, and leaders of charitable foundations. The guest speakers brought forth a real-time analysis of pandemic-related changes to their organizations while presenting a level of vulnerability that was appreciated. Many guest speakers were adjusting to the beginning of the pandemic and the changes accompanying COVID-19, and it was helpful to hear their thinking; this process made it feel as if we were taking part in a think tank about how to fundraise during the pandemic. Although the students were not involved in the decision to keep the guest speakers, after the course, many of the students reported that hearing from speakers throughout the course was an important part of their learning and networking.

COURSE GRADING

The pandemic-related policy change that most affected our course came with the University's announcement on March 20, 2020, that all spring semester courses would be graded pass/fail (Bollinger, 2020). This policy impact freed the instructional team to make significant changes to our course assignments and grading policies mid-semester, in collaboration with each other and with the students. Because the University moved to Pass/Fail grading for the semester, and because of a prediction that students would need accommodations to support their learning during the pandemic, the instructional team updated course grading, modified the final assignment, and increased overall support for students. These changes in particular demonstrated a prioritization of the trauma-informed teaching principle of physical, emotional, social, and academic respect.

Updated Grading Policy

To measure students' progress on the course objectives, in a normal year the instructional team would ordinarily administer weekly assessments, including discussion forum assignments and student presentations. Because of the University's shift to pass/fall grading for the semester and a sharp increase in collective stress, the team's proposal for the students included making some assignments optional, giving the students choices, and turning most assignments into complete/incomplete grading rather than grading with a points-based rubric. From the instructional team perspective, the students seemed to greet this proposal with relief; from a student perspective, it was a relief knowing that the instructional team cared for the students' total well-being and gauged capacity while sticking to the learning objectives. Our class discussion about the proposed updated course grading was a negotiation not based on percentage breakdowns but on intentional reflection about the course. Students expressed that the instructional team's trauma-informed lens fostered compassion and empathy in the course design. Figure 4.1 compares the original version of the grading policy with the proposed updates for discussion.

The instructional team opened the discussion about grading changes by talking about the context for making changes, the fact that students had chosen this course and wanted to learn the content, and the proposed changes to the grading. The instructional team framed this discussion by stating that every student will be treated with respect in this course and in the future, regardless of their grades and that the grades are intended to support learning by providing feedback on coursework, but are not a measure of anyone's worth as a human being.

Some of the students had not yet heard the University's announcement about the transition to pass-fail grading for the semester, so this included a discussion of this new policy and its implications, and space for students to process this. The students were receptive to the proposed grading change strategies and agreed to most of them, and the bulk of the discussion was around how to modify the final assignment. Students actively participated in the discussion via webcam, microphone, or in the typed chat, and expressed a lot of empathy for each other and everyone's changing situations. Afterward, students unanimously voted to accept the changes discussed. The discussion became a session of strategic planning and design thinking about sharing power and responsibility for course decisions. The members of the class balanced individual student learning goals while still maintaining academic integrity and rigor. For example, from the students' perspective,

Comparison of Grading Policy Proposals and Agreed-Upon Updates

Grading Policy - Original Version	Proposed Updates to Discuss	Agreed-Upon Updates
Attendance & class participation - 30%	Grading complete/incomplete, rather graded on a rubric	Students agreed to proposal
Discussion Forums - 30%	Choose any 4 of the 8; the rest are optional; Grading complete/incomplete	Students agreed to proposal
Presentation on a current issue in fundraising - 5%	Optional; Full credit for doing this; Exemption and full credit if you choose not to do this	Students agreed to proposal
Final group project - 35%	Let's discuss what's feasible & what will meet your goals for this course	Do either a written proposal or a pitch presentation (your choice), either individually or in a group (your choice)

Fig. 4.1 Comparison of grading policy proposals and agreed-upon updates

weekly engagement in discussion forums felt taxing while meaningful engagement on select posts still met our objectives and ability to bring forth critical analysis on various fundraising topics. These mid-semester changes reflected the instructors' commitment to defining the journey with consideration to students' capacity in a global pandemic.

The Final Assignment: Modifications and Student Feedback

The final assignment was originally a group project made up of several steps that culminated in a final paper and short class presentation. When the instructional team discussed the assignment with the class, students shared that everyone's hectic schedules made group projects difficult for the final assignment, particularly with students located in different time zones, and that individual projects would be more feasible. They also asked to eliminate some of the steps, such as submitting an early draft of the assignment for feedback, and to change the culminating assignment into a choice of either writing a paper or doing a longer presentation. The instructional team had originally created these steps to support student time management and scaffold the assignment into smaller steps with ongoing feedback, but it ended up being more supportive to simplify the assignment due to the emerging pandemic, concurrent crises, related impacts on the students' availability, and unprecedented stress levels. Because the COVID-19 pandemic necessitated certain assignments becoming optional, the final assignment carried more weight in assessing progress, as did the students' self-assessments on their progress toward mastery of each objective. Figure 4.2 describes the changes made to the original final assignment.

As part of the final assignment discussion, the instructional team pointed out that the students had all chosen this course topic and had specific professional goals in mind for the course. The instructional team asked how to meet student goals and maintain high standards, while also accommodating student needs during the tumultuous semester. The instructional team also shared the

Original Final Assignment Compared to Adjusted Final Assignment

Original Final Assignment	Adjusted Final Assignment
Group Project	Group OR Individual Project
Part 1: Group Contract	Deleted Completely
Part 2: First Draft	Deleted Completely
Part 3: Final Written Proposal	Final Written Proposal OR Pitch Presentation
Part 4: Pitch Presentation	Final Written Proposal OR Pitch Presentation
Optional extra credit: Meet with the Writing Center and submit the "session record"	Optional extra credit still offered
Grading: 100 points using rubric	Grading: 100 points using same rubric

Fig. 4.2 Original final assignment compared to adjusted final assignment

logic behind the original course design, which was intended to scaffold the assignment for the students in a supportive way, and discussed how to make changes to the assignment that removed some of the scaffolding without increasing stress. In this process, the instructional team reminded students about points they made when advocating for the course, including the skills they wanted to learn and also the value of keeping the integrity of the course. As we made decisions about what to cut, we considered as a group how to reduce stress without taking away from learning outcomes or the acquisition of skills the students originally wanted to gain from the course.

The discussion included consideration of whether to make the assignment rubric requirements less time-intensive for all involved, by letting students complete some of the assignment rubric components instead of all of them. Despite omitting some of the scaffolding steps, the cohort recognized the need to complete all original rubric requirements to ensure that the course objectives were met. Ultimately, the instructional team made all of the changes the students requested. During the final class, the instructional team also gave students a choice about whether their final presentation would be recorded.

STUDENT SUPPORTS

As mentioned earlier, we added a community agreement about giving each other grace during a global pandemic. This was an agreement that became embedded into the course framework. For example, if a student was late to class, their attendance was counted as complete, instead of losing a point for tardiness. If a student needed to step away to take care of a child or other unexpected need, there was no penalty to the participation grade. When one of CSSW's students, Susan Chuang, passed away from complications due to Covid-19, we held a moment of silence in class (Columbia University School of Social Work, 2020).

Being mindful of the unprecedented levels of stress and anxiety, the instructional team structured the course at a pace that allowed for smooth saturation. For example, the instructional team planned fewer breakout group activities and built-in cushions for sections of class that could be skipped if the class wanted to spend more time on an earlier part of class.

The instructional team took to heart "come as you are" as an expectation. For example, before the lecture, the instructional team did a presentation summarizing the readings to remind students of the key points. We also gave students time and choice to either briefly process their experience of the pandemic in class or opt to take their minds off of it by focusing on course content instead. For example, we used the "Check-in choice" activity from CSSW's webinar on trauma-informed teaching (Báez & Marquart, 2020) which lets students decide what they want to share during quick class check-ins; students could choose to share one thing that had brought them hope, one thing that had been difficult, one act of kindness they had seen or done, or one tasty snack they had eaten recently; the choice to respond to each prompt could change week to week. That brought in a sense of excitement, as we never knew what someone was going to share each week.

An additional support in the framework was facilitated by Katherine and Nicole, members of the instructional team. They both sent weekly announcements that included a combination of an affirming tone, encouraging language, and reminders for the upcoming class. Below are excerpts from weekly announcements to demonstrate their language and tone when supporting students:

- "I hope you each are well and healthy as you move into your final week of classes! Congratulations on all your hard work throughout this program, and this semester in particular, there is so much to be proud of."
- "And, of course, we have final presentations and paper discussions tomorrow! Remember that you will be on camera for your presentation/discussion as well as for our final class selfie!"
- "It was so wonderful to see you all the other night and hear about how you all are doing."
- "Please let me know if you have any questions! I hope you all have a lovely week and continue to stay well and safe."

As the course was heading to conclusion, the instructional team dedicated time to highlight the students' strengths and accomplishments, and affirm their resilience through adversity and global uncertainty. The second-to-last class included a design session to discuss what would be the most meaningful way to close out the course. Finally, in celebration of the final class, everyone participated in a group selfie via webcam and a reveal of the class quilt visual, a collection of images students and instructional team members emailed ahead of time that related to their experiences during the course (Counselman et al., 2018), which students verbalized during this activity.

STUDENT PERSPECTIVE

After the course ended, grades were submitted, and students had graduated, the instructional team invited the students to share their perspectives. One student became a co-author of this chapter and another student generously offered additional feedback to include.

Co-author Nykchasia S. Scott (CSSW '20) shared one final reflection, "The instructional team's ability to lead mindfully affirmed and honored the whole-person while exuding the humility that social work values. The collaborative process our instructional team modeled allowed all participants to share power in the direction of the course. The changes allowed the course to feel manageable and more enjoyable during a crisis. No matter what had happened previously or what would be coming after, I was able to be fully present and looked forward to engaging in the course because of how devoted the instructional team was in making it a supportive, brave space to learn."

Emilia Autin-Hefner (CSSW '20) shared, "The trauma-informed and collaborative process in redesigning the course left me feeling empowered to reach my educational goals. Despite the uncertainty of the world, I felt that the teaching team truly heard our needs as students."

INSTRUCTIONAL TEAM PERSPECTIVES

After the course ended, the instructional team reflected on the updates to the course in response to the pandemic, focusing heavily on how we applied the trauma-informed principle of collaborating and sharing power with students around course decisions, as well as how we implemented other trauma-informed principles, especially support and connection; empowerment, voice, and choice; and resilience, growth, & change. In an educational environment at a school of social work where social justice, transparency, and equity are so valued, the team found it refreshing to reflect and practice those values in the course. The team also agreed that the collaborative decision-making process supported students' engagement and empowerment in an already stressful and challenging time, and ultimately allowed the teaching team to receive invaluable input on how best to meet student goals and course objectives while making accommodations for challenges. It was evident that the students were experts on what would work best for them, and therefore discussing course changes with students made the course stronger. These changes provided students with options and choices, as a mechanism to give the students some element of control back, in a time when so much was out of our control.

Another common thread among the instructional team was a deep appreciation for each other's compassion, flexibility, and collaboration. Deeply parallel to the intentions for students, the cohesion and care among the instructional team amplified the importance of living and breathing values that align with the values and ethics of social work.

RECOMMENDATIONS

We hope that the lessons learned from this experience are applicable to other educators who want to partner with students and get class feedback on course content. In response to the COVID-19 pandemic, we noticed that our instructional team and students alike worked to be adaptive and to persevere in the face of uncertainty, adversity, and change. If the teaching team were to do this again, we might leave out assignments that we had made optional to possibly increase engagement in other areas because, understandably, no one did a presentation we had made optional. We also recognize some of the limitations to the strategies we employed if used in different contexts; for example, courses with a high enrollment of students or courses implemented asynchronously could present both different obstacles and strengths. The following recommendations are based on strategies that were helpful to navigate the significant course transitions and change.

- Prioritize equity and access relating to student learning needs during the course transitions. For example, when a student didn't have a strong internet connection to access the course site, the instructional team emailed that week's readings. Students were also allowed to choose whether or not to be on camera especially in consideration of internet connection challenges.
- Set the foundation of the course with community agreements and revisit the community agreements each class session to allow for the agreements to be a working document, easily adaptable, and responsive to changing needs.
- Keep lines of communication open through the change; this included allowing time for discussion to process change and proactively reaching out to students during the implementation through gentle reminders in class and via email.
- Employ trauma-informed strategies in consideration of our current environment; these strategies were used in class session outlines and major assignments.
- Maintain flexibility in making changes to major assignments by seeking feedback from students and each teaching team member. Invite students into the decision-making process and lean into making changes to assignments and the syllabus, while still maintaining learning objectives and course goals.
- Incorporate guest speakers to support student engagement with the material in a tangible way and to build networking and connections especially within the context of the pandemic.
- Embody tenets of mindfulness, self-awareness, and ethics as stewards of the course.
- Prioritize students' well-being, safety, and health to embody the social work core values of respecting the dignity and worth of the person as well as recognizing the importance of human relationships. While there is always an inherent power dynamic between an instructional team and students, it was important to shift communication and engagement with students to ensure that they felt that they were individuals surviving a pandemic first and students receiving grades second.

Acknowledgements The authors would like to thank Angelie Singla, Betty Newborn, Brian Anderson, Chung Wong, Doug Bitonti Stewart, Emilia Autin-Hefner, Erin Boss, Gary Scott, Hee Joo No, Janice Carello, Joan Cole Duffel, Johanna Creswell Báez, Jordan Posamentier, Julie Fisher Cummings, Kalyn Mattis, Khaled Yousfi, Kristin Garay, Laurel Hitchcock, Lauren Lee, Lauri Harrison, Leslie Newborn, Leta Obertacz,

Marty Englisher, Matthew D'Eredita, Phyllis Thompson, Rebecca Y. Chung, Robert Wong, Rubi Solis, Veterans Alternative, Wayne Marquart, and Whitney Humphrey.

References

Báez, J. C., Marquart, M., Garay, K., & Chung, R. (2020). *Trauma-informed teaching and learning online: Principles & practices during a global health crisis.* https://doi.org/10.7916/d8-gc9d-na95

Báez, J. C., & Marquart, M. (2020, March 24). *Webinar #2: Trauma-informed teaching & learning (TITL) online (Adobe Connect version)* [webinar]. Columbia School of Social Work Online Campus. https://doi.org/10.7916/d8-8z2a-ae81

Bollinger, L. (2020, March 20). Update on course instruction and university commencement. *COVID-19 Resource Guide for the Columbia Community.* https://covid19.columbia.edu/news/update-course-instruction-and-university-commencement

Carello, J. (2019). Examples of trauma-informed teaching and learning in college classrooms. *Trauma-Informed Teaching & Learning.* https://traumainformedteaching.blog/resources/

Carello, J., & Butler, L. D. (2015). Practicing what we teach: Trauma-informed educational practice. *Journal of Teaching in Social Work, 35*(3), 262–278. https://doi.org/10.1080/08841233.2015.1030059

Columbia University School of Social Work. (2020, April 7). In Honor of CSSW Student Susan Chuang. *Columbia University School of Social Work Communications Office.* https://socialwork.columbia.edu/news/in-honor-of-msw-student-susan-chuang/

Counselman Carpenter, B., Garay, K., & Spriggs, S. (2018, December). *Termination Quilt* [online presentation]. Columbia University School of Social Work Online Campus Faculty Development Session Lighting Round Teaching and Learning Showcase.

National Equity Project. (2008). *Developing Community Agreements.* https://www.nationalequityproject.org/tools/developing-community-agreements

Marquart, M., Creswell Báez, J., & Garay, K. (2019, August 21 and 22). *Intensive workshop on power, trauma and grading* [workshop]. Columbia University School of Social Work. https://doi.org/10.7916/d8-4fh7-zm92

Marquart, M., Seibel, K., & Wong, N. (2020, June 8). Fostering a spirit of collaboration with Social Work Students during the COVID-19 Pandemic. *Teaching and Learning in Social Work.* https://www.laureliversonhitchcock.org/2020/06/08/fostering-a-spirit-of-collaboration-with-social-work-students-during-the-covid-19-pandemic/

Marquart, M., & Verdooner, E. (2019, June 16). Sharing power with students by seeking their input on a grading rubric. *Teaching & Learning in Social Work.* https://www.laureliversonhitchcock.org/2019/06/19/sharing-power-with-students-by-seeking-their-input-on-a-grading-rubric/

Substance Abuse and Mental Health Services Administration. (2014). *SAMHSA's concept of trauma and guidance for a trauma-informed approach.* https://ncsacw.samhsa.gov/userfiles/files/SAMHSA_Trauma.pdf

World Health Organization. (2020, March 11). *WHO Director-General's opening remarks at the media briefing on COVID-19 - 11 March 2020.* https://www.who.int/dg/speeches/detail/who-director-general-s-opening-remarks-at-the-media-briefing-on-covid-19---11-march-2020

PART II

Trauma-Informed Teaching Across the Curriculum

CHAPTER 5

The Trauma of Privilege and Privileged Trauma in Tertiary Music Classrooms

John D. Perkins

During classroom discussions about cultural traumas, retraumatization and secondary trauma may occur. I have previously investigated (Perkins, 2021) different stressful-to-traumatic reactions from Black, Indigenous, People of Color (BIPOC) and White students. Due to a long North American history with African American and Indigenous oppression that presently continues, I feel compelled to emphasize the need for White educators to critically consider their engagement with BIPOC students, especially in primarily White institutions. Though I wish to avoid shifting the emphasis toward Whiteness, the two vignettes I provide below highlight an ongoing presence of ignorance, disengagement, pushback, and obfuscation demonstrated by White, privileged students. These difficult matters must be addressed. White privilege is corrosive, inflicts greater psychic wounds on survivors of racial trauma, and ultimately hinders the project of critical education.

In this chapter, I explore Britzman's (2009) view that narcissism and the loss of certitude result in a resistant, privileged ignorance (Garrett & Seagall, 2013) but constitute a form of student engagement. I suggest two simultaneous goals for educators: (1) educators must "contain" critical conversations (Berlak, 2004) from slipping away from honest engagement; and (2) while doing so, the "contained," or perhaps focused, space should be built as a place where students can make "mistakes" and feel loved during the process

J. D. Perkins (✉)
Butler University, Indianapolis, IN, USA
e-mail: jdperkin@butler.edu

P. Thompson and J. Carello (eds.), *Trauma-Informed Pedagogies*,
https://doi.org/10.1007/978-3-030-92705-9_5

(Allen & Rosatto, 2009; Applebaum, 2017). Such a framework may develop into an ongoing practice that honors self and other (LaCapra, 2004), rather than resulting in fixed notions of failure and success. The practice of noticing one's own feelings and those of others may draw students and educators to pose better questions about self and other. Digging deeper, this chapter will connect power and emotion, specifically how power manifests in the world (critical theory), coupled with an understanding of emotional transference (LaCapra, 2004) or how strong emotions operate between people. If students are given opportunities to reflect upon how their emotions engage with others, critical pedagogy may have a chance to sustain students, particularly minoritized students, in future situations. Therefore, I argue that culturally sustaining pedagogy (Paris & Alim, 2017) needs emotional practice to help survivors from being further traumatized and privileged students from creating trauma or feeling secondary trauma by hearing traumatic narratives.

Because these practices are not only for choral educators but also for educators who use artistic artifacts (music, novels, film, etc....), I draw on Frank (2010) and Gardner et al. (2021). As critical storytellers, they help me reconceptualize artistic artifacts as stories in order to open trauma-informed and emotionally hopeful spaces for critical dialogues.

The vignettes below demonstrate how students in higher education emotionally depart from each other during such discourse. Drawing on these two vignettes, the chapter shows how educators can use critical pedagogies to re-map discursive spaces into transformative ones.

Vignette 1

In the fall semester of 2020, I embarked on a partnership with a Brazilian choral conductor, Martha,[1] who was keen on her student-singers learning about power and privilege, specifically because many grew up in *favelas* (impoverished urban communities). At the time, at least two cultural traumas weighed on both choirs: The horror of George Floyd's murder (felt in Brazil as well as North America) and the global pandemic. Having embarked on research surrounding trauma-informed care and traumatic responses in the classroom, my colleague and I hoped that by employing some of these lenses and techniques, such as body scanning (Menakem, 2017), and discussing the implications of stress and trauma (Carello & Butler, 2014), we might facilitate a space where both groups grew their understanding of critical knowledge and used it as a tool for dialogue.

The choirs met via video conference for nine weeks on Friday afternoons. Differences between access and effort were noticeable. The North American students had access to campus internet, computers, and, often, multiple devices from which they could participate. The Brazilian students had phones, though had to travel for sometimes 30–45 min to reach secure internet

---

[1] The name "Martha" is a pseudonym.

hotspots. Some were dealing with food and electricity insecurity. Many had to work. This information was made known to the North American students, though not emphasized during mutual conferencing times since Martha felt that her students might feel ashamed of their economic situation.

During our planning, Martha and I expected that group video conferencing and translation could be issues to overcome but assumed that both groups, given the opportunity for cross-cultural exchange, would work to overcome these challenges. We attempted to build trust with fun team-building activities and provided opportunities for small groups to exchange ideas about their musical experiences, what they prioritized in their music education, and how their experiences in the pandemic were similar or different. They co-composed music in an effort to make music outside of the large videoconferencing space. Students shared music they frequently listened to, collected pictures from their local environment and related both to curricular themes. These artifacts were intended to spur dialogue. As video conference fatigue and individual pandemic stress waned on during the nine-week encounter, the North American students engaged less and less. The Brazilian students mostly maintained their attendance, with a few dropping out.

Following the curricular experience, I spoke to the Brazilian cohort who expressed dissatisfaction with their American counterparts. Though they had made an effort to meet and discuss the topics presented, the North American students would often not participate and would meet them with silence, muted screens, and an overall lack of engagement in the group projects. Some Brazilians left the cohort because they found it more necessary to earn income and others admitted that they felt alone in their effort. Some North American students who I spoke with also felt ashamed that many of their colleagues did not take it seriously and uncharacteristically disengaged when they entered a space with the Brazilian cohort. Others did not notice.

Vignette 2

During choral rehearsals for my university's annual Black History Month concert, I found it appropriate to contextualize Joel Thompson's *The Seven Last Words of the Unarmed* (2015) with two, eighty-minute dialogues. In the work, Thompson sets to music the last words of Black men who were unjustly murdered by armed guards and police. Before the dialogue began, a student visited my dean's office with "real honest concerns" after which the dean met with me to share the student's worry that we, a predominately White choir, would be coopting Black experience with our performance. During our first dialogue, the same White student reiterated his position, became red in the face and fought back tears. The Black students offered a more critical insight and shared how they had been racially targeted on our campus by the campus police. Some White students acknowledged how Thompson's music and their Black colleagues' experiences tied together, yet the two days of dialogue seemed to dwell on the White students' fear of being implicated as "incorrect" or not thoughtful. At the performance, we shared these fears as well as the ways in which the students were able to consider the educational impact of Thompson's gripping work. The student who spoke with the dean removed himself from that performance (Perkins, 2021).

Whether intentional or not, the conversation never stayed focused on Black lives. It shifted to White interpretation and even Black collegial coddling of White interpretation. By the end of the performance, many students still seemed divided over the issue.

CRITICAL DIALOGUE AND TRAUMATIC WITNESSING IN THE CHORAL SPACE

Researchers have found that singers experience increases (between 40 and 80%) in their oxytocin (hormone that encourages empathy and trust) levels (Kreutz, 2014) and decreases (up to 30%) in cortisol (stress-inducing hormones) levels following a choral rehearsal (Beck et al., 2000). One should not wonder why dialogue, especially concerning cultural traumas, are largely avoided in choral spaces. Conversations about cultural traumas, such as slavery or genocide, constitute "difficult knowledge" which can be "terrorizing to students and teachers" (Britzman, 1998, p. 2), yet are necessary as educators present a full reality of human existence. Ensemble directors often package and deliver the message of a musical work without allowing students to explore their "relationship with it" (Garrett, 2011, p. 337). Similar to many academic disciplines, due to the choral field's convention of a one-way dialogue from the director, students do not come to expect dialogue—a meeting point of identities. Oftentimes, if the space is opened up for dialogue, a lack of critical theory in choral curricula leaves the choral educator unable to make sense of the complexities of identity and power.

Secondary traumatization may occur without educators' knowing it (Zubriggen, 2011). For privileged students in the general fields of education, often privileged by their White ethnicity and/or family's income, learning about difficult knowledge can be shocking, like a "slap" (Zembylas et al., 2014, p. 310). Though this "slap" might be a crucial form of witnessing another's trauma, the brain's amygdala region can fire up trauma responses such as fight, flight, or freeze. The amygdala can partially or fully block the frontal cortex, the brain's rational processing area (van der Kolk, 1994). Zembylas' (2014) mention of a "slap" is not metaphorical. He aptly situates the body into a sudden feeling rather than the mind into a rational process.

The educator must pay close attention to the moment where identities meet, which is where students can experience fear of not being heard or a terror of implicating themselves in another's trauma (Britzman, 2009). Even partially feeling another's trauma is a type of witnessing, by which curriculum and pedagogy can be both a "window" and a "mirror" (Style, 1988)— a glimpse into the identities of others and, simultaneously, a reflection of one's identity. If the traumatized student, or a student who affiliates with a cultural trauma, looks for an empathetic witness and does not find one, the entire learning process can become one of survival, rather than rational and empathic dialogue. Though a moral imperative exists to prioritize the realities of those affected by historical racism and poverty (and all minoritized people), for instance, the privileged witness may still recede into a stance of non-participation, for fear of implicating themselves in or identifying with survivors of trauma and cultural traumas.

Fear of Loss

"[T]he difficulty resides not in the content but rather in the learner's relationship with it...We remind our student teachers that they are not teaching content, that they are teaching students *about* content" (author's emphasis, Garrett, 2011, p. 337).

Through his work on trauma research, LaCapra (2004) defines transference as "one's implication in the other or the object of study with the tendency to repeat in one's own discourse or practice tendencies active in, or projected into, the other or object" (p. 74).[2] Privilege has survived not only by overt protestations of privilege and engrained invisibility taught to privileged people but also by the covert side-stepping of the "task at hand" when discussing, for instance, issues of race and poverty. For this reason, Zembylas et al. (2014) wonder, "How do feelings of 'disgust' towards the 'other' (e.g., migrant), often concealed under false claims of empathy and caring, objectify and sentimentalise the other? How do claims of empathy and caring in fact perpetuate privileged irresponsibility and social inequalities?" (p. 201). Garrett (2011) refers to these privileged emotional movements as "re-routing" away from not only difficult knowledge and the students' "relationship with it" (p. 337) but also an emotional movement away from minoritized students. Not only do obvious slurs need to be addressed but more concerning are students' coopting of social justice concepts to subtly disengage a conversation due to privileged discomfort. Privileged silence also "projects into the other" (LaCapra, p. 74) without words. Privilege protects a critical understanding of transference—"one's implication in the other" (Garrett, 2011, p. 337)—however, it is more easily understood by the minoritized "other" who struggles under oppressive discourses.

For example, in a study on a secondary education course, Garrett (2011) shares how a student side-stepped away from a conversation on race by speaking about oppression in more generalizable, more "agreeable," terms.

Lynne: "I guess [race could be made] more of a general statement. Like the government doesn't seem to care about us. Or, the government is acting ineptly

---

[2] Within a position of privilege, I mention "other" as those who are minoritized or survivors of trauma, however, these instances are not limited to general notions of "self" and "other".

and people are dying because of their mistakes. I think that would have been a valid point of view." (Author) Notice that Lynne's recommendation for how to make a more constructive argument is to remove race altogether. Race is made silent; it is removed from the statement. (p. 340)

Certainly, Lynne demonstrates a privilege of not wanting/needing to address race. Why, however, is avoidance being employed, in her case and in the case of some of the students in the vignettes above? Perhaps the fear of losing that which was not previously known to be lost implicates privileged identities in the lives of minoritized others. For instance, if a White student suddenly realizes that a question they posed to a BIPOC student was harmful, they most often perceive their action as a "failure" on their part, resulting in a fear of losing one's status or even friendship. Britzman (2009) locates this fear within a type of narcissism that depends on certainty. North American culture, however, rewards certitude by recounting decisive, unflappable social and professional "success" stories. In the case of critical dialogue, certitude may rest on ignorance, and a privilege to remain silent in the face of uncertain trauma. Perhaps students have been trained to "master" education due to educators "banking" and assessing information without deep inquiry (Freire, 1970). If something as complex as racial understanding cannot be mastered by studying alone and must be experienced through dialogue and the sharing of identities, then fear may lead to avoidance or dismissal: "[Guilt] becomes a device to protect ignorance and the continuation of things the way they are, the ultimate protection for changelessness" (Lorde, 2012, p. 130).

Garrett and Segall (2013) suggest that privileged ignorance is often not a naïve action but an operationalized one. Likewise, it is also a type of active engagement. Students must have opportunities that maintain the focus on the issues at hand; reflexively, they suggest that teachers should not see it as their "goal" to solve students' reasons for avoidance. Instead, Garrett and Seagall (2013) propose "containing" difficult knowledge by not letting the discourse slip away, but also not using it as a tool to exacerbate students' heightened anxiety. As the conversations slipped away from anti-oppression in both vignettes, I contemplate how I can support my future students who might be engaging but also employing ignorance in a self-soothing reaction against the reality of "difficult knowledge." Simultaneously, I must lead students back to the problem at hand.

LaCapra (2004) compliments the discussion by offering a "heteropathic mode of identification in which the difference between self and other is recognized" (p. 76). In other words, this practice simultaneously engages students' empathetic listening skills and helps them stand apart at an analytical distance. At once, one practices a stance of openness and one that disassembles one's assumptions about the "other."

With analytical distance and empathy, space is created for an *emotion* of hope—one that may release one's narcissistic fears—that opens to the "other." Hope provides room to witness and not flee. With room for students to upend their fixed notions of self, the instructor may practice subjectivity as the "norm" and call on students to suspend previous beliefs (Butin, 2014). Within a hopeful, subjective framework, students may engage in emotional travel with another. Such a traveling together through discomfort offers what Applebaum (2017) calls a "critical hope" and manifests through what Freire (in Allen & Rosatto, 2009) calls "radical love":

> Loving the oppressor student requires that they be treated as capable of becoming more fully human once released from their investment in their oppressor status. Loving the oppressor student requires interventions that help them learn how to not dehumanize themselves and others. It requires not allowing them to take on the oppressor role in dialogue. And it requires letting them know that if they make a mistake they will still be loved. That is radical love. (p. 178)

Carello and Butler's (2014) warning that educators are not trained therapists should remain sharply present as educators take such actions against fear. Educators' interest in "healing," for instance, requires the skills and fieldwork learned through official certification, otherwise, students may be re-triggered in their trauma, for instance. Such acts may result in oppressive education due to an educator's ignorance. Britzman (2009), however, provides an example of a relational approach in which educators emotionally co-identify with students. After many meetings with a student who had great anxiety about teaching, she admitted that Freud called education the "impossible profession." This implication of both herself and the student in such an undertaking provided relief: "We could leave the classroom together" (p. 143). Her relational opening, what hooks (2014) identifies as a "location of possibility" (p. 207), with the student provides both her and the student the space, or vulnerability, crucial for critical hope and radical love. Such emotional work shifts the curricular content as a fixed outcome for banking knowledge (Freire, 1970) toward an intentional, critical awareness of self and other.

Garrett and Segall (2013) further provide educators with a glimpse of emotion-based questioning. They ask their students: "What just happened here? What was it that first made us feel more emotionally heightened? What was it that first made us say, 'no?' Did we really not know what we said we did not know?" (p. 301). I would add that the answers to these questions might be privately journaled and only shared publicly if students feel comfortable. If educators compel their students to share their emotions, vulnerability may turn back to fear. Perhaps, after students privately document their emotions, the difficult knowledge could be shared again. Students might then be asked, "Did you notice a shift in your emotions? If yes, how might you understand the process of engaging with difficult knowledge? If not, could you write some guesses as to why?" Such questioning identifies emotions and how they arose and allows students to explore their own roles in dialogue and relationships to difficult knowledge.

PROCESSING TIME

The emotional questioning above requires crucial processing time (Berlak, 2004) during which students practice suspending the certitude of their identities (Butin, 2014). If LaCapra's (2004) "heteropathic" practice becomes regularized, the classroom may manage expectations and (re)value relationships with greater complexity and fluidity. Making time to process allows for the distance that LaCapra calls for, which sits on the other side of fear (Britzman, 2009). Perhaps these relational ties are best built before or during the type of questioning that Garrett and Segall (2013) suggest above, and end with time to reflect (Berlak, 2004).

Despite time constraints that often conflict with pedagogical preparedness, the educator must also make time to reflect and process. Thoughtful attention to student-to-student emotions cannot occur if their navigator, the educator, is not emotionally attentive, or does not value emotional learning in the classroom. A critical theorist/educator can retreat into an emotionally unresponsive mode and become frustrated with privileged discourses that oppress minoritized students and reroute away from the topic at hand. Indeed, I am, as Britzman surmises, "surprised by what [I] do not really know" (2009, p. 141). This surprise feels both self-incriminating and could negatively project back on students. The educator's relationship to the students depends on one's ability to continue to wonder and hope how ignorance, narcissism, and active rerouting are understood as simultaneous inquisitive, engaging, and defensive measures.

ALIGNING EMOTIONAL PEDAGOGY WITH CULTURALLY SUSTAINING PEDAGOGY

The two vignettes and scholarship reviewed throughout this chapter highlight an intention to teach with a critical lens. I draw attention to the trauma and stress that may arise when teaching about cultural traumas. I argue that the purposeful alignment of empathetic connection, emotional questioning, and critical hope are part of a pedagogical approach that complements Britzman's (2009) concept of therapeutic action which "sustains and expresses the creativity of psychic survival and include[s] in this work the analysis of how it may be destroyed" (p. 137). To analyze how survival may "be destroyed" educators must examine emotional travel through a critical lens. Britzman's therapeutic action, therefore, aligns in the outcomes of culturally sustaining pedagogy (CSP) which not only supports students through culturally relevant pedagogy and content (Ladson Billings, 2014) but also focuses on providing students "with the opportunities to survive and thrive" (Paris & Alim, 2017, p. 14). If CSP is a lens, among many critical theories, then practicing heteropathic modes of identification is integral to any critical encounter. Emotional practice cannot be separated from CSP.

MUSICAL STORY-TELLING

As mentioned earlier, the choral space produces therapeutic qualities and may also cause stress and trauma, depending on the sung content. Due to a diversity of emotional responses present in a choir, the choral educator—among many other disciplines—cannot interpret the content as having one outcome or one meaning. Though musical pieces may be tied to historical situations, one might reconceive the music as not only an embodied oration (performance) of a story but, in the case of critical dialogue in the rehearsal space, a critical story-telling experience. Gardner et al. (2021) propose that critical story-telling connects students to "strands of their past in relation to the present" (p. 304). It also prompts students to think abstractly and temporarily suspend their connection to their fixed identities. Frank (2010) believes that stories have a life of their own due to the vast diversity of student identities. He advocates for educators to not let a single interpretation of the story prevail. "Stories make dangerous companions when they reduce too much complexity and are too good at concealing what they reduce" (p. 149). In relation to self and other, and to avoid reducing complexity, Frank contests that "two [or more] stories instigate dialogue" (p. 152). If a *single* story prevails, then hierarchies of self and other can creep in: "*our* stories are true and justified; *their* stories are biased, hateful, and unjustified" (p. 159).

For instance, in an undergraduate first-year music philosophy course I teach, a guest speaker critically narrated how race operated in the world of country music. He showed us three videos of contemporary country songs. The class analyzed the various messages based on the images, the lyrics, and even the instruments used—all through a critical race lens. Though students elicited many interpretations, the use of multiple stories (videos) provided students with an analytical space that helped them contextualize the country music genre as a system. Ultimately, students discussed how this system needed more nuanced discussions on race. The classroom finished with the question: "How else does racism operate in unseen ways?".

In music-making ensemble spaces—which have their own historical priorities of performance-first pedagogies, accompanied by little reflection and minimal dialogue—the educator-conductor may find pieces of music that act in a multi-storied approach to dialogue. In the case of Thompson's *Seven Last Words,* perhaps several other pieces were needed to provide emotional relief from the piece's intensity without diluting Thompson's critical musical narration of being murdered while Black and unarmed.

In Frank's work with story-telling, he lists three elements that constitute a narrative act: "a story, a storyteller, and a listener" (p. 16). In the case of choral singing, however, the storyteller is both the educator-conductor and the students who sing the story. The entire rehearsal space constitutes the story, the storyteller, and the listener. Self and other meld and are colluded into, often, uncritical and simultaneous projections and reflections. The space is one of hyper-emotion, and perhaps the most dangerous of all educational spaces to speak about difficult knowledge, and yet, if not iterated, the most likely of places to silence it.

Conclusion

I conclude by remembering my first pedagogical instruction in an undergraduate conducting course—one which I believed for more than a decade: "There are no bad choirs, only bad conductors." Such emotionally closed aphorisms once made me relive the phantoms of my own perceived failures as an educator and left me skeptical about my successes. As I attend to my skeptical narcissism (self-blame) and notice emotional closure in my former learning environment, I wonder about how loving pedagogy embraces student vulnerabilities—resistance, ignorance, trauma, and fear—as pedagogical outcomes. Students' relationships with their school environment, peers, educators, families, worship places, and other civic engagements all shape their relationship to the subject matter. Within their orbit of meaning-making, students' emotional journeys are as much unpredictable as discoverable. Attending to students' emotional travel is a loving and sustaining pedagogy that "avoid[s] a life of fading narrowness" (Allsup, 2016, p. 65). The possibility of opening the unpredictable and discoverable (predictably traumatic) through story-telling, musical works or dialogue about both, reveals tensions of supporting the vulnerable student while "containing" (Berlak, 2004) their privilege as a critical responsibility to the "other." Turning privileged attention back to the "task at hand," engaging, and suspending certitude, results in loving minoritized students. If pedagogy can be life-giving, the navigational tools that CSP cultivates in student's lives may only be realized through the development of a group consciousness of emotional travel—a spectrum of ecstasy, hope, discomfort and trauma. This work is mindful, full of practice, and ultimately, a trauma-informed approach.

Commonly, choral educators remark on the "magic" of choral music that "brings us all together." The field of choral music is full of shared goals, certainty, and agreement; however, Britzman (2009) challenges the fixity of the object (the music, in this case) by prompting educators to leave the classroom together. In this case, Britzman and her student experienced relief together but did not feel the same way. This type of unfixed, vulnerability that both exposes an emotional precarity and allows for failure may be the greatest gesture of love between student and "educator" and between student peers.

With the promise of ever-changing identities, there can be no "bad" students or educators. Maybe emotional closure occurs when classrooms silence the relationship between self and other, at the expense of driving home a point about critical theory. Perhaps the challenge of education is not only "moving the needle" toward a critical stance but cultivating students' emotional consciousness which "threads the needle" (Gibbs & Papoi, 2020, p. 101) of critical, traumatic knowledge between self and other.

References

Allen, R. L., & Rossatto, C. A. (2009). Does critical pedagogy work with privileged students? *Teacher Education Quarterly, 36*(1), 163–180.

Allsup, R. E. (2016). *Remixing the classroom: Toward an open philosophy of music education.* Indiana University Press.

Applebaum, B. (2017). Comforting discomfort as complicity: White fragility and the pursuit of invulnerability. *Hypatia, 32*(4), 862–875.

Beck, R. J., Cesario, T. C., Yousefi, A., & Enamoto, H. (2000). Choral singing, performance perception, and immune system changes in salivary immunoglobulin A and cortisol. *Music Perception, 18*(1), 87–106.

Berlak, A. C. (2004). Confrontation and pedagogy: Cultural secrets, trauma, and emotion in antioppressive pedagogies. *Counterpoints, 240,* 123–144.

Britzman, D. P. (1998). *Lost subjects, contested objects: Toward a psychoanalytic inquiry of learning.* State University of New York.

Britzman, D. P. (2009). *The very thought of education: Psychoanalysis and the impossible professions.* State University of New York Press.

Butin, D. W. (2014). *Teaching social foundations of education* (pp. 109–126). Routledge.

Carello, J., & Butler, L. D. (2014). Potentially perilous pedagogies: Teaching trauma is not the same as trauma-informed teaching. *Journal of Trauma & Dissociation, 15*(2), 153–168.

Frank, A. W. (2010). *Letting stories breathe: A socio-narratology.* University of Chicago Press.

Freire, P. (1970). *Pedagogy of the oppressed.* Continuum.

Gardner, R. P., Osorio, S. L., & McCormack, S. (2021). Creating spaces for emotional justice in culturally sustaining literacy education: Implications for policy & practice. *Theory Into Practice, 60*(3), 301–311.

Garrett, H. J. (2011). The routing and re-routing of difficult knowledge: Social studies teachers encounter when the levees broke. *Theory & Research in Social Education, 39*(3), 320–347.

Garrett, H. J., & Segall, A. (2013). (Re)considerations of ignorance and resistance in teacher education. *Journal of Teacher Education, 64*(4), 294–304.

Gibbs, B., & Papoi, K. (2020). Threading the needle: On balancing trauma and critical teaching. *Occasional Paper Series, 2020*(43), 101–112.

Hooks, B. (2014). *Teaching to transgress.* Routledge.

Kreutz, G. (2014). Does singing facilitate social bonding? *Music and Medicine, 6*(2), 51–60.

LaCapra, D. (2004). *History in transit: Experience, identity, and critical theory.* Cornell University Press.

Ladson-Billings, G. (2014). Culturally relevant pedagogy 2.0: Aka the remix. *Harvard Educational Review, 84*(1), 74–84.

Lorde, A. (2012). *Sister outsider: Essays and speeches.* Crossing Press.

Menakem, R. (2017). *My grandmother's hands: Racialized trauma and the pathway to mending our hearts and bodies.* Central Recovery Press.

Paris, D., & Alim, H. S. (Eds.). (2017). *Culturally sustaining pedagogies: Teaching and learning for justice in a changing world.* Teachers College Press.

Perkins, J. D. (2021). Approaching the "void of racism": Traumatic choral dialogues. In *Trauma and resilience in music education* (pp. 127–140). Routledge.

Style, E. (1988). Curriculum as window & mirror [Conference proceedings at Oak Knoll School of the Holy Child]. In *Listening for all voices: Gender balancing the school curriculum* (pp.6–12). Oak Knoll School.

Thompson, J. (2015). *The seven last words of the unarmed* [Musical score]. Music-Spoke.

van der Kolk, B. A. (1994). The body keeps the score: Memory and the evolving psychobiology of posttraumatic stress. *Harvard Review of Psychiatry, 1*(5), 253–265.

Zembylas, M., Bozalek, V., & Shefer, T. (2014). Tronto's notion of privileged irresponsibility and the reconceptualisation of care: Implications for critical pedagogies of emotion in higher education. *Gender and Education, 26*(3), 200–214.

Zurbriggen, E. L. (2011). Preventing secondary traumatization in the undergraduate classroom: Lessons from theory and clinical practice. *Psychological Trauma: Theory, Research, Practice, and Policy, 3*(3), 223–228.

CHAPTER 6

Stumbling My Way into Trauma-Informed Nursing Education

Andrea Alexander

I knew the moment I blew it.

A student raised her hand from the back furthermost corner of the lecture room. Thinking I was being appropriately interactive, I'd asked an open-ended question that was relatively benign. Her answer was correct, but seemed to be stated by rote.

"Yes, but that's pretty much straight out of the textbook," I replied.

Students muttered under their breaths and shifted uncomfortably in their seats. I was brand new to the university, teaching a class that was being removed from the curriculum after the current cohort completed it, and the subject matter wasn't even particularly interesting to me. To top things off, this was the single most difficult semester of nursing school for students in terms of workload.

This was only the second week of the semester. The tide shifted for the rest of the term. Discussions were dry, side conversations were frequent, and my frustration grew. At the end of the semester, student evaluations were harsh, some even cruel.

What did I expect? Nursing school, with its love for multiple choice tests, including the ever-dreaded *Select All That Apply*, reinforces students with the thought that there is only one right answer.

A. Alexander (✉)
Simpson University, Redding, CA, USA
e-mail: aalexander@georgefox.edu

George Fox University, Newberg, OR, USA

© The Author(s), under exclusive license to Springer Nature
Switzerland AG 2022
P. Thompson and J. Carello (eds.), *Trauma-Informed Pedagogies*,
https://doi.org/10.1007/978-3-030-92705-9_6

One different reply from me that day would have likely changed everything. "That's right. Go on?".

* * *

One year later, I was preparing to teach the same cohort in my Mental Health Nursing course. I panicked the entire summer, fearing that the atmosphere would be the same or worse as before.

While my mental health course had gone slightly better the previous year (with the cohort one year ahead), it was similarly dry and quiet in terms of engagement and discussion. Attempting to avoid triggering students with forced discussion or uncomfortable active learning activities, I rarely veered from my PowerPoints and the textbook.

Not wanting to make the class all about me, I opted to not self-disclose, particularly my own story relating to the subject: I am a survivor of chronic depression, and my first husband died by suicide.

End-of-semester evaluations were lukewarm; one student said they could have listened at home in their PJ's; another thought I didn't really care about mental health.

I was desperate to have a better semester.

* * *

I recalled a sign posted on every unit at one of our mental health clinical sites that highlighted the basics of trauma-informed care for patients:

- Realize the effects of trauma
- Recognize the impact on patients, families, and staff
- Respond with trauma-informed practices
- Resist re-traumatization

It dawned on me that the same mindset could help me as an educator. I decided to weave the pieces of my mental health nursing content together under the lens of trauma-informed practice. My primary objective shifted from covering content to building empathy within and between students.

The first day of class, I covered the basics (syllabus, assignments, schedule). Next, instead of moving directly to content, I asked students in groups of 3 to 4 to describe "deal-breakers" for class that were unacceptable behaviors by either students or myself, such as interrupting or using inflammatory language. We then had a class discussion, where themes were investigated between groups, such as respect. I shared my own main "deal-breaker": if there is a conflict, communicate directly with the person you have a disagreement with, whether that be another student, me, or anyone else. The room was quiet. I waited for a moment, then moved on, in more ways than one.

Next, I asked students to pass around colored Post-It notes. Each person took several, and the fun began. I asked them to have the people in their small groups write down one word to describe them and give it to them. There were giggles in the room. Then I asked students to roam around the room and ask at least one person they didn't talk to often. Some students excitedly asked for more Post-It's. Some stayed in their seats. A few moments later, I asked students to return to their seats and place their collection on their desk in front of them.

While they looked at their personality profile, I played a brief reading by a theater professor from a memoir I had read on depression. The gist: depression is just one part of my personality, and you can't define a person by a word.

The room felt intimate. Holy almost.

By gaining their trust, the ice was broken.

* * *

To the students' surprise, many of the rules were thrown out that semester. No more participation points, and therefore less pressure to self-disclose. Attendance was encouraged but not required. Lectures were recorded, or "captured," (Krautscheid et al., 2019, p. 97) on an interactive whiteboard called Explain Everything. Instead of reciting slides verbatim, they became a discussion outline when possible. Sensitive topics were given an introduction prior to being discussed, which I called "hot spots." Does anyone else find the phrase "trigger warning" an ironically hard thing to hear?

To my surprise, students not only came to office hours, but came just to talk! When it became a near-weekly event to have a student share their difficult stories with me, I realized that my new approach had a deeper effect than I could have anticipated. Students who no one would have expected to be suffering were barely hanging on just below the surface. Knowing that it was key not to assume the role of therapist, I encouraged students to get connected with a mental health professional. While I knew that many mental health conditions are diagnosed in late adolescence and early adulthood, I didn't realize that many students who had experienced trauma several years before would be ready to seek help near the end of their college career.

At the end of the semester, students reported in their evaluations that they most appreciated the option of not being in class, while many never took me up on the offer. It seems that just having the possibility reduced their stress. And, while it was gratifying to have my quantitative evaluation scores significantly improve, that paled in comparison to hearing one student say that they were feeling relief from pain they had held onto for years in silence, partly due to our course.

That shift, from "my" to "our" course, is the best way I can summarize what happened. I didn't fear my students or dread going to class; I was excited to teach again.

One discovery from my new foray into trauma-informed teaching and learning was that students who had no (disclosed) trauma also benefited from my approaches. I've never been much of a theory gal, but as I began to dig into the science behind trauma-informed practices, I realized a simple truth: it's better for everyone. Similar to Universal Design principles, which were designed with students with disabilities in mind, accessibility has benefits for all. And, unfortunately, most of us will face a traumatic event at one point or another in our lives. By being informed, we can prepare.

I was connected with a psychology doctoral student with common interests who mentioned a study investigating uncertainty. While I can't help but wonder how they secured Institutional Review Board (IRB) approval, the researchers found that people had higher anxiety when the *threat* of an electric shock was present than *knowing* for a fact that one was going to receive one (Piray & Daw, 2020).

After my jaw was lifted back to my mouth, I realized why trauma-informed nursing education was just plain good education. You don't need to be in pain (such as a survivor of trauma) to benefit from clarity.

Other evidence is equally intriguing. Learning is adversely affected by both instability and stress. A very recent study by two Princeton researchers (not yet peer-reviewed) found that unpredictability increased "noise" and decreased the speed of learning (de Berker et al., 2016). Gagnon et al. (2018) found that acute stress impaired the recollection of details of past experiences (such as information from previously-attended lectures!) and that memories expressed with a high level of confidence were less accurate under stress.

Uh-oh. My trademark teaching moves were spontaneity and developing group activities that encouraged student creativity. No wonder students felt stressed instead of excited to come to my class. I had no idea that students lost trust in me with each unexpected, informal group presentation, inconsistent date (between syllabus, learning management system, and schedule), and ambiguous rubric. It's a constant struggle to sift between what constitutes a meaningful and innovative strategy versus an activity that is fun, yet frivolous, and not pertinent for any exam questions.

The challenge for me was (and will be indefinitely) to capture the best parts of my approach—creativity, humor, and multiple modes of formative assessment—balanced with increased structure, consistency, and clear expectations.

Small changes have made a big difference:

- Triple-check due dates prior to posting assignments
- Allow for non-speaking participation in group exercises, such as a "researcher" or "artist"
- Include clear rubrics and provide excellent samples of work by previous students (examplars) for assignments
- Connect activities to rationales such as course outcomes
- When in doubt, send a clarification email.

- Have realistic, non-jargon-filled learning objectives to guide studying

  - Tie summative assessment directly to these

- Have short, sweet, and understandable lecture slides, and provide students with an electronic copy

In candor, this felt like over-communicating. Students disagreed with that sentiment and stated that they felt significant relief and an increased capacity to engage in the course.

* * *

That was 2019. Pre-COVID-19.

I did not see the pandemic coming—who could? In fact, in my medical-surgical nursing course, I omitted covering SARS (a type of coronavirus) in my respiratory lecture because it was so rare.

The triple-checked dates, creative active learning strategies, and discussion-heavy (versus lecture-based) class periods were thrown out the window. In their place: asynchronous online lectures. Optional, yet recommended Zoom meetings with poor attendance. Learning in isolation.

While my colleagues and I tried to keep a personal element in our courses, we found that the overall climate was one of disengagement.

Perhaps the hardest adjustment was being unable to deny my "double life." With one college freshman, a 7th grader, a 3rd grader, and a preschooler suddenly at home 24 h per day, we were a full, frantic, emotional house My husband and I had to trade off caring for children who were also taking classes on Zoom.

We were incredibly fortunate; my husband was essentially placed on paid leave for the month of April. His baseline is already being an active dad, and he stepped up this role even more. My institution thankfully finished the academic year in late April. I had some stockpiled childcare hours that I was able to utilize. Summer was full of adventures, hikes, and more time than usual with my husband, who was back to work but with a greatly reduced workload.

* * *

Fall loomed. My university staunchly held to its promise to return to on-campus learning in August 2020. I was excited; I longed for face-to-face teaching, office hours, brainstorming with colleagues, walking to coffee with friends after a long day in the classroom. I was also terrified; how did social distancing mix in?

A few weeks prior to returning to campus, I developed a survey to gauge the temperature of student's attitudes and readiness to return to the clinical setting. I added an open-ended question about how students had been or could be supported by faculty.

My hypothesis: I expected to read that students were nervous to begin clinical practice after an extended break and virtual clinical. I anticipated appreciation by students of the efforts made by faculty with some helpful suggestions.

Reality: I received angry, frustrated responses. Students felt unprepared to return to school and clinical and didn't feel like they had been kept in the loop of what the fall would entail. They were disappointed in the lack of frequent communication over the summer.

When my university suddenly announced that the semester would begin a week early, notifying students, staff, and faculty together, I better understood the students' sentiments. So much was unknown.

As I made final plans for my mental health course, I revisited my trauma-informed teaching guidelines (traumainformedteaching.blog/resources— thank you Dr. Carello!

I added a new "student choice" assignment, knowing it would be a bit of a gamble. Students who needed black-and-white examples would be frustrated, yet the rubric and guidelines needed to be flexible to reflect the wide variety of topics and frameworks students could use. I made sure the rubric had clear expectations for the key aspects of the assignment, and reassured students that the grading would be fair as long as these were met. Additionally, I emphasized the rationale for the assignment: a way to allow students to study something they found personally meaningful. A way to assess student learning outside of a multiple-choice test. A way to celebrate their fellow students and learn from each other.

I also added extra optional quizzes, allowing students to have more practice with application-level exam questions, and told them that I would take the higher of two scores for 10% of their grade: the average top four out of five quiz scores, or their score on the end-of-the-semester standardized test. This exam tends to cause anxiety, and some students historically get low grades, despite doing fine on the unit exams. Students were surprised and relieved.

Due to a requirement to have the class have a hybrid component (I'll spare the long backstory), the students would have approximately one hour of online learning added to the course per week. This was a sudden change for students. They were also faced with learning in a gym that had been converted into four classrooms, using an app to listen to professors using headphones. Instead of implementing a completely "flipped" classroom, I asked students for their input. Would they rather have the online component prior to class, or after? Students overwhelmingly preferred to have as much material covered in-person as possible, with supplemental online lectures afterward.

This year was plain hard. I'm thankful to teach in person, but it's vastly different to teach students who are masked and up to 100 feet away from me. It's been difficult to connect with students. I opted to add an "exit ticket" to my classes, where students jot down key takeaways and/or "muddiest points." My favorite part is the tiny segment on the bottom where students can either give a discreet update, prayer request, or jot a note to me. While it's not the

Select Student Survey Answers from the Perceived Stress Scale

	Fairly often	Very often
Upset because of something that happened unexpectedly	38.8%	26.9%
Unable to control the important things in your life	31.3%	31.3%
Felt nervous and "stressed"	25.4%	61.2%

Fig. 6.1 Select student survey answers from the Perceived Stress Scale

Survey Results of Level Of Satisfaction with Support Received from Professors

Very unsatisfied	Unsatisfied	Neutral	Satisfied	Very satisfied
1.5%	14.9%	28.4%	44.8%	10.4%

Fig. 6.2 Survey results of level of satisfaction with support received from professors

same as having a heart-to-heart in my office, it helps me keep a pulse on the class and be a starting point with students who are struggling. Students have been vulnerable, reaching out with unexpected transparency.

* * *

Results from an anonymous survey I collected after IRB approval from both undergraduate and graduate students (75 responses and counting) in November 2020 confirmed my fears: my nursing students' responses of anxiety and frustration in August 2020 reflected students at my university as a whole. Unfortunately, the situation did not apparently improve with being on-campus in fall 2020. Using the Perceived Stress Scale, a validated and reliable tool, students rated the frequency in the past month of several statements (see Fig. 6.1). The majority of students reported they either "fairly often" or "very often":

- Felt upset because of something that happened unexpectedly
- Felt unable to control the important things in their life
- Felt nervous and "stressed"

I also asked about the level of satisfaction overall with the support received from professors. The majority felt rated this as "satisfied" or "very satisfied." Over one-fourth rated this as "neutral." (See Fig. 6.2).

Call me an idealist, but I see a great wealth of opportunity in the "neutral" category. We can and should do better.

When asked what behaviors by professors helped decrease distress, the most common themes were:

- Communication and clear expectations
- Extending deadlines
- Not requiring in-person attendance
- Encouragement
- Flexibility
- Giving space to talk about stressors
- Asking for student feedback
- Reaching out to check in with students
- Praying in class or individually

Behaviors that increased distress:

- Last-minute changes
- Ignoring stressors
- Lack of communication
- Slow response rates
- Unclear expectations
- Disorganization
- Vague feedback
- Requiring in-person learning

In their own words:

"The professors who make it clear that they care about me and my health have made it much easier to go easy on myself during this difficult semester."

"More support = better outcomes"

Question: if there was one thing you wish professors knew about what it's like to be a student under stress?

"I wish they [faculty] knew how close some of us are on having to give up our dreams of finishing graduate school."

"We are going through a lot more than just school, be understanding that we have a lot to cope with unrelated to academics."

"I wish they knew that we're trying our very best to focus on academics, but that at least a quarter of us had shattered worlds that are crumbling on all sides."

* * *

I play the role of cheerleader best (I'm a Myers-Briggs ENFP). I am at a loss when my enthusiasm is low. I don't like to be a downer. I'm not a big "feelings" person.

Unfortunately, life happens to all of us. So, when COVID-19, being isolated, stress of blending a family and having a friendship end, and chemistry collided in late spring, I fell. Hard. Depression does not discriminate, even for mental health nursing professors. I hid my exacerbation from my superhero husband, and I don't even really know why.

Thankfully, medication, therapy, and leaning on him and friends helped. I didn't feel hopeless anymore. It has also always helped to stay busy, which was a no-brainer this academic year. Being out of the depression "woods," I am always at risk for my runner-up mental health challenge: anxiety.

Enter Fall Semester 2020. I accepted my spot in a Doctor of Nursing Practice program just before COVID-19 hit and started the fall 2020 semester both as a professor and a student. I rarely call "uncle" from stress; it helps me stay afloat and gives me purpose. However, this year was so far beyond stress. I found myself suddenly crying several times. I felt guilty or suspicious whenever I laughed or did something just for fun. Times with my daughters were brief and typically centered around necessities: getting ready for school or bed; eating dinner; showers. My house was held together by my husband, who never complained, stating, "I got you. I got you."

I thought it was just me. I thought it was my fault for adding school to the mix.

Then my work friends couldn't hold back the tears, either. We all felt so alone. We felt inadequate. Exhausted. There was no end in sight.

Then, Jennifer Moss' essay in the *Harvard Business Review* on "Preventing Burnout is About Empathetic Leadership" came up on my news feed. Moss discusses the idea of margin, and the ways that the pandemic has taken away our abilities to cope with challenges. She describes:

> How many of us are currently living without margins – the space to handle life's simplest stresses…It can happen after being mentally stretched and dealing with chronic stress for too long. Basically, we are left with zero margin for error. It also means that we don't realize we're at our max until it's too late. Before we know it, we've hit the wall. (Moss, 2020, n.p.)

My breaking point came at 4:57 p.m. on a Tuesday. We had abruptly lost a clinical site earlier that day, and 14 students would not be able to have on-site mental health experience at all. I was adamant that the students deserved a quality experience. As a faculty team, we worked quickly to make a plan for the students prior to notifying them to minimize distress. I was waist-deep in this process when the email came: it was my month to be a "birthday buddy," and it was getting late in the month. This would have normally been a minor stressor, and the reminder would have been appreciated. Today, it was just. Too. Much. It didn't help that it was also my second wedding anniversary. As I worked alone until 7:00 p.m., crafting the finalized plan and notifying students, I felt the end of my rope.

* * *

Something's gotta give, or our bodies and brains will. As a nurse practitioner, I know that chronic stress can cause permanent changes to our bodies, particularly the brain. "Allostatic overload" occurs when body systems, such as neuroendocrine, cardiovascular, and psychological, become persistently activated, which leads to accelerated disease progression (Peters et al., 2017). Furthermore, stress decreases the brain's ability to process complex information, even causing brain structure changes, including atrophy of the prefrontal cortex (the key to higher-level brain functions) and hippocampus (key in episodic and spatial memory as well as mood regulation) (Peters et al., 2017). Interestingly, the amygdala, the "emotion center" of the brain (particularly fear and anger), hypertrophies with early stress, and later atrophies (McEwen et al., 2016). Like us, the amygdala can only take so much, and eventually burns out!

If I had to choose one lesson learned from the pandemic, it's that it was unwise to assume that it would be short-lived. My supervisor likened teaching during the pandemic to "sprinting in a marathon." Sprinters would never be considered out of shape if they got tired after a few miles. Students and faculty are no different. We cannot run without a rest. While I don't have the answers to this riddle, I know that it's okay to ask for help. Advocating for patients comes easy to us as nurses. Asking for and accepting help for ourselves is harder, but the only way forward.

References

de Berker, A. O., Rutledge, R. B., Mathys, C., Marshall, L., Cross, G. F., Dolan, R. J., & Bestmann, S. (2016). Computations of uncertainty mediate acute stress responses in humans. *Nature Communications, 7*, 10996.

Gagnon, S. A., Waskom, M. L., Brown, T. I., & Wagner, D. W. (2018). Stress impairs episodic retrieval by disrupting hippocampal and cortical mechanisms of remembering. *Cerebral Cortex, 29*(7), 2947–2964. https://doi.org/10.1093/cercor/bhy162

Krautscheid, L., Williams, S., Kahn, B., & Adams, K. (2019). Untethered lecture capture: A qualitative investigation of college student experiences. *Journal of Educational Technology Systems, 48*(1), 97–111.

McEwen, B., Nasca, C., & Gray, J. (2016). Stress effects on neuronal structure: Hippocampus, amygdala, and prefrontal cortex. *Neuropsychopharmacology, 41*, 3–23. https://doi.org/10.1038/npp.2015.171

Moss, J. (2020, September 3). Preventing burnout is about empathetic leadership. *Harvard Business Review*. https://hbr.org/2020/09/preventing-burnout-is-about-empathetic-leadership

Peters, A., McEwen, B. S., & Friston, K. (2017). Uncertainty and stress: Why it causes diseases and how it is mastered by the brain. *Progress in Neurobiology, 156*, 164–188.

Piray, P., & Daw, N. D. (2020). Unpredictability vs. volatility and the control of learning. *bioRxiv*. https://doi.org/10.1101/2020.10.05.327007

CHAPTER 7

Humanizing Social Work Education: Resetting for Healing

Alexis Jemal

During the pandemic, I was a master's student of Applied Theatre and a professor of Master of Social Work (MSW) education. Consequently, I observed education from a student's perspective and received student feedback about my teaching methods during the COVID-19 pandemic. Reflecting on both experiences facilitated my definition and implementation of humanizing social work education. Effectively, the pandemic operated like an x-ray of my teaching methods, exposing a brokenness that I am committed to setting right. Specifically, as I attempted to ignore the pandemic and carry-on business as usual, I exposed my training, socialization, and dominant ideology (e.g., white supremacy, patriarchy, capitalism, etc.) programming to perpetuate the oppressive status quo. For years, I've understood privilege to mean unearned, systemic advantage bestowed on those who occupy dominant social identities. However, my perspective expanded to include people who could continue living uninterrupted during a global pandemic. Like a cocoon, privilege insulates and protects persons from harm. As I cocooned within some of my social identities, many students (my fellow peers and the students in my class) existed and survived direct and indirect exposure to COVID-19.

Along with intersectionality, critical theory and restorative justice, my work as a critical social worker, researcher and community/cultural practitioner is informed by Bronfenbrenner's (1977) social-ecological model and Maslow's

A. Jemal (✉)
Silberman School of Social Work at Hunter College, Manhattan, NY, USA
e-mail: aj1423@hunter.cuny.edu

P. Thompson and J. Carello (eds.), *Trauma-Informed Pedagogies*,
https://doi.org/10.1007/978-3-030-92705-9_7

(1943) hierarchy of needs. Imagine Bronfenbrenner's stacked Venn diagram transforming into a bull's eye. The closer you are to the center based on the number of valued social identities (e.g., white, male, cisgender, able-bodied, educated, etc.) you occupy, the more protected/privileged you are, the more valued you are, and thus, harder to hit or harm. Those closer to the center are more likely to have their needs met on Maslow's (1943) pyramid. Conversely, a social location closer to the periphery increases the likelihood of harm (Jemal, 2018), translating to less needs met, and thus, perpetuating the victim/survivor status of a dehumanizing society. Crises, like COVID-19, disproportionately place people (e.g., differently abled bodies, gender fluid persons, racial minorities) on the margins at great risk and in perilous conditions. As such, systemically disadvantaged groups will bear the weight of this pandemic and all future crises and catastrophes as has been the historic pattern.

The pandemic reiterated the lesson that we live in a US society that targets and threatens humanity on a daily basis (not only during global pandemics) by exposing the false narrative of choice that perpetuates and justifies inequity. The choice myth does not acknowledge how white supremacy, anti-Blackness, racism, transphobia, sexism, ableism, xenophobia and other forms of oppression at the systemic and institutional levels remove agency in decision-making. The pandemic revealed that the choices one has are not usually of their own choosing. How do people, including students, choose between leaving young children at home while they go to work or staying home and losing their job/income? A clear indication of a dehumanizing society is when a person's choices leave no other options but to be harmed.

As I attempted to balance teaching and learning (including parenting/homeschooling) during the COVID-19 pandemic, I realized that the measures I take to survive a dehumanizing culture also facilitate the survival of a dehumanizing culture. I have been programmed, perhaps bribed with tokens of "success," to dehumanize myself and others, and to allow others to dehumanize me. When working from home while simultaneously homeschooling my seven-year-old and caring for my eighteen-month-old, I was bombarded with internal questions, such as: should I grade papers or go for a bike ride with my family? While debating, I pondered how I and many colleagues break our backs to prove we have the backbone to perform at high levels of productivity that drain us of our life force, identity, and imagination, such that we transform into mutated and muted beings (Freire, 2000). As these imposters of ourselves, we perpetuate dehumanization: cultivating institutions, practices, policies, and culture in our own image that then shapes who we are to ourselves, others, and in community. As we dismember ourselves—breaking down into pieces of our identities—we disrespect our authentic selves and invite others (students, colleagues) to follow our example. When did it become a badge of honor to send the 2 a.m. email or to look like what we've been through, such that "You look tired!" became a compliment? We detach parent from professor and divide daughter from student to specialize in one role as an effective and productive division of self and labor. The hypothesis is that if I'm only a professor at a certain time, then I'd be a better professor. Except this doesn't work.

The pandemic shattered the illusion of separate social identities when working from home commenced and schools closed. How will I be an effective worker and educate my children? Socialized in a society that customarily pits social identities against each other—to be a better professor, I am a worse mother, and to be a better activist, I am a worse student—I realized that I combined the impossible expectations of perfection from all my various identities, which made me not only ineffective, but also sick and tired (a typical social work client), and ultimately, broken. To heal, I reset standards and expectations that support the integration of my identities—such that my role as a student supports my role as a professor—according to my individual circumstances. This healing process supports my humanity, growth, needs, and my ability to self-actualize in a way that does not leave me depleted, but instead, replenished. When we interact with slices of identity rather than the wholeness of our humanity, we cut ourselves off from our authentic selves, genuine connection, support, sense of belonging, and healing opportunities. Every person is intersectional, and to deny that complexity is to dehumanize. Thus, part of the humanization process is to "re-member" who we are. Reassemble the pieces of identity to integrate oneself. When I finally remembered myself, mirroring my refined values, I recognized that my reflected priorities shifted. Priorities for my students also changed. Suddenly, meeting deadlines was much less important when compared to caring for loved ones, meeting basic human needs, or enjoying life. With these ideas in mind, I sent a reflection note to my students acknowledging that,

> I'm doing my best to relax these [unreasonable] standards that I have in my head. I want to be able to do what I can and that be good enough; meaning, I don't want to feel guilty about not doing more, or incompetent or less than a stellar student-scholar-academician. So, I want to offer the same support to you that I am trying to give myself.

This reflection cemented the epiphany that the illusive work–life balance is an impossible standard that we're socialized to believe is possible. Ironically, by pursuing this myth to make it a reality, we do more and more and get less and less. Then we do more with less and set a precedent that we don't deserve more. And since the standard is unrealistic and unattainable, but believed to be achievable, failures to achieve are attributed as an individual deficit: *What's wrong with you* (the oppressive question) versus *What happened to you* (the trauma-informed question) (Bloom, 2013) or *What do you need to support your humanity in this moment* (the healing-centered question).

As COVID-19 wreaked havoc and wrecked the elective course that I created and was piloting for the first time, I kept the pandemic's differential impact in mind and tried to respond in a way that would support students through the experience of colliding identities. I eliminated assignments, extended deadlines, and noted that if the revisions were insufficient, we could identify additional strategies to support their well-being. Students asked to receive extra credit for completing eliminated assignments. I was transparent about my reluctance to give extra credit that would essentially reward people who were most likely not directly or disproportionately impacted by the pandemic, and thus, had the privilege of time and mental capacity to spare to complete the extra credit. The decision to allow extra credit would have demonstrated how inequity (i.e., privilege and/or oppression)—especially inequity within decisions that are seemingly race neutral on the surface but have a disparate impact on marginalized populations)—is baked into systems, procedures, and operations, with no one person being held accountable or taking responsibility (Jemal, 2017).

In some ways, remote learning created the environment to know students/peers as multi-faceted persons as we entered (somewhat uninvited) people's homes and private spaces, but for the most part, remote learning made it difficult to build relationships with and between students/peers. History and the present-day penal system demonstrate the importance of names and how being unnamed or known by a string of numbers is a component of the dehumanization process. In addition to knowing names, I want to know students' interests and ambitions, so I can see them as whole people. Do students know and see me as a whole person: a mom, daughter, life partner, researcher, woman of color, and exhausted? Imagine if interactions in educational spaces were positioned from a humanizing stance to communicate love, respect, and appreciation. The student-professor relationship could extend beyond the point of evaluation—professors evaluating students on learning and students evaluating professors on teaching—to understanding commonalities, appreciating shared narratives, and celebrating our differences. These humanizing relationships could be manifested in an infinite number of ways. However, it is easier to provide an example of the dehumanizing norm. I was appalled and saddened when a friend, who's a Black woman and adjunct professor, told me that she had 35 students in her Spring 2020 class that had a stated max capacity of 25, and the school's administration did not provide the promised grading support. Then, in the middle of the semester, eleven people in her inner circle passed away from COVID-19 and her father was on a ventilator. When the students complained to the administration that they weren't being taught because this professor canceled a class and was not responding to emails within 24 hours about a graded assignment, the administration emailed the professor several times on behalf of the students.

For me, the pandemic reinforced radical teaching practices that transformed education into a humanizing experience rather than a "mental hazing to see who can survive" experience. I considered how to apply the assumptions, values, and commitments of critical participatory action research (CPAR) to my educational philosophy and style. Relevant CPAR principles include: decentering white, colonial perspectives; valuing knowledge that has been historically marginalized and delegitimized; finding strategies to build collective capacity and to use the collective's resources and strengths to create an enriched experience; using a variety of educational approaches to meet the diverse learning needs; excavating and exploring multiple approaches for relationship building; and, creating an educational space in which individuals and the collective can express multiple aspects of their identity to inform the educational experience. Certainly, these changes include the practice of radical imagination (tapping into the unknown) and creative risk-taking to generate collective knowledge and then identify, develop, and implement innovative alternative strategies for participation. Moreover, the incorporation of transformative teaching methods requires the interrogation and engagement of power relationships within and outside of the classroom (or Zoom room). Importantly, the educational institution must support humanizing education and extending similar practices to the Academy and life, in general, for faculty and staff. From my experience learning and teaching during a pandemic, I discovered that I could not do business as usual. The more I tried to ignore the disruption, the more harm I potentially caused to myself and my students/peers. The changes I made responded to the central question posed by the pandemic: How can social work education be trauma-informed, healing-centered: a humanizing force? Clearly, humanizing anything requires a transformative healing experience that promotes liberation to disrupt the status quo—that is, mitigates the harm of dominant ideologies and advances social justice and equity.

Potential humanizing social work education revisions include the elimination of grades in favor of grade-free assessments or other holistic and relationship-based systems of evaluation; smaller class sizes; a malleable syllabus that can respond to complexity and humanely adapt to constant change; co-teaching; greater investment in who's admitted; free tuition; integrated education that bridges the micro, meso, macro divides; interacting with students as intersectional beings; more opportunity for group work that builds relationship and community; implementing institutional anti-racism action plans and methods of evaluation; encouraging innovation and radical imagination; and establishing the norm of interrogating oppressive systems throughout the curriculum because there can be no effective action without a radical understanding of root causes of societal issues. Humanizing (trauma-informed and healing-centered) social work education is intersectional, critical, restorative, and teaches practices to repair the damage of living in a dehumanizing society. As such, it makes space for people to show up as their authentic selves, build community, reestablish identity, engage empathy and compassion. It supports the growth of all involved to reach full potential. Surely, the full potential of humanizing social work education will prepare future social workers to reset their thinking and practice to provide humanizing service to people and communities on a daily basis, and especially during global crises.

REFERENCES

Bloom, S. L. (2013). *Creating sanctuary: Toward the evolution of sane societies* (2nd ed.). Routledge.

Bronfenbrenner, U. (1977). Toward an experimental ecology of human development. *American Psychologist, 32*(7), 513–531. Retrieved 7 June, 2020 from https://pdfs. semanticscholar.org/a5f5/a4f4a4545519d84c5c57095b4bcc685d7dd9.pdf?_ga=2. 187704936.1360170486.1594077583-468122225.1594077583

Freire, P. (2000). *Pedagogy of the oppressed* (30th anniversary edition). Continuum (original work published 1970).

Jemal, A. (2017). Critical consciousness: A critique and critical analysis of the literature. *Urban Review, 49*(4), 602–626.

Jemal, A. (2018). Transformative consciousness of health inequities: Oppression is a virus and critical consciousness is the antidote. *Journal of Human Rights and Social Work, 3*(4), 202–215.

Maslow, A. H. (1943). A theory of human motivation. *Psychological Review, 50*(4), 370–396.

PART III

Approaches to Working with Specific Populations

Trauma-Informed Approaches to Teaching Students with Marginalized Identities During Times of Crisis

Megan Paceley, Sarah Jen, Michael Riquino, Sarah Cole, Kortney Carr, and Kelechi Wright

As social work educators, trauma is a central component of our teaching. We are responsible for teaching students to approach social work practice from a trauma-informed lens—to understand and recognize the multisystem effects of trauma among the clients, families, and communities with whom they will work. We aim to integrate trauma-informed principles into our teaching. Further, as practitioners with values and ethics rooted in social,

M. Paceley (✉) · S. Jen · M. Riquino · S. Cole · K. Carr · K. Wright
University of Kansas, Lawrence, KS 66045, USA
e-mail: mpaceley@ku.edu

S. Jen
e-mail: srjen@ku.edu

M. Riquino
e-mail: mriquino@ku.edu

S. Cole
e-mail: s478c894@ku.edu

K. Carr
e-mail: k_carr@ku.edu

K. Wright
e-mail: kelechiwright@ku.edu

P. Thompson and J. Carello (eds.), *Trauma-Informed Pedagogies*,
https://doi.org/10.1007/978-3-030-92705-9_8

racial, and economic justice, we recognize the importance of viewing oppression and injustice through a trauma-informed lens and we advocate naming marginalization for what it truly is: trauma.

The importance of trauma-informed teaching became even more relevant during the early months of the COVID-19 pandemic. As we rapidly shifted into teaching during a global crisis, existing sources of disparity among our students with marginalized identities became even more stark. We witnessed how marginalization made changes related to COVID-19 more challenging, such as attending online classes, navigating practicum changes or endings, being isolated from support systems, and managing competing family, work, and personal obligations. While we struggled to teach during this global crisis, we also aimed to attend to our students' needs as they attempted to learn during the same crisis. We could see the disparities in challenges faced by students who are Black, Indigenous, and people of color (BIPOC) and students with disabilities, and we felt that there must be a better way to support and educate them. Despite a growing literature base on trauma-informed pedagogy, not surprisingly, this literature does not situate or explore teaching within a global pandemic. We could anecdotally understand our students' experiences based on our own and what they shared with us, but we had few resources to guide our teaching. Therefore, we aimed to identify trauma-informed approaches to teaching students with marginalized identities during times of crisis. We developed a student-centered research team to qualitatively explore student experiences during the early months of COVID-19. We situated our study in trauma-informed principles and centered the voices of students as experts with unique perspectives and insights to offer.

This chapter provides a reflexive and empirical examination of student and faculty experiences during the early months of COVID-19, with an emphasis on the narratives and experiences of students who are BIPOC and/or Disabled. We first define and explore trauma-informed pedagogy. Next, we discuss our experiences with teaching and learning during the pandemic. After this introduction, we share student narratives from our study on the experience of marginalization and its intersections with learning during COVID-19. We end by situating trauma-informed pedagogy and teaching during a crisis with related literature with the intention that these strategies will inform teaching across higher education in a transformative and meaningful way during and beyond the COVID-19 pandemic.

Trauma-Informed Pedagogy

Trauma-informed pedagogy builds on aspects of trauma-informed care to specify teaching practices that recognize and center the impact of trauma on individuals and communities. Trauma-informed care includes safety, empowerment, trustworthiness, collaboration, and choice (Harris & Fallot, 2001), as well as recognition of cultural, historical, and gender issues (Substance Abuse & Mental Health Services Administration, 2014). Trauma-informed pedagogy includes considering how class content, course policies, and teaching practices may reactivate trauma or challenge survivors (Carello & Butler, 2015). Without these trauma-informed principles, students may be at risk of vicarious traumatization or retraumatization in the classroom, particularly among Disabled students and students who are BIPOC who face marginalization and oppression due to trauma shaped by living in a racist and ableist society. A global pandemic adds its own layers of trauma, making it critical that we explore and identify how to implement these trauma-informed principles and identify other strategies to use in our teaching.

Teaching and Learning During the Early Months of COVID-19

It was mid-March when our university announced that Spring Break would be extended and classes would transition to online delivery through the remainder of the semester. As faculty, we quickly adjusted our syllabi and course content to an online format, as well as our expectations for student engagement and learning. We changed assignments, spent class time processing student fears and concerns, and checked in on students who seemed to disappear. Simultaneously, we attempted to balance our own family, work, and personal obligations with our new reality of being fully remote, separated from our colleagues, and amidst growing uncertainty. We balanced parenting, pre-tenure workloads, health concerns, wedding planning, service work, mental health challenges, supporting students and colleagues, supporting anti-racism efforts, and our own fears and concerns surrounding COVID-19. As we move into the ninth month since classes moved online, these challenges have not changed and, in many ways, have increased. And yet, as faculty, we sit in places of privilege with tenure-track positions, steady incomes, the ability to work from home, and consistent health insurance. The experiences of the students with whom we work and who serve as co-researchers on this project emphasize even greater disparities and challenges.

The initial extension of Spring Break came with a wave of emotions for us as students. An extra week off from classes, spending time with family, friends, and traveling brought an initial excitement; however, this excitement quickly turned to confusion, fear, stress, and hurt as the reality dawned on us that something significant and impactful was happening in our lives. To quickly transition from spending time learning in-person with our peers and faculty to a new virtual space created anxiety and confusion. Many students had to transition off-campus or move back home with family, and practicum placements were shut down with no opportunity to end services with our clients. Many students had to navigate caring for families, loss of employment, addressing health and mental health, and caring for children. Despite these significant life changes, there was pressure to show up for synchronous classes, be engaged, complete assignments, and move forward, but it was impossible to adhere to the normal standards and expectations of learning while navigating these critical life changes. The exhaustion that came with online learning and limited interaction with others quickly became a burden, and a source of loss and sadness for many. Although we are nine months into this reality as we write this chapter, it cannot be said that things are easier or "normal." Barriers to technology continue to be an issue. For some, access to equitable learning due to preference, learning style, and ability status is a concern. Some students feel that they are being taken advantage of due to being charged tuition rates and fees without campus access. There seems to be minimal relief and continued struggles for students navigating their life and learning amid COVID-19.

These experiences highlight some of what we all likely know by now— teaching and learning during a global pandemic is challenging at best and impossible at worst. Additionally, students with marginalized identities, such as students who are BIPOC and students with disabilities, are managing the impacts of a global pandemic with marginalization and oppression. We are in critical need of literature addressing and identifying trauma-informed approaches to teaching Disabled students and students who are BIPOC during times of crisis, whether it be a global pandemic, natural disaster, community crisis, or personal crisis. And yet, we hope such approaches can be used in our regular teaching to better support and engage with the students with whom we work during non-crisis times, as well.

Social Work Students and COVID-19

As we shifted our teaching to the new and growing demands of a global pandemic, it became clear that we were doing so with little empirical guidance. With the goal of centering and highlighting students' voices and concerns, Drs. Jen and Paceley connected with three social work students (two graduate, one undergraduate) to develop a qualitative study to explore social work students' experiences during COVID-19. Originally, we anticipated completing 15–20 interviews, as we were uncertain what time and energy students would have to dedicate to something new or "extra." However, within two days of emailing students to assess interest, we received over 100 responses requesting an interview. In response to the outpour of interest, we quickly added two PhD students and another faculty member to the team. The final team of eight conducted interviews via phone or video chat with 67 social work students during May 2020. Interviews were open-ended and included questions about their academic, professional, and personal experiences during the early pandemic, as well as their hopes for and messages to other social work students, educators, and practitioners.

Student Narratives

A sub-set of interviews with students who are BIPOC and students who reported chronic health or mental health disabilities were examined by part of the research team and grouped into preliminary themes. This analysis was applied to transcripts of 25 students who are BIPOC and 33 students who reported disabilities. Of these individuals, 11 identified as both BIPOC and Disabled. The experiences and stories shared by students with disabilities and/or who are BIPOC highlight critical issues and concerns faced among both groups during the early months of COVID-19. We present these stories in narrative form to center their lives, voices, and experiences. We also present these narratives separately from those of the full sample and without comparing them to the experiences of students with more privileged identities. By doing so, our goal is to view and present these stories as important and worth understanding in their own right.

Illuminating and Deepening Existing Marginalization

Students often described COVID-19 as exacerbating existing disparities in experiences of race, health, and access as well creating new or deepening existing physical and mental health challenges. While students recognized and expressed appreciation for the efforts of some faculty and administrators to improve access (e.g., through virtual offerings, ensuring equitable and multiple access points), they also named ways in which the crisis brought contrasts in safety, access, and ability into sharp focus. One of the most commonly reported experiences related to the pandemic was new or worsened struggles with mental health. One biracial student with a history of posttraumatic stress disorder described using a busy schedule as a coping mechanism prior to the pandemic, but remarked how the slowed, stagnant feeling of quarantine brought up previous traumas, the impacts of which were worsened by social isolation:

The busier you are, the less time you have to really think about things. There was one week that I noticed that I had gotten really sad…Without the busyness of life like I usually have…sometimes I feel like I've been triggered more.

Other students described the impact of challenges related to pre-existing mental health symptoms on their ability to fulfill academic requirements and responsibilities. For example, one biracial student described this impact as stemming from an overall decreased capacity for mental and emotional processing: "I don't have the mental stability or strength that I normally do…and it affected me academically." This participant also stated that triggers from past traumas kept them from being able to fully engage during class discussions or complete course readings, leading them to anticipate a much lower grade than usual. Despite the need for support, this student reported not reaching out to their instructor regarding these challenges, stating that the emotional labor and vulnerability of reaching out felt above and beyond their current capacity, whereas "normally I would have been able to."

Students also saw physical disabilities or medical vulnerabilities as being exacerbated by the pandemic. When asked what kinds of support would have been helpful during this time, one Asian American student living with multiple medical conditions replied:

I don't think there is too much problem solving that can be done for my situation in particular. I just am really vulnerable to getting sick and getting sicker than most people... I went through a process of a little bit of mourning because before that I was able to work to an extent that I cannot do anymore.

The same student described experiences of anti-Asian sentiment as an added source of strain during the pandemic. They remarked, "I feel like I've never really had anything racist happen to me until this pandemic started" and went on to describe negative interactions that made them feel unsafe in public spaces, including the grocery store: "It makes it a little bit harder for me to do things...I've seen a lot of people who have glared or who will say things if I'm alone. I don't really get the opportunity to just...be safe."

In response to these stressors, students requested that such tensions be discussed explicitly in their class settings, with one biracial student stating, "Asian Americans are being targeted because of racist rhetoric...just all of these things that have been brought to the forefront [are] things that I wish we honestly talked about more in class." Students also requested greater access to mental health supports. Although mental health services were often offered, students remarked these services are not realistically accessible due to busy schedules and affordability. Students also called for more sensitive messaging from their school's administration. One white student with mental and physical health concerns described negative emotional reactions to school announcements, which seemed to push an expectation of resilience onto students in an unwelcome way:

It's not that there was a lack of communication. I think just sometimes how it was portrayed, it just felt like it was salt on the wounds of something that was already going on. I think one [email said], 'As social workers, we're supposed to adapt. This is a crisis.' And I'm just like, you know what, it is, but also as social workers we would not be saying this to a client... like, 'This is a crisis. You better just suck it up and adapt to it,' which is how I took [the email].

Another Disabled student simply asked for validation of their experiences, specifically through connections with other students living with disabilities or medical vulnerabilities. They remarked, "It would just be nice to...have that camaraderie of, 'You are not a bad social worker. We really are doing the best we can.' Just to have somebody who just knows, who can just get it." Given that these students were training to become social workers, students expressed feelings of social responsibility, to be the "good man in the storm," and to support those most vulnerable. These sentiments were internalized and verbalized by students to such an extent that some felt the need to justify or explain their inability to work in social service or medical settings as their—often invisible—conditions put them at higher risk for medical complications from COVID-19.

Intersections of Marginalization: Finances, Immigration, and Isolation
Beyond deepening existing stressors, students also described ways in which their financial situations and familial or personal immigration backgrounds informed their experiences of the pandemic. These added intersectional stressors exacerbated feelings of social isolation, as many felt alone in these experiences. The most commonly cited intersection was the added stressor of making ends meet financially while being a student, which included descriptions of low-wage positions and being terminated due to the pandemic. As one student who is both BIPOC and Disabled described, "Being a student is just expensive. Tuition is expensive. Being laid off and being in the middle of the pandemic, I have felt a kind of shrinkage of my life...literally and figuratively." For this student, losing their job was just another way that their world grew smaller and more contained during a countywide stay-at-home order during the first months of the pandemic. Another multiracial and Disabled student described being on the verge of losing their housing: "The extra $600 a week for unemployment [is] pretty much the only thing keeping me from being homeless." The depth of the impact of this financial stress was described as shaping this student's entire experience of the pandemic and when asked if anything positive had come out of the experience for them, they reiterated their financial situation and concluded by stating, "Everything's been really awful. I don't have any positives."

Students who are BIPOC, particularly students who identified as Asian, Asian American, and Hispanic or Latinx, described specific concerns that created additional layers of stress on top of social isolation. Three students described deep sadness leading up to Ramadan, informed by the recognition that this celebration—one typically spent with family—would be spent in isolation. They remarked how fasting would be an individualized and isolating ordeal with which many of their friends could not empathize. Students with family members living outside the United States expressed fears of not knowing when they would be able to visit with them. Some also described different cultural experiences of the pandemic that seemed to separate them from their peers, such as one Asian American-identified student who stated:

> I feel the crushing weight of the collectivism of our culture and how it doesn't matter if one of us is doing well if the others are suffering...I don't have any friends in my direct circle that I think feel the same way. And so sometimes I feel really alienated.

While many students spoke to the disappointment of having their graduation ceremonies canceled, this was particularly evident among and differently experienced by first-generation students who are BIPOC. In responding to a question about the impact of missing graduation, one Latinx student replied, "It broke my heart. I knew it was coming. It wasn't a shock. It was just the fact that I'm the first person in my family to get a Master's and this was supposed to be the big thing." Another Latinx student remarked, "Graduation was a big, emotional smack in the face because I am a first generation. My parents were really looking forward to that...I think this graduation was more important to them than it was to me." One Asian American student spoke to the importance of graduation, not only for themselves, but as a family celebration:

> My family, it was really important to them to see me graduate. They had invited a lot of family...It was supposed to be really special...My parents have had a lot of their dreams die. I realize they have sacrificed many of them for mine. And I think that would have been a really great culmination to see that I tried. I tried my best, I care about their feelings, I care about what they want out of life.

In this narrative, the loss of graduation meant more than an individual marking of accomplishment but was also seen as a way to honor their parents' efforts in life, which likely made the associated grief complex as well.

Adaptation and Resiliency

While students named negative experiences such as deepened risks, vulnerability, financial and cultural struggle, isolation, loss, and grief, they also named the ways in which their marginality had shaped them to be adaptable, resilient, and impactful in their communities. For both students with disabilities and students who are BIPOC, simply being in a higher education program was described as a meaningful contribution to the academy as well as in the delivery of social services. When asked what she wanted to convey to other social work students, one woman of color described a recent experience in her practicum placement:

I think as a student, especially as an [undergraduate student in social work], we undervalue our worth constantly...[I'm] one of the only social work practicum students at the [after school program] that is of color, and I never really thought about [what] that even meant...And I remember once one of the students was like, 'You know, I feel like I can tell you this because you're not white,' and all of the administrative staff and all of the supervisors are all white...I just think you forget that you offer a lot to the agencies and places that you give your time.

Similarly, a student who is living with a physical disability said that their life had prepared them for resiliency and adaptation, stating:

> I've thought about this a lot in my life, actually just how being born and growing up with a disability or just having a disability, you have to learn...I had an occupational therapist in high school tell me I hold my pencil kind of weird. I have pretty good handwriting, but she kind of analyzed it and she's like, 'Wow, you found a way to adapt to that challenge without anybody having to tell you.'...I think you learn a lot of problem solving, and persevering.

Despite the disparities described by students who are BIPOC and students who reported disabilities, they were able to repeatedly identify ways in which their identities and related experiences had prepared them to adapt in times of crisis. Their narratives highlighted an ability to hold space for multiple tensions, including acknowledging resiliency and adaptability without dismissing disparities and finding common ground in experiences of marginalization without ignoring unique lived experiences.

Trauma-Informed Strategies for Teaching During Crisis

Trauma-informed pedagogy offers hope for teaching during times of crisis and beyond. When we center an understanding that global pandemics, natural disasters, or other types of crises are forms of trauma, we can approach students with grace, understanding, and flexibility. Clearly, there are aspects of trauma-informed pedagogy that directly translate to the ways in which we teach students experiencing marginalization during a crisis. We can establish safety in our classrooms by checking in with students, providing space for them to decompress, and addressing harms caused by other students related to marginalization. We can emphasize choice and flexibility in assignments, learning methods, and due dates. We can approach students from a place of trust and inherent worth rather than distrust and skepticism. We can meet them where they are, rather than where we are.

These aspects of trauma-informed pedagogy are essential components to teaching, regardless of global, local, or even individual crises. Indeed, we may never know when individual students are experiencing a crisis and, thus, approaching our classrooms and teaching in a trauma-informed manner is critical. As indicated by our own experiences and those of the students we interviewed, teaching during a large crisis may require more from us as educators. Our teaching may need to shift to more explicitly center and meet the needs of students experiencing marginalization within the context of crisis. To do this, we propose utilizing these principles derived from trauma-informed pedagogy, as well as other frameworks or lenses that offer promising strategies for teaching marginalized students during times of crisis: trickle-up social justice and complex hope.

Trickle-up social justice was born out of advocacy and activism related to both gender-based violence and queer and trans justice (Mehrotra et al., 2016; Spade, 2009). In traditional advocacy movements, justice was presumed to trickle down, with the assumption that if rights were obtained by some of a marginalized group, they would trickle down to others. For example, in the lesbian, gay, bisexual, transgender, and queer (LGBTQ+) rights movement, the fight for marriage equality took center stage for many years and largely benefited middle-upper class white gay, and lesbian people, yet failed to "trickle down" to rights for more marginalized sub-groups, such as youth who are queer and trans homeless BIPOC. Alternatively, trickle-up social justice argues that we must center the most marginalized in our advocacy efforts because obtaining rights, equity, and justice for those individuals and communities will trickle-up to people with less marginalization.

Although trickle-up social justice is situated in advocacy and activism, it can be translated to education and how we teach during crisis and non-crisis times. When we craft our syllabi, assignments, tests, policies, and interactions with students with the most marginalized identities in mind, they will translate to students without or with fewer marginalized identities. For example, students in our study who would have reached out to instructors to ask for extensions or assistance during "normal" times were not able to do so during the pandemic—it was too emotionally exhausting and taxing. This may mean that although we have a policy in our syllabus to contact the instructor if there are problems or concerns, we may need to reach out individually to students who have stopped showing up for class or are behind on their work. We cannot assume our students will have the emotional or physical capacity to get their needs met during a large crisis. This is especially important during times of crisis as we know marginalization is often a factor in who is most impacted by a crisis. We see this repeatedly within the COVID-19 pandemic as well as other large-scale disasters, such as Hurricane Katrina. Trickle-up social justice calls us as educators to consider how crisis and other factors are affecting our students who experience marginalization regularly and more so during crisis and center them in our planning and decision making.

Complex hope is primarily situated within education research and suggests that while it is the job of educators to instill hope in their students, this hope must also be situated in an understanding of the realities of historical and societal challenges (Webb, 2010). Hope cannot just be an overly optimistic belief that everything will work out, but rather grounded in the realities of systemic and historical oppression. Duncan-Andrade (2009) discusses the role of complex hope for educators teaching students who have experienced historical and contemporary marginalization. They argue for educators to move away from eternal optimism and hope as a method of slowing down or stifling progress and instead engage in three types of critical hope: material, Socratic, and audacious. Material hope includes resource provision to help students access personal agency and empowerment change aspects of their lives. Socratic hope requires an understanding of pain and anger as normal, expected reactions to marginalization and oppression. Audacious hope "demands that we reconnect to the collective by struggling alongside one another, sharing in the victories *and* the pain" (p. 190, emphasis theirs).

Although situated within primary and secondary schooling, the ideas related to complex and critical hope translate to the work of educators in college and university settings, particularly during times of crisis and with marginalized students. Duncan-Andrade (2009) argues that the biggest material resource educators can provide to their students is "quality teaching." Quality teaching is often equated with rigor and firm structure which is then seen as in opposition to social justice and flexibility in teaching. Alternatively, we argue that quality teaching and justice-oriented teaching can and should co-exist. When we relinquish power and control as educators and meet our students where they are, we may be able to identify creative and quality strategies for teaching concepts that are directly related to their lives. We must dismantle the idea that quality equals inflexiblity and that justice is antithetical to quality. For example, an educator could tie in current events and the crisis into the class content, making the material highly relevant to the students' current lives and realities.

Hope and social justice work as educators are messy and complicated. When we aim to engage with marginalized students, particularly during times of crisis, we must allow ourselves to sit in the mess and discomfort with our students. By doing so, we can move away from attempting to reduce students' anxieties and challenges and instead lean in to supporting them in a collaborative manner. We do not need to manage our students' feelings of rage, anger, discontent, sadness, or fear. They deserve and get to feel these things. Rather, as educators, we can sit with them in these feelings and identify collective goals for how to channel them into a place of hope. This requires us to BE with students rather than DO for students. It requires us to model vulnerability and authenticity and move beyond the confines of our syllabus. It requires us to reach out to individual students to express concern, support, and complex hope. It requires us to move away from mass emails or communication that seem like marketing strategies and engage in authentic interactions with our students. As Duncan-Andrade (2009) stated, "At the end of the day, effective teaching depends most heavily on one thing: deep and caring relationships."

We recognize that these approaches are not concrete strategies or a to-do list of teaching practices. We do so intentionally to avoid suggesting that a list of strategies will ever fully be trauma- or social justice-informed. Rather, we advocate for a conceptual shift in how we approach and frame our teaching during times of crisis with an explicit emphasis on the needs and experiences of students experiencing marginalization. Further, we argue that these strategies and this conceptual shift should inform our teaching and pedagogy broadly, within and beyond small and large crises. Doing so will promote a more inclusive and justice-oriented learning experience for all of our students and, subsequently, will require fewer shifts when unexpected crises emerge.

REFERENCES

Carello, J., & Butler, L. D. (2015). Practicing what we teach: Trauma-informed educational practice. *Journal of Teaching in Social Work, 35*(3), 262–278. https://doi.org/10.1080/08841233.2015.1030059

Duncan-Andrade, J. M. R. (2009). Note to educators: Hope required when growing roses in concrete. *Harvard Educational Review, 79*(2), 181–194.

Harris, M. E., & Fallot, R. D. (2001). *Using trauma theory to design service systems.* Jossey-Bass.

Mehrotra, G. R., Kimball, E., & Wahab, S. (2016). The braid that binds us: The impact of neoliberalism, criminalization, and professionalization on domestic violence work. *Affilia: Journal of Women in Social Work, 31*(2), 153–163. https://doi.org/10.1177/0886109916643871

Spade, D. (2009). Trans politics on a neoliberal landscape [video file]. http://bcrw.barnard.edu/videos/dean-spade-trickle-up-social-justice-excerpt/

Substance Abuse and Mental Health Services Administration. (2014). *SAMHSA's concept of trauma and guidance for a trauma-informed approach.* Author. https://store.samhsa.gov/system/files/sma14-4884.pdf

Webb, D. (2010). Paulo Friere and 'the need for a kind of education in hope.' *Cambridge Journal of Education, 40*(4), 327–339.

CHAPTER 9

How Trauma-Informed Care Principles Can Contribute to Academic Success for Students in Hispanic-Serving Institutions

Joy Patton and Lauren Cortez

The Hispanic population is one of the fastest growing populaces in the United States, however, in comparison to the general population, the least likely to have, at minimum, an undergraduate degree. According to a report for the US Census Bureau (2016), of the general population ages 25 years and older, 36.2% of all non-Hispanics, 22.5% of all Blacks, 53.9% of all Asian, and 15.5% of all Hispanics reported having at least a bachelor's degree. Efforts to increase the education level of Hispanics began with the Department of Education offering federal funds for Hispanic-Serving Institutions (HSI) as a result of Title III of the Higher Education Act of 1965. However, it was not until 1992, with the Hispanic Association of Colleges and Universities (HACU) leading the efforts, that Congress began to formally recognize campuses with high Hispanic enrollments as federally designated HSIs in order to direct federally appropriated funds to these institutions (HACU, 2020).

HSIs are one of the many federal Minority-Serving Institution (MSI) designations from the US Department of Education, which refer to degree-granting institutions that improve the academic attainment and success of Hispanic

J. Patton (✉)
Our Lady of the Lake University, San Antonio, TX, USA
e-mail: jpatton@ollusa.edu

Burleson, TX, USA

L. Cortez
Castroville, TX, USA

© The Author(s), under exclusive license to Springer Nature Switzerland AG 2022
P. Thompson and J. Carello (eds.), *Trauma-Informed Pedagogies*,
https://doi.org/10.1007/978-3-030-92705-9_9

students (Palmer, 2019). Through the reauthorization of the Higher Education Act of 1992, HSIs were designated by federal legislation (Hannah, 1996). To be eligible for HSI designation, 2-year or 4-year, degree accredited, not-for-profit institutions must have at least 25% of their enrolled undergraduate students be of Hispanic descent and more than 50% be identified as low-income individuals (Contreras et al., 2008).

Also through the Higher Education Act of 1992, funding is provided to eligible HSIs from Title III and Title V programs (US Department of Education, 2020). Title III programs provide funds to manage financial stability and support educational quality improvements to institutions that enroll large percentages of minority and low-income students. The Title V program provides funds specifically for designated HSIs to help strengthen the institution, support fiscal operations, and assist in building endowments. These are the principal sources of federal support for HSIs.

HSIs represent about 13% of all higher education institutions in the United States, but, unfortunately, persistent underfunding continues, even though HSIs enroll more than two-thirds of all Hispanic college students across the nation. According to the HACU (2020), an analysis of data collected by the Integrated Postsecondary Education Data System in 2016–2017 revealed that, of all federal funds allocated to HSIs, on average, HSIs receive much less funding than all other colleges and universities annually; $3,117 per student annually in HSIs compared to $4,605 per student for all degree-granting institutions. This indicates a significant gap in funding and resources for a disproportionately low-income student population.

Student learning and success are shared universal core values by the nation's higher education institutions. HSIs undoubtedly share this same goal of fostering student learning and success; however, the HSI designation strengthens the importance of actively serving Hispanic students and students overall through the promotion of academic success and not just educational access. HSIs have a vested interest in ensuring their students receive the academic preparation and ongoing support for degree completion and, in the process, a cultural environment inside and outside the classroom that cultivates students' self-efficacy (Gasman et al., 2008).

EFFECTS OF COVID ON HSIs

There is no doubt that COVID-19 has had a tremendous impact on all colleges and universities across the nation; however, the virus has had a much greater impact on HSIs because these institutions tend to be smaller in size, have fewer resources and infrastructure to support distance education, and historically do not have the funding to address the inequalities in higher education institution (HEI) settings (HACU, 2020). All HEIs across the nation had to move classes online and, most often, close the campus down completely, along with the closing of the nation, as that was crucial in curtailing the spread of the virus. Understanding the challenges that HSIs already faced, prior to COVID-19, it is not unexpected then that many Hispanic college students have reported a loss of access to technology, broadband internet, and workspaces, as well as loss of income and internships, at a far greater rate than the general college population as a result of COVID-19 HEI policies (Gates, 2020).

Effects of COVID on Students in an HSI

The COVID-19 pandemic has had and continues to have, many profound economic, psychological, and health consequences that, when taken together, can be characterized as a large-scale, traumatic, global event. The discovery of the extensive and long-lasting consequences of the pandemic is still unfolding and could quite possibly take decades to fully realize. Understanding the effects of COVID-19 for students in HSIs is especially important because research has shown that traumatic events increase the negative consequences of mental health among marginalized populations because of a significant number of daily stressors already present (Gruebner et al., 2017; Moore et al., 2015). Furthermore, the transactional model of stress and coping suggests that an individual's judgment of stressors determines how coping strategies will be used and, this, in turn, predicts the outcome of an event, whether that be negative or positive (Lazarus & Folkman, 1984). The outcome strived for among students in their academic studies is successful completion of classes that move them closer to their academic degree. Therefore, if administrators, faculty, and staff in HSIs desire to assist students toward their goal of successfully completing classes to reach the goal of an academic degree, realizing factors that both hinder and support students during this time of a global pandemic is essential.

Hispanic Student Experiences with COVID-19

A recent exploratory study was conducted by Caffrey et al. (2020) to help understand the most salient factors that led to student academic success during the COVID-19 pandemic. A secondary analysis of the data from this study revealed statistically significant differences between Hispanic students and students from all other races combined in experiences with COVID. For example, Hispanic students were more likely to have a diagnosis of COVID; to have had a close friend or family member who had a diagnosis of COVID and to have had a close friend or family member who had died from COVID. Furthermore, Hispanic students were more likely to report increased levels of stress, depression, and anxiety compared to students from all other races combined. Interestingly, the most significant finding for academic success for all students who participated in the study was the role of the instructor in their classes. Students who had an organized instructor who provided a safe environment and interesting learning activities were more likely to receive a final grade they expected to receive by the end of the semester in which COVID-19 transpired. This suggests then that faculty could hold the key to facilitating academic success for students, even in the midst of a global pandemic.

Hispanics and Trauma

Before the experiences with COVID-19, which, on its own, has shown to be a source of significant stress and trauma for college students, prior research has demonstrated that Hispanics tend to have high rates of PTSD, anxiety, and panic disorders, suicide, and suicidal ideations, substance use, and other mental health disorders, with increasing rates among second and third-generation Hispanics due to experiences of marginalization and acculturation (Fortuna, 2020). In a study by the National Child Traumatic Stress Network (2017), it was found that Hispanics experienced higher incidences of domestic violence, impaired caregiving, and community violence compared to Caucasian children. Additional environmental factors such as poverty, inadequate housing, single-parent households, substance abuse, stress related to discrimination, lower levels of education, and a history of oppression were found as contributors to the traumatic experiences of Hispanic children and families, leading, often-times, to what is known as complex trauma. Furthermore, research has shown that minority groups are significantly less likely to seek treatment for trauma and trauma-related symptoms than Whites because of widely held perceptions of stigma (Yamashiro & Matsuoka, 1997); mistrust of physicians (Almin et al., 2006); perceptions of bias in caregivers (Johnson et al., 2004), and reduced access to mental health care due to poverty and financial constraints (Chow et al., 2003).

Trauma-Informed Care Principles Applied in HSIs

What is known about individuals who live in conditions of ongoing exposure to trauma and who have recurrent experiences of trauma such as the COVID-19 pandemic, is that traumatic stress impairs the ability to maintain stable routines, creates a sense of vulnerability, anxiety, confusion, uncertainty, and helplessness, and can affect the ability to adjust to new challenges and stressors (Lahav, 2020). When looking at Hispanic students through this lens, the difficulties and challenges that class attendance and assignment completion poses is easily understood. SAMHSA (2014) has identified four key assumptions for organizations and six key principles for trauma-informed practice that can be drawn upon by administrators and faculty when working with Hispanic students experiencing overwhelming struggles of disengagement in classes due to additional traumatic stressors posed by crises such as the COVID-19 pandemic. The four key assumptions for organizations include:

- realizing the widespread impact of trauma and its role in recovery,

- recognizing the signs and symptoms of trauma for all employees and students within the university,
- responding to the trauma by changing policies, practices, and procedures to support those who are experiencing trauma and,
- actively resisting practices that will re-traumatize.

The six key principles for trauma-informed practice include:

- safety
- trustworthiness and transparency
- peer support
- collaboration and mutuality
- empowerment and choice
- cultural, historical and gender issues

The main focus here, however, will be on two of the key principles for faculty to practice in a trauma-informed approach with Hispanic students in an HSI. These two key principles are (1) collaboration with students by bringing them into the process to discuss mutually agreed upon goals and (2) being sensitive to the racial, ethnic, and cultural background and gender identity of students.

The key principle of collaboration and mutuality involves the partnering and leveling of power differences between faculty and students for meaningful sharing of power and decision-making. Applying this principle in HSIs, faculty would be willing to work collaboratively with students who may be experiencing challenges with assignment deadlines and, come to a mutual agreement on a different assignment deadline that is more manageable and attainable. Additionally, faculty could find alternative ways for assignments to be completed through the collaboration and mutual agreement of students. For example, in a class where a weekly written reflection journal was required, faculty could instead incorporate a video conference with students to reflect upon topics instead. This could prove to be especially important for Hispanic students who, due to additional stressors associated with COVID-19, might lack the ability to maintain the stable routines essential in providing the time and space necessary to complete writing assignments.

The second key principle is being responsive to the racial, ethnic, and cultural needs of students in ways that recognize and address historical trauma. In order to provide a trauma-informed approach based on this key principle, faculty must first learn about the cultural and historic trauma Hispanic students have experienced. Quite often, Hispanic children are taught the cultural value of *respecto*, which emphasizes obedience and dictates children should be highly considerate of adults and those in positions of authority and they are taught to not interrupt or argue. Hispanic students often see their instructors as those in authority and drawing from their value of *respecto*, find it difficult to approach the instructor to ask for assistance or extensions on assignments. Keeping this cultural value in mind and recognizing the Hispanic student's historical trauma, coupled with additional stressors such as COVID-19 that could lead to feelings of vulnerability and helplessness, instructors working from a trauma-informed approach would be more likely to pay close attention to students who are underperforming in their classes and be willing to reach out to the student for assistance instead of expecting the student to connect with the instructor first. For example, instructors could actively engage one-on-one with students who are underperforming through email, phone calls, and video conferencing, actively listening to the needs, concerns and challenges the student is facing. Through respectful and compassionate communication, the instructor could seek to re-engage the student in the class and assignments, finding collaborative and mutually agreed-upon solutions that are unique to the student's situation.

CONCLUSIONS

It is becoming clearer that trauma-informed approaches must not only be provided by professionals working directly with clients and students but must also be included in organizational policies and culture to be most effective. In an issue brief by the Robert Wood Johnson Foundation (2016) it was stated, "trying to implement trauma-specific clinical practices without first implementing trauma-informed organizational change is like throwing seeds on dry land" (p. 3).

Although no individual's situation is equivalent in experience, the COVID-19 pandemic has created a collective human experience of considerable mental health and trauma-related consequences. Hispanic students appear to be experiencing negative effects from the pandemic at a higher rate than other students because of the stressors that were most likely present prior to the pandemic. Equipped with the knowledge of disparities in US higher education matriculation among Hispanic students prior to the pandemic, and the negative impact of pandemic-related trauma on Hispanic students, administrators, faculty, and staff can provide their Hispanic students academic support and a path toward a higher quality of life through trauma-informed practices.

Extra time and care from administrators, faculty, and staff are needed as COVID-19 continues to rage on around the world. Considering the effects of trauma from the pandemic will not dissipate for many years after the pandemic has come to an end, HEIs would benefit from transforming policies, procedures, bylaws, and strategic plans to incorporate trauma-informed approaches that best support faculty and staff in providing trauma-informed care to all students, but especially to Hispanic students to ensure an increase in the number of university-educated Hispanics.

REFERENCES

Almin, T. N., Charney, D. S., & Mellman, T. A. (2006). An overview of posttraumatic stress disorder in African Americans. *Journal of Clinical Psychology, 62*, 801–813.

Caffrey, T., Viverette, A., & Patton, J. D. (2020). *Effects of the COVID-19 pandemic on student academic success* [unpublished manuscript]. Worden School of Social Service, Our Lady of the Lake University.

Chow, J. C., Jaffee, K., & Snowden, L. (2003). Racial/ethnic disparities in the use of mental health services in poverty areas. *American Journal of Public Health, 93*, 792–797.

Contreras, F. E., Malcom, L. E., & Bensimon, E. M. (2008). Hispanic serving institutions. *Understanding minority serving institutions*, 71–90.

Fortuna, L. (2020). *Working with Latino/a and Hispanic patients*. American Psychiatric Association https://www.psychiatry.org/psychiatrists/cultural-compet ency/education/best-practice-highlights/working-with-latino-patients

Gasman, M., Baez, B., & Turner, C. S. V. (2008). *Understanding minority-serving institutions*. SUNY Press.

Gates, Q. A. (2020). *Impact of COVID-19*. Computing alliance of Hispanic-serving institutions. NSF Committee on Equal Opportunities, El Paso, TX.

Gruebner, O., Rapp, M., Adli, M., Kluge, U., Galea, S., & Heinz, A. (2017). Cities and mental health. *Deutsches Arzteblatt International, 114*, 121–127. https://doi.org/10.3238/arztebl.2017.0121

Hannah, S. B. (1996). The Higher Education Act of 1992: Skills, constraints, and the politics of higher education. *The Journal of Higher Education, 67*(5), 498–527.

Hispanic Association of Colleges and Universities. (2020). About Hispanic-Serving Institutions (HSIs). https://www.hacu.net/hacu/HACU_101.asp

Johnson, R. L., Saha, S., Arbelaez, J. J., Beach, M. C., & Cooper, L. A. (2004). Racial and ethnic differences in patient perceptions of bias and cultural competence in health care. *Journal of General Internal Medicine, 19*, 101–110.

Lahav, L. (2020). Psychological distress related to COVID-19: The contribution of continuous traumatic stress. *Journal of Affective Disorders, 277*, 1129–1137. https://doi.org/10.1016/j.jad.2020.07.141

Lazarus, R. S., & Folkman, S. (1984). *Stress, appraisal, and coping*. Spring Publishing.

Moore, T., MacDonald, M., Carlon, L., & O'Rourke, K. (2015). Early childhood development and the social determinants of health inequities. *Health Promotion International, 30*, ii102–ii115. https://doi.org/10.1093/heapro/dav031

Palmer, R. T. (2019). Examining effective practices at minority-serving institutions: Beyond a deficit framing of leadership and overview of chapters. In *Examining effective practices at minority-serving institutions* (pp. 1–10). Springer.

Robert Wood Johnson Foundation. (2016). *Issue Brief: Key ingredients for successful trauma-informed care implementation*. Center for Health Care Strategies.

Substance Abuse and Mental Health Administration. (2014). *SAMHSA's concept of trauma and guidance for a trauma-informed approach*. HHS. Publication No. (SMA) 14-4884.

The National Child Traumatic Stress Network. (2017). Preliminary adaptations for working with traumatized Latino/Hispanic children and their families. *Culture and Trauma Brief, 2*(3), 1–8.

United States Department of Education. (2020). *Higher Ed Grants*. https://www.hig heredgrants.info/GrantDetails.aspx?gid=54383

United States Census Bureau. (2016). *Educational attainment in the United States: 2016.* https://www.census.gov/data/tables/2016/demo/education-attainment/cps-detailed-tables.html

Yamashiro, G., & Matsuoka, J. K. (1997). Help-seeking among Asian and Pacific Americans: A multiperspective analysis. *Social Work, 42,* 176–186.

CHAPTER 10

Naming the Urgency: The Importance of Trauma-Informed Practices in Community Colleges

Jeanie Tietjen

Before clicking on the link that starts the video conferencing meeting for an online synchronous early morning college writing class, I receive an email from a student apologizing for turning in the last two assignments late. The student's family and community life have been disrupted due to rioting and heavy gunfire in which an estimated 45 people were shot dead and 800 arrested in response to electoral factors thousands of geographic miles away from the community college where I teach. Another student, an immigrant from Haiti who fled after the catastrophic 2010 earthquake, enters the in-person physical classroom in a security guard uniform having just worked a ten-hour overnight shift. After class the second week of the semester, a student veteran who served tours in both Iraq and Afghanistan quietly hands me accessibility accommodation paperwork in response to diagnosed PTSD and a mild traumatic brain injury. Despite living in close proximity to a community college in his neighborhood, another student commutes to my college's campus from a city approximately 30 miles away to avoid gang activity and people who, in his words, make bad choices. A woman in her early forties resumes college education after leaving a decades-long abusive marriage. Snapshot profiles such as these represent lived experience and also signify how

J. Tietjen (✉)
Faculty of English, Institute for Trauma, Adversity, and Resilience in Higher
Education, MassBay Community College, Wellesley, MA, USA
e-mail: jtietjen@massbay.edu

© The Author(s), under exclusive license to Springer Nature
Switzerland AG 2022
P. Thompson and J. Carello (eds.), *Trauma-Informed Pedagogies*,
https://doi.org/10.1007/978-3-030-92705-9_10

trauma and adversity appear and impact the learning process in higher education, how resilience behaviors are remarkably common and provide insight into obstacles that can derail educational plans.

An estimated 41% of undergraduates in the United States attend community college, and these open-access institutions represent remarkable diversity in demographics, levels of academic preparation, and educational and career goals. Just under 30% of community college students are first generation, 15% are single parents, 9% are non-U.S. citizens, 5% are veterans, and 20% have documented disabilities (American Association of Community Colleges, 2021). As gateways for both traditional and post-traditional students and characterized by a unique fluency between campus and the community, these colleges serve as sites of potential academic, career, and personal transformation. Higher education also forms a gateway to socioeconomic mobility, empowering individuals to make the kind of meaningful progress the United States critically needs for its workplaces, and civic and domestic life, and community colleges represent an exciting setting for emerging and next-generation workforce and citizenry.

Yet it's important to recognize that community college students undertake their educational pathways often with more challenges and fewer resources to manage. For example, the Hope Center's 2020 survey of basic needs in higher education including 247 community colleges reports that 42% of community college students were food insecure in the last month, 50% experienced housing insecurity, and 17% experienced homelessness in the previous year (Baker-Smith et al., 2020). In addition to the equity gap, many community college students have also been exposed to traumatic or potentially traumatic experiences: veterans returning from Iraq and Afghanistan, students and families displaced by political and social upheaval, by natural disasters, by domestic and community violence, by addiction, by issues in mental health (Arnekrans et al., 2018; Ashford, 2020; Brogden & Gregory, 2019; Davidson, 2017; Edman et al, 2016; Hinojosa et al., 2018; Metzler et al., 2017; Ogul, 2020; Read et al., 2011; Shalka, 2015; Verschelden, 2017). Further, the community college student body is constituted by those identified as academically vulnerable in post-secondary education—LGBTQ+ individuals, BIPOC/people of color, women, students with uncertain immigration status, first-generation students, veterans, and students with disabilities (Davidson, 2017). Those same individuals are also at higher risk for trauma including identity-based systemic violence and marginalization (Davidson, 2017; Edman et al., 2016; Gomez, 2019; Verschelden, 2017). Recognizing this data and its demographics aims neither to pathologize community college students nor embrace a deficit model of pedagogy and student services. Rather, it seeks to challenge or destabilize the notion that somehow most people have little or no violence in their normal lives, and those who do must in some way exist outside the realm of the ordinary. The truth is that while traumatic experiences used to be thought of as uncommon, leading health organizations such as the Centers for Disease Control (CDC, 2019) and Substance Abuse and Mental Health

Services Administration (SAMHSA, 2019) now recognize trauma as not only commonplace but prevalent.

As a college writing professor, my colleagues and I are natural witnesses to narratives conveying the lived experiences of students. In composition classes across the nation, we address common modes of rhetorical writing including description and narration, working with students on various competencies in research and writing. In my own classes, the narrative and descriptive essay functions as an effective on-ramp between the personal and the newly evolving academic voice. Nearly a third of community college students are first-generation, so beginning with content students know (their own experiences) often increases relevance and engagement. In response to a generic writing prompt offering options to reflect upon meaningful experiences or individuals it is not uncommon for students to relate experiences that are painful:

> *I was 16 years old when I found myself homeless.*
>
> *I was so afraid to leave my home but my family had to desert our culture and roots and everything that was ours in the midst of the war to escape being murdered, put into prison, or to starve along with all the other people of my country. It's hard to explain.*
>
> *He wasn't allowed in our house because my mom said he was lying in court saying she was planning to kidnap my brother and me.*
>
> *All my friends around me were people who used drugs and did so many criminal things and every single day I was afraid to get into trouble because of their way of life.*
>
> *She's stiff so stiff I couldn't move her and couldn't find a pulse and I call Katrina and she tells me to call the police right now.*
>
> *I didn't tell anyone for years because he said he would hurt me and nobody would believe me anyway it'd be my word against his.*

These particular examples are fictional composites. However, they fairly represent some of the range of traumatic events regularly disclosed in the community college classroom: homelessness, political violence, family dysfunction and discord, the violence of drug culture and the opioid epidemic, and childhood sexual assault. Moreover, often an essay represents not just one but a concurrence or co-morbidity of potentially traumatic factors such as mental illness, addiction, poverty, and a loved one's early death. How to appropriately respond to student disclosure of traumatic or adverse experiences in the context of academia, what Jeffrey Berman characterizes as "risky writing" (Berman, 2001), has been the subject of a good number of books and essays over the years precisely because the phenomenon is so widespread.

Traumatic experience as subject matter in personal narrative is also not unfamiliar to me as a writing instructor. When I started teaching in January 2009 at the community college, I had already at least ten years of teaching experience ranging from English language learners both in the United States and overseas, teaching writing in homeless shelters and a women's prison, plus a usual palette of college composition and literature courses as a graduate student at university. What stunned me in 2009 and continues to be remarkable today is not that a few folks in a class of just over twenty choose to represent traumatic content. Rather, it is that proportionally so many of these essays make this decision and also that a single essay often presents multiple experiences categorizable as violent, traumatic, or adverse. Given that that an estimated 70% of adults in the United States have experienced a traumatic event at least once in their lives (only around 20% of these people go on to develop PTSD), any surprise at this proportion has more to do with mistaken assumptions about adversity and violence than it does with the actual pervasiveness. "Unless education at all levels acknowledges the violence in the lives of women and children along with its impact on learning," writes literacy instructor and author Jenny Horsman (2000) in *Too Scared To Learn*, "many students will not only fail to learn, but may also experience the educational setting as a silencing place or another site of violence, where they are controlled and diminished by institutional structures or classroom interactions and shamed by their failure to learn" (p.7). Violence is commonplace, and yet educators have been conditioned to categorize individual, familial, community, and systemic traumas as extraordinary and largely absent from the learning process, thus constructing a failure of recognition that undermines teaching and learning.

Naming the Problem: Trauma, Adversity, and Violence in Higher Education

The 1998 Adverse Childhood Experiences (ACE) public health study established trauma and adversity as common and prevalent factors influencing public health, correlating trauma to adult health and well-being outcomes including lowered educational attainment. In fact, the classroom was one of the first places in which researchers saw the impact of childhood adversity with "more than half of those with ACE scores of four or higher reported having learning or behavioral problems, compared with 3 percent of those with a score of zero" (van der Kolk, 2014). In the same year the ACE study was first published, an interdisciplinary group of parents, educators, experts in trauma, lawyers, and social services professionals headed by the nonprofit Massachusetts Advocates for Children examined how domestic violence created learning and behavioral difficulties for children and adolescents (Cole et al., 2005). They did so in response to an expulsion crisis involving children with behavioral difficulties including acting-out behaviors in the classroom (Cole et al., 2005). What they learned is that a history of exposure to trauma, violence, and toxic stress produces neurobiological changes that adversely impact academic and social functioning. Essentially, when neural functions that regulate the fight/flight/freeze in response to perceived threat are continually stimulated, the stress response becomes over-active. This matters because while the stress response functions adaptively in the short term, its overactivation works against the kind of self-regulation, cognition, and interpersonal skills critical to academic and social well-being (Cole et al., 2005). This critical recognition of the prevalence of trauma and adversity coupled with understanding the impact of these on the developing brain form the cornerstone of the now well-established trauma-sensitive schools movement K-12 nationwide. Trauma-informed educational practices in elementary and secondary schools affirm the ubiquity of violence and trauma and orient their practices based on knowledge of the learning brain.

But trauma likewise matriculates, affecting traditional benchmarks of post-secondary success including retention, course completion, and graduation rates (Davidson, 2017; Read et al., 2011). While not yet as established as the K-12 trauma-sensitive schools movement, research indicates that as in the general population, experiences of adversity and trauma in college students are common, increasing the risk for physical and mental illness, substance abuse, and risky behaviors (Oehme et al., 2019). Substance abuse, psychological distress, and risky behaviors can in turn impact persistence, completion, and GPA (Arnekrans et al., 2018; Brogden & Gregory, 2019; Davidson, 2017; Hinojosa et al., 2018; Kerka, 2002; Metzler et al., 2017; Read et al., 2011). Research summarized by Education Northwest's *Trauma-Informed Practices for Postsecondary Education* posits that trauma impacts attention, self-regulation, and stress management as well as access to higher-order skills necessary for academic success such as abstract thinking and problem solving (Davidson, 2017). In contrast to the acting out behaviors that in part gave rise to the K-12 trauma-sensitive schools movement, concerning behaviors in higher education present more often as disengagement. Students with trauma histories may struggle with poor attendance, for example, or become easily overwhelmed and emotionally dysregulated with anxiety about deadlines, exams, group work, or public speaking. They may be more prone to isolation and withdrawal, less likely to seek out supports to solve inevitable challenges, have difficulty focusing on and retaining content, and resist the risk and ambiguity inherent in the learning process (Davidson, 2017; Hallett & Crutchfield, 2017; Hoch et al., 2015).

Cognition at the post-secondary level is in some ways the most expendable of human brain functions. Successful college students attend class with regularity, structure time outside of class to study, and negotiate peer and educational relationships for personal and academic support. They write essays, perform calculations and experiments, and navigate technology tools and platforms. Abstract thinking, delaying gratification, and setting goals are examples of higher order cortical functions that can be eclipsed or hijacked when the threat and fear mechanisms in the brain get activated. The fight–flight–freeze or Arousal Response (Perry, The Child Trauma Academy, 2011) has historically saved our lives for thousands and thousands of evolutionary years. Its calibration to finely differentiate types of threat (an actual tiger versus the paper tiger of an upcoming exam) is more rough-hewn, however. Once the arousal system activates, neurochemical messaging urgently recruits physiological stress responses that "flip the lid" (Siegel, 2012) of the cortex, as Daniel Siegel characterizes, rendering those higher order functions largely inaccessible until normal, baseline reactivity is restored. Students with trauma histories can have threat response systems that are pitched or "tuned up" making them more reactive to stressors and to unfamiliar and potentially therefore threatening situations and encounters (Perry, The Child Trauma Academy, 2011). "The key to understanding the long-term impact of trauma on an adult learner," offers Perry, "is to remember that he or she is often, at baseline, in a state of low-level fear. This fear state reflects either hyper-arousal or a dissociative adaptation pattern, or a combination of both" (Perry, Fear and Learning: Trauma-Related Factors in the Adult Education Process, 2006). Ambiguity and contradiction—hallmark features of complex subjects, phenomenon, and human relationships—carry a higher arousal potential than simplicity and congruity. Higher order cognition necessary to learning in post-secondary life depends upon the ability to access the cortex, and the ability to manage or regulate the arousal response is why mindfulness practices are often referred to as the *Einsteinification* of the brain (EOC Institute, 2021). Brains that are less alarmed are quite literally and organically thinking better and with more facility.

In nearly all the composite writing presented earlier in which the students describe trauma, adversity, and violence, the writers in their essays unanimously concluded that the experiences ultimately taught important lessons and insights, and resulted in personal growth, strength, and empowerment. While psychological resilience and posttraumatic growth are thankfully the norm and given that community college students often demonstrate extraordinary personal resilience, the disruptive impact violence has on academic resilience is at the same time clear and consequential. Academic resilience refers to the "capacity to overcome acute and/or chronic adversity that is seen as a major threat to a student's educational development" (cited in Chisolm-Burns, 2019). Academic resilience indicates the ability to persist with one's studies in the face of adversity, difficulty, obstacle, failure, and stress. Many community college students face adversity that is complex, serious, and consequential: for example, how does the notion of homework change when a student has no home in which to do the work and counts among the 14% of community college students nationwide who are housing insecure and homeless (Baker-Smith, et al., *#RealCollege 2020: Five Years of Evidence on Basic Needs Insecurity*, 2020). And for those students who before the pandemic closures, for example, depended upon libraries and college cafeterias as predictably open, safe sites in which to do the work away from an abusive partner or homophobic family environment, loss of those spaces further saps what Cia Verschelden (2017) calls the "cognitive bandwidth" available to learn. Poverty, racism, homophobia, transphobia, discrimination, and stereotype threats are costly because they demand cognitive resources to manage. When the arousal system discussed earlier is constantly being activated in response to very real threats, higher order cortical functioning becomes, in Verschelden's vernacular, less affordable.

> Students whose bandwidth is depleted are less able to "keep their head in the game." When they're worried and broke and feel isolated, it's difficult for them to focus on long-term goals … Students' capacity for persistence is diminished, and school might lose out to life's other demands. Even if students somehow find the self-control to focus on academics, they may do half as well with only half of their cognitive resources available for the task. It is easy to understand why they might give up altogether. (Verschelden, 2017, pp. 29–30)

Indeed it is. I've lost track of how many students with whom I've met over routine issues in composition who end up disclosing the actual story behind a late assignment, failed quiz, and missed class. One such student was responsible for dropping off his two younger siblings at elementary school before coming to campus, and he missed a class and assignment. When he showed up at my office to explain that his siblings had been delayed in getting ready, thus holding him up, he ended up talking about how his mother had years ago left a cigarette burning that caught fire and seriously damaged the apartment in which they lived. She had problems in her mind, my student explained, and he had to take care of his siblings. Though the actual danger had long ago passed, its memory continued to register in the present, and when forced to choose between his own schedule and the safe delivery of his siblings, he chose the latter. In other words, past trauma-informed current decision-making for this student which in turn affected his ability to be present in class.

The point here is not that students miss class or turn in assignments late. The point is that traumatic experiences in the past inform present decision-making and were very much part of this student's active cognitive bandwidth. Further, as an instructor I did absolutely nothing but listen to this student's memories. I was not responsible for fixing his schedule or finding transportation for his siblings and was neither social worker nor therapist. And yet in my role as instructor for a class in which this first-generation citizen and college student is enrolled, the simple act of listening for all of twenty minutes facilitated a recognition of the decisions he made to achieve his academic goals. And this attentiveness makes a difference because sharing that story creates a connection between the student, me as faculty and representative of higher education as institution, and the uneven path to completion. In a small but not insignificant way, he forged a link between his non-academic personal life and the responsibilities of the classroom and was seen and heard in a way in which he could recognize himself as on an authentic post-secondary trajectory. He later fulfilled the requirements for his program and graduated with an associate degree.

However, data on persistence culminating in graduation can be frankly depressing. Thirteen percent of community college students graduate in two years, according to the National Center for Education Statistics, 22% of students graduate in three, and within four years, the rate stands at 28% (Chen, 2020). While these numbers actually have serious flaws (for instance, they don't count the significant percentage of community college students who transfer before graduation and then graduate with significant credits earned from the community college from which they transferred without graduating), the reality is that many community college students drop out. Yet faculty and staff familiar with the everyday lives of these students are often more surprised at how students manage to persist given the many obstacles.

> Another report by New American Foundation explores the specific needs of community college students and relates those to dismal graduation rates. The report explains that many high school graduates that come from low-income families or are first-generation college-goers may find community college to be the best option for them. However, life circumstances for these demographics, including financial constraints, transportation, and child care needs, can hinder goals to finish the educational process and obtain a degree in a traditional time-frame. Therefore, many of the students who show up in reports as "dropouts" did not leave school because they wanted to, rather, they were compelled to by some uncontrollable life event. While it is difficult to determine the exact number of students who fall into this category, it is sure to be a large portion of the total number of students who do not complete their two-year degree. The American Community College Association contends that if this and other factors were taken into account, graduation rates for two-year institutions would be closer to 40 percent. (Chen, 2020)

In other words, practical obstacles that overwhelm academic resilience and influence educational outcomes frequently originate outside the classroom, and educational pathways are derailed by factors beyond individual control. Further, the vast majority of student crises at the community college do not come to the attention of relevant resource providers on campus, or come at a crisis point and often too late, or far exceed the resources of a student development office. Additionally, federal and state funding mechanisms for public higher education and especially for community colleges fail to adequately allocate resources to the scope of need. For example, a recent *Center on American Progress* analysis revealed a funding gap of $78 billion between education revenue for community colleges as compared to four-year institutions (Yuen, 2020). And despite the educational services provided to an extraordinarily diverse student body with wide-ranging needs across the nation, stereotype and stigma regarding community colleges and their students persist. Community colleges perform a vital service in our nation precisely because they are open access and affordable, because they meet students exactly where they are. Curriculum from nursing and allied health to automotive to early childhood education and the first two years of liberal arts operates as a dynamic and vibrant network with countless points of connection between students representing a diverse range of academic experiences and their educational, career, and personal goals.

Higher education must consider how it does or does not recognize the pervasive, serious ways in which violence, trauma, and adversity undermine academic resilience. Misperceiving and misnaming a prevalent underlying problem leaves the educational community cycling through well-intentioned interventions that ultimately fall short of desired outcomes. Epidemiologist and one of the authors of the landmark Adverse Childhood Experiences study, Robert Anda offers that:

> our society has tended to treat the abuse, maltreatment, violence and chaotic experiences ... as an oddity instead of commonplace, as the ACE Study revealed...And our society believes that these experiences are adequately dealt with by emergency response systems such as child protective services, criminal justice, foster care, and alternative schools. "These services are needed and are worthy of support — but they are a dressing on a greater wound," he says. (cited in Stevens, 2012)

In her critical *Too Scared to Learn: Women, Violence, and Education*, Jenny Horsman argues against what she calls the "privatization of pain" at the site of education. What Horsman describes here is the conceptualization of violence and pain primarily as an individual, personal experience. She returns to this concept later when discussing the difference between therapy and literacy education with battered women in Canada. "The conception of violence as a private medical issue separate from education is a major barrier to programs and instructors recognizing issues of violence" (Horsman, 2000). Seeing the violence and pain that sap or derail development—including academic progress—as primarily individual misapprehends the scope and maintenance of historical, systemic violence as one person's problem. Being trauma-informed in higher education necessitates collective awareness of how trauma, adversity, and violence impact academic resilience. The focus is not on diagnosis of individuals as in a therapeutic context, but rather intentional awareness of the personal and systemic violence already present in the lives of campus members and also in the institutional history and practices. Working against the privatization of pain does not mean invalidating personal therapeutic work. What it refuses in the ecology of higher education is how violence is too often conceived through a prism that is individual and private rather than public and shared: not surprising in view of a highly individualistic culture in which pulling oneself up by the bootstraps is shorthand for the viability of the American dream.

A foundational precept in trauma-informed practice across human services formulated by Sandra Bloom and Sarah Sreehar's (2008) "The Sanctuary Model of Trauma-Informed Organizational Change" necessitates asking the right question: not "What's wrong with you?" but rather "What happened to you?" *What's wrong with you?* signifies a lexicon of deficit and pathology, and in the educational context, sets students up as broken, defective subjects in need of correction by expert authority. *What happened to you?* generates inquiry and recognizes that education occurs in a holistic context. To be clear, trauma informed education does not mean that faculty and staff diagnose students as patients: the educational alliance is fundamentally different from that of a trained, professional clinician. Being trauma-informed in higher education means that every area of the educational community—from pedagogy to campus security, advising to financial aid, facilities to college policies and administration—can be informed by understanding: the basics of the learning brain, the prevalence of trauma, adversity, and toxic stress, how resilience as skill can be encouraged through best practices and meaningful supports, and evidence that just one relationship can powerfully bolster productive and resilient behaviors. Rather than a rigidly prescriptive list of teaching or institutional practices, trauma-informed education instead describes a perspective or lens through which practices are evaluated and refined, revealing ways in which policies and practices might unconsciously exacerbate trauma, and pursuing academic rigor and inquiry in a supportive community informed by knowledge of lived experience. Revision of educational practices in higher education will not have a monolithic format, but will require local re-conception based on campus climate, resources, and needs. The trauma-informed educational movement K-12 and many of the authors in this collection offer much by way of precedent and possibility to interpret and scale to higher education. And this is the urgency, this is the core of the movement beginning to take hold nationwide in postsecondary education: trauma-informed higher education means seeing that trauma, adversity, and violence already exist as consequential forces in the lives of students as well as in the culture and practices that constitute higher education. Inadequate recognition of this prevalence undermines educational reform because it fails to see in whole or in part the fundamental mechanisms that either support or dysregulate cognition, relationship, and behaviors. Incorporating awareness of trauma and adversity also reveals strategies that contribute to academic resilience vital to authentic equity and inclusion in higher education and the health and well-being of our national workforce, citizenry, and community.

References

American Association of Community Colleges (AACC). (2021, January). *Fast facts 2021.* American Association of Community Colleges. https://www.aacc.nche.edu/wp-content/uploads/2021/03/AACC_2021_FastFacts.pdf

Arnekrans, A. K., Calmes, S. A., Laux, J. M., Roseman, C. P., Piazza, N. J., Reynolds, J. L., … Scott, H. L. (2018). College students' experiences of childhood developmental traumatic stress: resilience, first-year academic performance, and substance use. *Journal of College Counseling, 21*(1), 2–14.

Ashford, E. (2020, May 11). Pandemic compounds inequities. *Community College Daily.* https://www.ccdaily.com/2020/05/pandemic-compounds-inequities/

Baker-Smith, C., Coca, V., Goldrick-Rab, S., Looker, E., Richardson, B., & Williams, T. (2020). *#RealCollege 2020: Five years of evidence on campus basic needs insecurity. The Hope Center for College, Community, and Justice.* Temple University.

Berman, J. (2001). *Risky writing: Self-disclosure and self-transformation in the classroom.* University of Massachusetts Press.

Bloom, S. L., & Sreedhar, S. Y. (2008). The sanctuary model of trauma-informed organizational change. *Reclaiming Children and Youth, 17*(3), 48.

Brogden, L., & Gregory, D. E. (2019). Resilience in community college students with adverse childhood experiences. *Community College Journal of Research and Practice, 43*(2), 94–108.

Center for Disease Control. (2019, November). *Adverse childhood experiences (ACEs): Preventing early trauma to improve adult health.* CDC Vitalsigns. https://www.cdc.gov/vitalsigns/aces/pdf/vs-1105-aces-H.pdf

Chen, G. (2020, June 15). The Catch-22 of community college graduation rates. *Community College Review.* https://www.communitycollegereview.com/blog/the-catch-22-of-community-college-graduation-rates

Chisholm-Burns, M. A., Spivey, C. A., Sherwin, E., Williams, J., & Phelps, S. (2019). Development of an instrument to measure academic resilience among pharmacy students. *American Journal of Pharmaceutical Education, 83*(6), 6896. https://doi.org/10.5688/ajpe6896

Cole, S., O'Brien, J., Gadd, M., Ristuccia, J., Wallace, D., & Gregory, M. (2005). *Helping Traumatized children Learn: Supportive school environments for children traumatized by family violence.* Massachusetts Advocates for Children Trauma and Learning Policy Initiative.

Davidson, S. (2017, August). *Trauma-informed practices for postsecondary education: A guide.* Retrieved from Education Northwest. https://educationnorthwest.org/sites/default/files/resources/trauma-informed-practices-postsecondary-508.pdf

Edman, J. L., Watson, S. B., & Patron, J. D. (2016). Trauma and psychological distress among ethnically diverse community college students. *Community College Journal of Research and Practice, 40*(4), 335–342. https://doi.org/10.1080/10668926.2015.1065211

EOC Institute. (2021). *The "High Intelligence" prefrontal cortex: How meditation makes you smart, healthy.* https://eocinstitute.org/meditation/prefrontal-cortex-how-meditation-forges-an-einstein-brain/

Gomez, J. M. (2019). Isn't it all about victimization (intra)cultural pressure and cultural betrayal trauma in ethnic minority college women. *Violence against Women, 25*(10), 1211–1225.

Hallett, R. E., & Crutchfield, R. (2017). Homelessness and housing insecurity in higher education: A trauma-informed approach to research, policy, and practice. *ASHE Higher Education Report, 43*(6), 1–129.

Hinojosa, R., Nguyen, J., Sellers, K., & Elassar, H. (2018). Barriers to college success amongh students that experienced adverse childhood events. *Journal of American College Health,* 1–10.

Hoch, A., Stewart, D., Webb, K., & Wyandt-Hiebert, M. (2015). Trauma-informed care on a college campus [Slides]. *American College Health Association.* https://www.acha.org/documents/Programs_Services/webhandouts_2015/TH2-322_Hoch.pdf

Horsman, J. (2000). *Too scared to learn: Women, violence, and education.* Lawrence Erlbaum Associates, Publishers.

Kerka, S. (2002). *Trauma and adult learning. ERIC Digest.* ERIC Resource Center. Digest Number 239. http://www.ericacve.org/pubs.asp

Metzler, M., Merrick, M. T., Klevens, J., Ports, K. A., & Ford, D. (2017). Adverse childhood experiences and life opportunities: Shifting the narrative. *Children and Youth Services Review, 72*, 141–149.

Oehme, K., Perko, A., Clark, J., Ray, E. C., Arpan, L., & Bradley, L. (2019). A trauma-informed approach to building college students' resilience. *Journal of Evidence Informed Social Work, 16*(1), 93–107.

Ogul, D. (2020, November 5). Struggling through a pandemic. *Community College Daily.* https://www.ccdaily.com/2020/11/struggling-through-a-pandemic

Perry, B. (2006). Fear and learning: Trauma-related factors in the adult education process. *New Directions for Adult and Continuing Education* (110).

Perry, B. (2011, September 26). *The child trauma academy.* Neurosequential Model of Therapeutics: Clinical Practice Tools. https://therapistuncensored.com/wp-content/uploads/2019/11/ChildTraumaAcademyClinicalPracticeTools-Psychoeducation.pdf

Read, J. P., Ouimette, P., White, J., Colder, C., & Farrow, S. (2011). Rates of DSM-IV-TR Trauma Exposure and Posttraumatic Stress Disorder Among Newly Matriculated College Students. *Psychological Trauma: Theory, Research, Practice and Policy, 3*(2), 148–156. https://doi.org/10.1037/a0021260.

Shalka, T. (2015, Nov/Dec). Toward a trauma-informed practice: What educators need to know. *About Campus, 20*(5), 21–27.

Siegel, D. (2012, February 29). Dr Daniel Siegel presenting a hand model of the brain. https://youtu.be/gm9CIJ74Oxw

State Council on Child Abuse and Neglect. (2016, January). *Maryland State Council on child abuse & neglect annual report.* https://dhs.maryland.gov/documents/Data%20and%20Reports/SSA/Annual%20Progress%20and%20Services%20Review%20Report/2017%20-%202018%20APSR%20Reports/Appendix%20AE.%202016%20SCCAN%20Annual%20Report%20FINAL%206-14-17.pdf

Stevens, J. (2012, October 3). *The adverse childhood experiences study—The largest, most important public health study you never heard of—Began in an obesity clinic.* Aces Too High https://acestoohigh.com/2012/10/03/the-adverse-childhood-experiences-study-the-largest-most-important-public-health-study-you-never-heard-of-began-in-an-obesity-clinic/

Substance Abuse and Mental Health Services Administration. (2019). *Trauma and violence.* www.samhsa.gov/trauma-violence

van der Kolk, B. (2014). *The body keeps the score: Brain, mind, and body in the healing of trauma.* Penguin Books.

Verschelden, C. (2017). *Bandwidth recovery: Helping students reclaim cognitive resources lost to poverty, racism, and social marginalization.* Stylus.

Yuen, V. (2020, October 7). *The $78 billion community college funding shortfall.* Center for American Progress. https://www.americanprogress.org/issues/education-postsecondary/reports/2020/10/07/491242/78-billion-community-college-funding-shortfall/

CHAPTER 11

Not a Hero and Not a Stranger: Serving Veterans in Higher Education

Jay A. Breneman

Military veterans face many of the same barriers and traumas as other populations and non-traditional students, while simultaneously encountering problematic—and even contradictory—societal expectations and stigma around perceptions of heroism and trauma. This chapter explores the internalized and externalized pressures which student veterans may face and discusses perspectives which educators and administrators can integrate into their practices, policies, and programming to build a learning environment that is responsive to the strengths and interests of their student veterans.

Key to this approach is the critical analysis of existing narratives about military service and a recognition that institutions of higher education play an important role in a veteran's transition from the military to civilian communities in ways which can supplement their sense of belonging and being or cause friction or tension in an environment they have no choice but to endure.

I offer the considerations in this chapter as just one veteran, shaped by my own experiences as a student veteran and as someone who has led and collaborated on a multitude of veteran and student-veteran reintegration programming. I recognize that my experiences and perspectives may not be universal; it is my hope that they are informative and enlightening for those who wish to do more for other student veterans as they navigate their own journey of reintegration.

J. A. Breneman (✉)
Edinboro University of Pennsylvania, Edinboro, PA, USA
e-mail: jbreneman@edinboro.edu

© The Author(s), under exclusive license to Springer Nature
Switzerland AG 2022
P. Thompson and J. Carello (eds.), *Trauma-Informed Pedagogies*,
https://doi.org/10.1007/978-3-030-92705-9_11

What Makes a Veteran?

While there are certain parallels between experiences of community integration by veterans of recent conflicts and those of prior service periods, the population explored in this chapter are those who have served during the time of America's longest wars: the Post-9/11, or Global War On Terror veterans following the declarations of open war by the United States after September 11, 2001. More specifically, the use of the term *veteran* is reflective of individuals defined by Title 38 of the US Code of Federal Regulations (1996) as "a person who served in the active military, naval, or air service and who was discharged or released under conditions other than dishonorable," including a "reservist or member of the National Guard called to Federal active duty or disabled from a disease or injury incurred or aggravated in line of duty or while in training status." Some veterans might more readily discuss or feel connected to their veteran identity than others, just as their military experience can vary dramatically from person to person. Not every veteran has served overseas or has seen combat, and not every veteran had much of a choice of where they served or what jobs and tasks they performed, so it is important not to treat the veteran identity as a fixed experience let alone a uniform label worn by all or an experience that should be measured against that of other veterans.

Veterans: A Community of Identity in Transition

Like others, the veteran community originates from some sort of a shared experience, beginning with one unifying experience of having served in the Armed Forces, and varying considerably thereafter by such things as duty assignments and military occupations, gender, race, ethnicity, country or community of origin, sexual orientation, dates of service, and combat experience. The common connection is having served in an environment where members formed and adhered to a unique lifestyle and value set. As veteran is an identifier for those who no longer serve on active duty, this also means this community shares one other common experience: that of transition and reintegration to a civilian society upon completion of their duty. This transition experience can shape both the externalized and internalized identity and the well-being of the veteran.

Community itself is not limited to geography, though identity and geography may be intertwined. Whether a community of place or a community of identity, both forms of community have at their foundation a sense of established being or belonging (a shared history), as well as a sense for prospective being or belonging (a shared future), influenced by a person's ideal or self-orienting purpose. It defines, is defined, builds, unifies, and separates. Community is the portrait of our manifest or desired existence, our latent or acknowledged connections, and our inter-reliance with one another. Throughout our lives, we find ourselves members of—or desiring access to—multiple communities; for instance, we may recognize geographic boundaries as a placeholder that represents an association, we give value to while concomitantly appreciating an experience or history-based connection that extends beyond place. These parallel (though not always intersecting) community memberships can supplement each other, or seed friction within us. This role of community as a source of friction or supplement to a sense of belonging is key to understanding how we can better foster a veteran's reintegration.

When woven together in a coherent or desired way, community interactions can strengthen our self-image and empower our interactive capacity or capability. When frayed or disconnected, community interactions can cause dissonance or detriment within us and unto others. While someone could—and many do—survive on that which is traumatic or deleterious, we depend upon that which is confluent or in harmony with our ideals to thrive. A thriving student veteran is undoubtedly a stated goal by many institutions of higher education, and it is essential that colleges and universities become better prepared to recognize the barriers to veteran reintegration and determine whether and where they are supplementing belonging or fostering friction. Adaptation is an unavoidable requirement for veterans, but it should be a burden they do not have to shoulder alone. Often, it is more than the veteran who suffers from the frictions of reintegration: it is also their families and the communities they belong to (or strive to belong to) that experience unrealized potential. It is only through a purposeful and shared effort that veterans with and within their civilian communities, including academic institutions, can achieve the capacity to thrive.

According to the US Census Bureau's 2020 report titled "Those Who Served: America's Veterans From World War II to the War on Terror," the number of U.S. adults who were veterans declined from 18% in 1980 to 7% in 2018. This new generation of veterans—comprising more than 3.7 million people—are demographically different than veterans from prior service eras, and the future composition of our Armed Forces is expected to follow this trend:

- Currently, about 1 in 8 men in the United States are veterans, possibly falling to about 1 in 14 by 2040; comparatively, 9% of veterans—or 1.7 million—are women, possibly rising to 17% by 2040.
- Among veterans of all eras, Post-9/11 veterans represent the highest proportion with a disability, have more education, and are more diverse, with 34.9% reporting some other race and ethnicity than non-Hispanic White.

There is a broader benefit to an institution's full participation in this reintegration effort, as shown in the Veterans Civic Health Index, published by the National Conference on Citizenship (2017), which reports that veterans are more likely to volunteer, vote, donate, and belong to civic organizations than their non-veteran peers. If a student veteran desires to serve and give back beyond their time in uniform, then the very institutions that are shaping their future should focus on building a sense of belonging, while reducing any friction within the academic environment itself both physical and social. The veteran subculture might be defined by a unique set of experiences, language, cues, values, and norms, but it is also apparent that it is one defined largely by an orientation—not necessarily an obligation—toward service.

MODERN PRESENCE OF VETERANS IN HIGHER ED

According to the Veterans in Higher Education Factsheet by the Postsecondary National Policy Institute (2020), student veterans are older (24–40) and reported higher GPA and completion rates than their non-veteran peers, and they are also more likely to be first-generation college students; however, they also report challenges in adapting to higher education and are also less likely to participate in campus activities. Though student veterans face many of the same barriers and traumas as other students, sometimes these may be exacerbated by the built environment and institutional culture, even unintentionally. All students experience internalized and externalized pressures to conform, challenge, or create within these spaces, and for students who relocate to attend a university, they do so having lost a measure of the social capital they had accrued or inherited in their previous communities. In this light, veterans experience a loss or thinning out of those capitals, as the experience of the veteran community is that of a diaspora. Where can a student veteran go to leverage the relationships, connections, and resources once all around them, other than to start again? Such a re-building of social and other capitals—or at least a bridging—necessitates an interactional relationship with the institutions that are at the forefront of the veteran's reintegration. All too often, however, they are met with transactional solutions, often in the form of benefit counseling. We must recognize that veterans need more than a connection to resources: they and we as educators need a connection to one another and to recognize that reintegration is a shared journey.

THE AUTHOR'S PERSPECTIVE

My life is inexorably tied to this era of wars and the role of higher education in reintegration. At the age of 18, and not long after the terror attacks of September 11, 2001, I called the US Army recruiter and began a nearly year-long journey to become a soldier. I enrolled in 6-months of GED courses, participated in pre-enlistment training, evaluations, and activities, and ended up serving for 6 ½ years across two-enlistments. I would go on to serve over 3 years overseas, to include a year in South Korea and nearly 2½ years deployed to Iraq. I had a successful military career and achieved much more than I thought possible when I swore my first oath. I won't recount those experiences in this chapter, other than to say that when I wasn't deployed or in training, I frequently experienced jarring interactions with civilians who regarded me as some sort of hero who needed a hug, a free beer, cash in my hand, and thankful handshakes or backslaps. Even though I was honorably discharged in 2009, I still haven't figured out a response to those interactions—which often felt transactional—that I am completely comfortable with, given that there are those with whom I served who came back injured or who were killed in action, and my own choice for service in the military was not for the glory or greatness but for that essential Army value of selfless service. If I was a hero—which I most certainly was not—what does that make those who paid a higher sacrifice or put more on the line for the sake of others?

In a way, this question guided what would become nearly a decade of direct or supportive work for veterans. I enrolled in college classes just two-weeks after my discharge and witnessed what it was like to be a student veteran at two different universities in a time when veteran benefits were changing, when universities were trying to figure out how to serve a growing number of student veterans, and when the Department of Veterans Affairs was under scrutiny for delaying or denying benefits to student veterans in the years during and following the Great Recession. After earning both my undergraduate and graduate degrees in social work, I found myself serving as the first veterans coordinator for a small private college, and then later as the veterans coordinator for a larger public university.

At both institutions and in collaboration with others, my first and ongoing goal was to convince the administration that we needed to do more than process benefits or refer student veterans to healthcare services, and that we should meet them with more than symbols and events of patriotism, gratitude, cliché displays of militarism, or treating every veteran event as a Memorial Day service.

Between the Pit and the Pedestal: Challenges to Community Integration

As we acknowledge the diverse experiences and representation of student veterans, as well as their need to reintegrate into a civilian community, what good were we doing by constantly anchoring their experiences and environment to a stereotyped past or an endless "Welcome Home Parade"? How might a student veteran feel about constant reminders of those killed in action or being treated as fragile shadows of their former selves because of perceived wound they endured?

As illustrated in Fig. 11.1, such pathologizing and acculturalization of personhood and traits marginalize the student veteran with separate, unattainable, or objectifying expectations: a veteran must be a hero of achievement to be put on a pedestal or a warrior broken by unspoken horrors to be pitied. To relate and build community with student veterans, we must re-align our language, practices, and beliefs, to see ourselves as peers in a community that is yet to be fully actualized.

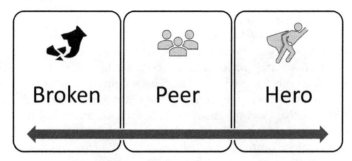

Fig. 11.1 Between the pit and the pendulum

PRINCIPLES FOR CHANGE

The mechanism for change lies in an interactional approach with the student veterans in collaboratively witnessing and creating a shared identity and emphasizing a sense of being and belonging on and off campus. In what follows, I outline three main principles to help educators and policy-makers create college learning environments that support a sense of belonging for student veterans.

Fostering an Environment of Mutuality and Belonging

- *Challenge*: overcoming identity conflict and marginalization from unfair and unrealistic portrayals (such as a broken hero), and past-oriented stereotypes.
- *Approach*: develop a community which fosters veteran-civilian identity amalgamation, focusing more on similarities in present and future-oriented interests through the physical and social environments.

    - Physical environment—design spaces which do not segregate veterans or overemphasize symbology of militarism and armed conflict; keep memorial events separate from veteran-oriented events.
    - Social environment—focus on interactional engagement, events, and programming which emphasize belonging and an openness, striving for exchanges informed by cultural humility.

Supporting Student Veterans in the Co-discovery of Their Future Selves

- *Challenge*: student veterans are often anchored in the past because of the social or physical environment on campus and maybe encouraged or feel obliged to stick to academic programs or social events that are

aligned with their military experience; student veterans may find themselves unsatisfied with their field of study, or disinterested in the social activities, and thus alienated from the campus environment.
- *Approach*: encourage and support student veterans in exploring broader educational and career options as well as social and cultural experiences, enabling a more holistic civilian-veteran identity transition that might not even be related to their military occupations, experiences, and expertise.

Bridging Communities Beyond the Campus

- *Challenge*: student veterans experience a loss or thinning out of military-community capitals as they reintegrate into civilian life; approaches to ameliorate this are largely transactional, consumer-oriented, or focus on referring student veterans to health or educational benefits, rather than meaningful interactional opportunities to build new capitals.
- *Approach*: develop a purposeful exchange with student veterans that stresses community self-examination, exploration of social networks, social structure, modes and elements of community membership, and opportunities for community engagement. Think beyond veteran-only organizations, such as pathways to civic and board service, wellness and recreation, housing, and family-oriented opportunities.

Consider utilizing approaches that serve as a means toward attaining social and environmental integrations as both an outcome and as part of the process itself. Simply put, the process should be earnest and rewarding for everyone involved. We want veterans to know that they mean more to an institution than the GI BILL and mean more to a classroom than stories from their service. Ultimately, an established sense of belonging on campus is just as beneficial to the academic community as it can be for the student veteran. Furthermore, bridging those linkages beyond the campus will help realize long-term benefits for the broader community, stability, and opportunity for the veteran, and relationships with the university never before explored.

CONCLUSION

Applying some or all of these perspectives will look different from institution to institution and community to community. My hope is that academia serves as a space of bridging opportunity for veterans and a facilitator for integration of veterans and non-veterans alike. The end goal is two-fold: a rewarding academic experience and a successful bridge to a thriving future. One does not need to be a veteran to have a meaningful impact on a student veteran's reintegration, nor is it necessary to understand the lingo or to have shared histories. Simply put, with so few Americans serving in the Armed Forces, it is unrealistic to assume that reintegration can be done by veterans alone or to move forward while always looking in the rearview mirror. If we are to establish and build community on campus and beyond its boundaries, then civilians and veterans must co-create that shared future together, and there is no better place to start than academia.

References

National Conference on Citizenship. (2017). *Veterans Civic Health Index*. https://www.ncoc.org/wp-content/uploads/2018/08/2017-Veterans-Civic-Healh-Index.pdf

Pensions, Bonuses, and Veterans' Relief, 38 U.S.C. § 3.1. (1996). https://www.ecfr.gov/current/title-38/chapter-I/part-3#3.1

Postsecondary National Policy Institute. (2020). *Veterans in higher education factsheet*. https://pnpi.org/veterans-in-higher-education/

United States Census Bureau. (2020). *Those who served: America's veterans from World War II to the War on Terror*. American Community Survey Report. https://www.census.gov/content/dam/Census/library/publications/2020/demo/acs-43.pdf

The Benefits of Reflective Journaling During COVID-19: Contingent Faculty Examine Impacts on Academic Lives and Student-Centered Teaching

Óscar Fernández, Dana Crosby, Maureen Hickey, Sam Settelmeyer, and Ami Sommariva

Faculty in contingent positions are generally overlooked in department and institution-wide planning (AAUP, 2018), and higher education's 2020 COVID-19 response was no exception. As U.S. colleges and universities moved to "emergency remote teaching" (ERT; Hodges et al., 2020) during the spring of 2020, higher education leaders emphasized the impact that ERT would have on student learning, enrollment, and tuition remissions due to COVID-19-related dormitory closures, graduation rates, and the professoriate (Mangan, 2020; McMurtrie, 2020a). However, a discussion on how ERT impacted contingent faculty in their teaching practices during the first few months of the pandemic was mostly unexplored. Such data and perspectives are needed, as contingent faculty hold 73% of all instructional positions

Ó. Fernández (✉) · D. Crosby · M. Hickey · S. Settelmeyer · A. Sommariva
Portland State University, Portland, OR, USA
e-mail: osf@pdx.edu

M. Hickey
e-mail: Mhh3@pdx.edu

S. Settelmeyer
e-mail: Sette12@pdx.edu

A. Sommariva
e-mail: ami7@pdx.edu

P. Thompson and J. Carello (eds.), *Trauma-Informed Pedagogies*, https://doi.org/10.1007/978-3-030-92705-9_12

133

at post-secondary U.S. institutions (AAUP, 2018). This point-in-time, action research study grounded in reflective journaling (RJ), documents and examines the teaching experiences of four contingent faculty members during spring 2020 (the first quarter of ERT and stay-at-home government orders due to COVID-19). RJ is defined as written documents that practitioners create "to think about various concepts, events, or interactions over a period of time for the purposes of gaining insights into self-awareness and learning" (Thorpe, 2004, p. 328). We argue that RJ during the pandemic is beneficial for two reasons: RJ provided ethnographic insight into how ERT impacted contingent faculty during this crisis and enabled study participants to identify negative assumptions regarding student-centered teaching (SCT). Specifically, RJ generated new insights about how remote teaching during this crisis affected contingent faculty's professional/personal lives and their practice and understanding of SCT. These findings will be helpful to university planners in incorporating the needs and aspirations of contingent faculty as they prepare for and respond to future crises.

The co-authors acknowledge that we are writing about a pandemic from a relatively privileged employment space as contingent faculty in the U.S. (i.e., as of date, we are employed and teach online). Nevertheless, COVID-19 has affected the lives of students and educators around the world in ways that this study alone cannot address. Therefore, we urge other teacher-scholars to join us in documenting their experiences during this crisis.

INSTITUTIONAL CONTEXT

Co-author Fernández initiated the study as part of his inaugural role as diversity, equity, and inclusion (DEI) coordinator (2017–2020) in University Studies. "University Studies" refers to Portland State University's general studies program, including Freshmen, Sophomore, and Senior Capstone courses built on four learning goals (Hamington & Ramaley, 2019). To create future DEI workshops focused on teaching during this pandemic, he wanted faculty to describe their ERT experiences. During late winter quarter 2020— and as Portland State University announced it was moving to ERT starting spring quarter 2020— Fernández sent an invitational email to approximately 240 members of University Studies' all-faculty-staff listserv. The current five co-authors decided to join the study.

We conducted our research within three academic units: (1) Department of International and Global Studies—IGS (Hickey), (2) the School of Social Work (Settelmeyer), and (3) University Studies (Fernández and Sommariva). Except for Settelmeyer, all other contingent faculty also teach in University Studies. The study utilizes data from the four contingent faculty. "Contingent faculty" is defined as follows: "Depending on the institution, contingent faculty can be known as adjuncts, postdocs, TAs, non-tenure-track faculty [NTTF], clinical faculty, part-timers, lecturers, instructors, or non-senate faculty" (AAUP, 2020). Fernández and Hickey were non-tenure-track faculty (NTTFs); Settelmeyer and Sommariva, adjunct faculty. Since co-author Crosby, a Masters of Public Health (MPH) candidate at that time, was not an instructor of record during the spring quarter, we did not analyze her RJ when we coded for themes. For this study, Crosby assisted with analysis and writing. As a University Studies graduate peer mentor, she joined the study to understand the challenges facing University Studies' faculty. "University Studies peer mentor" (or "peer mentor") refers to undergraduate and graduate students working with faculty partners to mentor undergraduate students in University Studies' Freshmen and Sophomore courses (Fernández et al., 2019). All co-authors collected and analyzed data through the methods that we designed.

Literature Review

The benefits of RJ are often drawn from studies about students (i.e., in schools, colleges, and medical programs) and how RJ fosters critical thinking, develops self-understanding, enhances cultural competence, and helps capture changes in students' perception (Alt & Raichel, 2020; Dunlap, 2006; Schuessler et al., 2012). Other scholars also discussed the benefits of RJ for pre-service teachers and K-12 educators, which generally focus on how RJ is a tool to bolster professional development (Dreyer, 2015; Kremenitzer, 2005; LaBelle & Belknap, 2016). Although pre-service educators practice teaching-related reflection, such reflection "stagnates or vanishes over time" for veteran teachers (Dreyer, 2015, p. 334). Although it is critical to understand how K-12 educators utilize RJ, this study addresses a literature gap about RJ in higher education.

Although much has been written already about the near- and long-term impacts of the COVID-19 crisis in higher education in the United States and abroad, much remains to be explored (*Boston Review*, n.d.; *The Chronicle*, n.d.). For example, the authors of *Academe's* fall 2020 issue identified challenges facing American higher education: concerns over university budget short-falls; staff and faculty lay-offs; mandated returns to in-person teaching without COVID-19-related health safety protocols in place; teaching practices informed by care; discussions about racism as it relates to healthcare access; creation of communities of care among faculty; COVID-related deaths and injuries of Black and Latinx communities; expressions of gratitude to first responders; and demands by contingent faculty for employment and healthcare access (Stommel et al., 2020). In addition, news writers reported how the pandemic laid off hundreds of thousands of higher education workers, including tenured professors and contingent faculty (Bauman, 2020; Pettit, 2020). While it is critical to discuss these near- and long-term impacts, university leaders also need to understand what contingent faculty experienced as the 2020 spring quarter of mandated ERT unfolded.

Other scholars have examined the ways post-secondary educators modified their teaching as both students and faculty lived, worked, and adjusted to crises in the recent past (e.g., terroristic attacks in Oklahoma on April

19th, 1995 and in New York and Pennsylvania on September 11th, 2001; gun-related suicides and mass murder in private and public places, including schools, colleges, places of worship, LGBTQ bars, and at other events); hate crimes; police violence against Blacks; Central American refugee crisis; and natural disasters (Adedoyin et al., 2019; Arar et al., 2019; Doe & Langstraat, 2014; Fox & Savage, 2009; Giroux, 2004; Gramlich, 2019; Masucci & Langton, 2017; Smawfield & Brock, 2012). Emerging scholarship directly describes how COVID-19 changed how faculty deliver ERT and modify their pedagogical approaches (McMurtrie, 2020a; Youmans, 2020). Although the scholarship about university teaching during the COVID-19 crisis includes necessary discussions on the personal and employment challenges facing non-tenure-track faculty, there is less understanding of how contingent faculty re-examined their teaching during those first months of the pandemic.

Much has also been written about the value of SCT in higher education before the pandemic, especially around de-centering lectures and grading as the primary form of instruction by engaging students through simulations, unconventional writing exercises, peer teaching, and self-paced and cooperative (team-based) learning (Felder, 2016; Felder & Brent, 1996). SCT, or "learner-centered teaching" (LCT), is defined as a teaching philosophy that shifts the instructional focus from the educator to the student, including active learning, cooperative learning, and inductive learning (Felder, 2016). Scholars focused on ways that general and discipline-specific workshops help tenure ladder faculty modify their teaching from teacher-centered (i.e., lecture-based) to SCT in STEM (science, technology, engineering, and math) and the humanities (Kember, 2008; Murray et al., 2019). The scholarship also discusses how STEM disciplines need to foster SCT to improve retention (Mack, 2019). Although the literature discusses the importance of SCT for tenure ladder faculty, there is less understanding of the contingent faculty's professional challenges as they continue to hone their student-centered practice.

METHODOLOGY

To address the literature gap on what contingent faculty experienced with ERT during spring 2020, co-author Fernández first invited all University Studies faculty and affiliates to form a writing group during late March 2020. Next, the writing group kept a reflective journal during the spring quarter's ten weeks (March 30th–June 7th, 2020). We then developed three research questions and answered them based on our RJ. Next, we used in vivo coding (Saldaña, 2016) to determine themes and findings. Finally, we reviewed the findings and created additional focus group questions to explain our findings. Three themes emerged: (1) faculty over-reported on students' emotional states while minimizing their own; (2) faculty focused on SCT; and (3) faculty identified negative assumptions about SCT.

Reflective Journaling

Our research focused on ten weeks of unstructured RJ, guided by three questions meant to trigger broader metacognitive awareness (Alt & Raichel, 2020):

1. What challenges, if any, did you experience with ERT during the spring quarter of 2020?
2. What opportunities, if any, did you experience with ERT during the spring quarter of 2020?
3. What recommendations, if any, do you have for faculty, academic professionals, staff, peer mentors, graduate students, and administrators, for example, who are interested in ERT?

Research Approach: Participatory-Social Justice Design

The research design followed a participatory-social justice framework "to give voice to participants and collaborate with them in shaping the research and to build evidence from both quantitative and qualitative data" (Creswell & Creswell, 2018, p. 230). All co-authors designed the three research questions, the focus group interview questions, and the data collection methods.

Research Procedures: Reflective Journaling and Focus Group Interviews

During spring quarter 2020, all co-authors kept a reflective journal based on three research questions. For three quarters (spring, summer, and fall quarter of 2020), we met via Zoom once a month for one hour to check-in regarding our study. Given that in 2020 we were reflecting on teaching during many crises (i.e., COVID-19, sustained social protests in downtown Portland, and forest fires affecting Oregon), the monthly meetings also became a space for sharing non-academic experiences. Overall, the co-authors participated in six types of interactions:

1. Reflective journaling (spring quarter 2020 only);
2. Monthly check-ins (spring–summer–fall of 2020);
3. In vivo coding process (summer 2020);
4. One meeting to share themes and findings from in vivo coding results (summer 2020);
5. One meeting to come up with additional focus group interview questions based on findings (summer 2020); and
6. Focus group interview questions via Google Docs and our monthly check-ins (summer–fall of 2020).

Minimizing Power Dynamics

During our first meeting in spring 2020, Fernández initiated the group-writing collaboration by discussing ways to minimize power dynamics. The co-authors did not know each other before this study, and we held different ranks at the university. We avoided "a hired-hand mentality" by actively involving all co-authors in formulating the "research questions, deciding on-field strategies, and making sense of the data" (Taylor et al., 2015, pp. 96–97).

Data Analysis

Data analyses included in vivo coding and open coding (Saldaña, 2016; Seidman, 2019). In vivo coding consisted of using participant-generated words or short phrases from "the actual language found in the qualitative data record" (Saldaña, 2016, p. 105). Open coding consisted of looking for patterns and themes in the transcriptions of responses to three research questions and responses to the author/participant-designed focus group interview questions. To interpret the categories derived from the analysis, we used Luborsky's (1994) thematic analysis to isolate prominent themes. In addition, we conducted constant comparative data analysis (Glaser & Strauss, 1967) using two data sources (RJ responses to three research questions and author/participant-designed focus group interview responses) to analyze our research data from multiple perspectives.

The co-author/participants used triangulation in this study to improve internal validity and establish the study's trustworthiness (Merriam & Tisdell, 2016; Taylor et al., 2015). To ensure triangulation, we utilized data from two sources: RJ responses to three research questions and answers to co-author/participant-designed focus group interviews.

RESULTS: EXPLORING OUR THEMES

Explaining the Use of "Name Withheld"

In some instances, direct quotes from co-authors appear as "name withheld" and "they." As contingent faculty members with precarious employment contracts—and despite how academic freedom protects "full freedom" in research and publication" (AAUP, 2020/1940)—we were concerned that specific quotes might impact us negatively in contracts and promotions.

Theme 1: Faculty Over Reporting on Students' Emotional States

Whenever the co-authors reported on emotional states related to ERT, we overwhelmingly reported students' emotional states. In sum, we described their emotional states as "terror-fear-apprehension" and "rage-anger-annoyance" (Plutchik, 2001). One of the co-authors, for example, noted that they were "genuinely disturbed by students' emotional states" and then went on to elaborate on students' emotions without further commenting on their own (name withheld):

- "Terror, fear, apprehension" language: "Students appeared petrified with anxiety about infection and feared anything from outside their homes." (name withheld)
- "Rage, anger, annoyance" language: "Some were (righteously) angry that they had to choose between their health and service industry jobs that provided for their basic needs. Many were (righteously) angry that people in prisons and detention centers were not being protected from the virus and that BIPOC [Black, indigenous, people of color] folks were being brutalized and arrested for going around outside without a mask. Most felt isolated." (name withheld)

In contrast, when we identified our emotional states, we expressed feelings of "rage-anger-annoyance" and "admiration-trust-acceptance" (Plutchik, 2001). For instance, co-author Fernández expressed anger at faculty and departmental policies that did not prioritize culturally inclusive teaching before the pandemic. Fernández wrote:

I feel anger. If faculty had not figured out doing culturally inclusive teaching in the classroom before COVID-19, why are they asking for this diversity training now? And amidst a global crisis? COVID-19 reveals fissures in higher education: not prioritizing inclusive teaching in any classroom setting, whether online or on campus.

Alternatively, when co-authors Hickey and Sommariva reported on their feelings, they described their compassion to self and their students as "admiration-trust-acceptance" (Plutchik, 2001):

- "Digging deeper within myself to find compassion and understanding for both myself and my students has been one important challenge and opportunity." (Hickey)
- "I felt both compassion and the urge to try to convince them that getting outside and going for a walk would be good for their health." (Sommariva)

Theme 2: Identifying Emotional Labor

Although the co-authors were practitioners of SCT before COVID-19 in on-campus and online courses, including being emotionally available for students, our RJ described a higher level of emotional labor with our students. A co-author wrote:

I spent much one-on-one time talking to students over email and in Google-Meet about their situations and challenges and figuring out the best way to pass or otherwise succeed in the class. I was happy to do it, as I care about my students, and such work is central to my teaching philosophy, but it was time-consuming and did, at points, take an emotional toll on me. (name withheld)

Theme 3: Identifying Negative Assumptions About Student-Centered Teaching

The co-authors identified how teaching during this pandemic brought back debates about SCT's academic rigor (i.e., SCT focuses more on the process of learning and less on discipline-specific content, skills, and methodologies). More importantly, in our RJ, we reflected on how students and colleagues negatively perceive SCT—and how that perception contributes to negative student evaluations and, therefore, uncertain employment prospects whenever departments only use student evaluations to assess our teaching performance. One co-author wrote, "The reality of the pandemic made me feel more comfortable being flexible and generous with students and grading" (name withheld).

DISCUSSION

RJ created a space for faculty to develop self-analysis and increase awareness of our work and life experiences. Our journals became a "permanent record of our thoughts" (Schuessler et al., 2012) during those first ten weeks of mandated ERT and quarantine lock-down. Our findings confirmed that RJ during the pandemic is beneficial for two reasons: RJ provided ethnographic insight into how ERT impacted contingent faculty during this crisis and enabled study participants to identify negative assumptions regarding SCT. Without RJ, these insights may not have come to light.

Naming Contingent Faculty's Emotional Labor

As suggested by Schön's (1983) reflective practitioner model, RJ during a crisis allows practitioners to make new sense of situations marked by uncertainty. During the first ten weeks of COVID-19-related teaching, our RJ identified a dimension of higher education employment difficult to express as faculty committed to SCT: We experienced a higher level of emotional labor exhaustion. Like on-campus teaching, teaching remotely with a student-centered lens meets two characteristics of jobs requiring emotional labor: The job requires "face-to-face or voice-to-voice contact with the public" and requires "the worker to produce an emotional state in another person" (Hochschild, 1983, pp. 147, 156). Although co-author Fernández, a queer Latinx immigrant scholar, has been emotionally supporting his students of color for the past seventeen years (his first academic post started in 2003), he was emotionally drained by the end of spring quarter 2020. Evans and Moore (2015) assert that faculty of color do experience an unequal distribution of emotional labor in higher education due to negotiating everyday racial aggressions and dominant ideologies that deny the relevance of racism in society and academia.

However, ERT increased the level of emotional labor exhaustion in ways that the co-authors had not felt before as online educators. In looking back at our RJ, we recognize a life out of balance (was it ever?): As we helped students make sense of the pandemic, we also navigated the emotions of loved ones. Moreover, for Latinx co-author Fernández, the pandemic reveals to more faculty the reality of emotional labor that faculty of color were already doing pre-COVID-19. Professor Michelle Moyd affirms this hidden labor by proposing that the pandemic "has peeled back all the layers of things that are in some ways masked" (McMurtrie, 2020b).

For co-author Sommariva, the pandemic also highlights the higher level of emotional labor that woman-identified faculty have been expected to do, even before the pandemic. For decades, studies have shown that students hold instructors to gendered expectations (MacNell et al., 2015; Sandier, 1991; Sprague & Massoni, 2005). Women faculty are expected to provide students with more personal attention and warmth than their male colleagues (Sprague & Massoni, 2005). If they do not provide this to the level expected by students, they will hear about it on end-of-term student evaluations (Sandier, 1991). Women faculty also face more student requests for special favors than their male colleagues (El-Alayli et al., 2018). These requests are most likely to come from students with higher degrees of academic entitlement, who are also more likely to be upset if the favors are not granted (El-Alayli et al., 2018).

Moreover, regardless of what teaching practices they utilize, women faculty are penalized on student teaching evaluations simply for being perceived as women. A 2014 controlled research experiment about gender and student teaching evaluations has shown that the average penalty for being perceived as female is 0.5 points on a 5-point scale (MacNell et al., 2015). Contingent faculty's dependence on student evaluations for continued employment generates anxiety every quarter. However, the burden of increased emotional labor during spring 2020 had a disproportionate effect on contingent women faculty. They were already being held to higher personal interaction standards, handling a more significant number of student requests for special favors, responding to more angry students, and facing a higher risk of receiving inadequate student evaluations regardless of what they do.

Undoubtedly, universities need to do more to address emotional labor by minoritized faculty. As our campus went remote for spring 2020—and as we prepared for ERT for fall quarter 2020—the co-authors did not see the university organizing workshops on recognizing work/life imbalances and emotional labor. Instead, our university offered necessary workshops on using online tools to engage students in discipline-specific course needs and learning objectives. We urge universities to provide workshops on work/life balance as remote employees, including identifying and reducing stress and emotional labor. A fall 2020 survey among college and university presidents already shows that the mental health of faculty and staff is third on their list of most pressing issues facing higher education (Turk et al., 2020).

Consequently, we urge universities to provide material investment in all faculty's well-being, including contingent faculty, given that initial care-related resources were only inspirational. For instance, university leaders emailed faculty and staff messages affirming the care-related work faculty were doing and encouraging faculty to find ways to care for themselves and each other. Although the co-authors appreciated the words of encouragement during spring quarter 2020, we do not see a formal structure for providing care to contingent faculty (e.g., access to temporary mental health care, transparency about the employment process, and emergency stipends).

Examining Faculty's Underreporting of Our Emotional States

In our RJ, the co-authors had difficulty sharing what we were feeling during the pandemic. We only named two emotions: compassion (to self and others) and anger. To clarify, as faculty committed to students' well-being, we unabashedly prioritized their emotional needs over ours during the first weeks of the pandemic. In this section, we examine why our ten-week RJ lacked self-reflection on our emotional states.

Co-author Settelmeyer proposes that faculty's misconceptions regarding SCT may cause the underreporting of our feelings: Some faculty may think that SCT means prioritizing the emotional needs of the students while avoiding faculty's. Lee and Hannafin (2016) similarly omit faculty/staff emotions within their comprehensive framework to operationalize SCT. Additionally, higher education *disciplines* faculty to prioritize discipline-specific intellectual reflections (i.e., content, research methodologies, and teaching techniques) over affective and cultural ones (i.e., how our experiences and cultures should shape disciplinarity). Palmer (2007) argues that "emotions are the enemy of objectivity and must be suppressed in higher education. As a result, educated people tend to compartmentalize their feelings, acknowledging them in private, perhaps, but regarding them as dangerous to professional life" (p. 209). Without a doubt, exposing our emotional lives as contingent educators is also dangerous for employment and professionalization reasons. Two questions underlie our hesitance to share feelings in academic spaces—including this study:

- Will department chairs renew our contracts if they assume all we teach is emotional intelligence? (Rendón & Nepo, 2009)
- Will colleagues devalue our teaching, research, and publications if our contributions are categorized as "me-search"? (Sumerau, 2016)

Then, it is not surprising that our RJs feature lists of adjectives for our students' emotional states—and just two emotions for ourselves (compassion and anger). In short, by overly describing students' emotional states in our RJ, we practice what professional academic life taught us to do well—compartmentalize feelings and protect notions of objectivity.

Indeed, compartmentalizing feelings is a survival strategy, especially for women and minoritized faculty who already struggle against stereotypes of being too emotional or lacking objectivity. In fact, as contingent faculty members with intersectional positions, we purposefully do not share feelings in academic spaces as a self-preservation mechanism. In our graduate student years and postdoctoral appointments, the profession's hidden curriculum was explicit: Do not reveal weakness or doubt. Some colleagues would consider such revelations as a sign of mental health problems or unprofessional behavior. For instance, co-author Fernández avoids talking about complicated feelings (such as anger) to avoid the stereotype of the angry faculty of color and minimize derailing conversations around his feelings when the goal is to critique academe's systems of oppression.

As graduate students and faculty, we learned that academia, in general, is not a safe space to share emotional and culturally specific challenges we face in society (e.g., racism, sexism, ableism, and White supremacy). Moreover, we suspect that academic spaces will never be safe as long as there is an overfocus on competition and publishing, combined with the academy's neo-liberalization and the active devaluing of teaching as a central part of the mission and profession of higher education. Thus, well beyond the current pandemic, the question of how universities and disciplines consider the emotional and culturally specific needs of their tenure ladder and contingent faculty will remain.

Identifying and Disrupting Assumptions: Student-Centered Teaching Lacks Academic Rigor

> The pandemic provided some institutional 'cover' to move in a more student-led learning direction during spring quarter.
> —Name withheld

Although we named SCT as our pedagogical lens for the spring 2020 quarter, our RJ also revealed that we worked through a longstanding critique of our teaching: SCT lacks academic rigor. The phrase "academic rigor" calls to mind academia's history of sexist, racist, and ableist standards that prioritize specific skills and quantitative results over the quality of one's learning process, initiative, resilience, or ability to collaborate. Our classrooms present students (and faculty) with a range of options for intellectual and personal growth. Each student faces different challenges and brings different strengths to bear upon their learning. So, why would it make sense to impose a "universal" standard on a diverse group of learners?

In recalling past teaching evaluations, the co-authors notice how some students see the absence of formal lectures as evidence that we do not know our content. While some students appreciate that we incorporate their feedback in *how* we teach them and *what* we teach them, other students view this inquiry-based approach as a waste of time and indicate the faculty's lack of content-based knowledge. Given the banking model of education that students often experience before coming to our classrooms (Freire, 2003), we acknowledge their frustration: SCT requires students to think differently about *how*—and *what*—they learn. Students' misconceptions about SCT are not the only factor impacting our teaching evaluations. Given that some of the co-authors self-identify as women faculty and faculty of color, we acknowledge studies that describe how racism and gender bias negatively impact students' teaching evaluations of minoritized faculty (MacNell et al., 2015).

Likewise, some colleagues critique the value of SCT in our disciplines. Their concerns generally focus on (1) norming disciplinary knowledge (i.e., faculty may be deviating from accepted discipline-specific standards), (2) evaluating the "actual knowledge" students learn (i.e., SCT compromises discipline-specific sets of skills and knowledge), and (3) refusing to acknowledge the student and the university as socially constructed (i.e., by focusing on the individual, faculty do not acknowledge the socially constructed nature of students' cultural identities and universities' practices) (Mckenna, 2013). In contrast, many scholars have addressed the value of SCT (Felder, 2016; Kember, 2008; Murray et al., 2019). As contingent faculty, such criticism from colleagues regarding our teaching is concerning. Given the absence of protections associated with tenure related to our teaching methods, student evaluations and colleagues' review letters impact our employment prospects. Despite our efforts to be transparent with students and colleagues regarding our SCT lens—including citing the relevant scholarship supporting SCT—, we cautiously navigate how we teach students as it impacts our teaching evaluations. In writing our employment-related self-appraisals, we are strategic: We highlight discipline-specific methodologies and downplay SCT to minimize negative employment reviews.

CONCLUSION

Faculty and students alike are coping with a series of crises in 2020 (e.g., COVID-19, police violence, environmental collapse). This study was designed to examine how RJ creates a space for contingent faculty to describe COVID-19's disruption of our personal and academic lives during the spring quarter of 2020. Our study indicates that creating such a contained space for reflection brought forth new insights into the practice of SCT, the effects of ERT on contingent faculty, and the emotional labor required of contingent faculty. We examined personal and pedagogical concerns that we usually do not share with colleagues from the various institutions that employ us—let alone during a pandemic. We also identified professional growth areas to recognize contingent faculty's hidden emotional labor. Lastly, we named key negative assumptions regarding SCT.

Utilizing RJ during a crisis allows faculty to practice what Freire calls "authentic reflection"—a reflection that refutes the concept that humanity is "abstract, isolated, independent, and unattached to the world" (Freire, 2003, p. 81). RJ is one tool educators can utilize to find meaning and insight as we experience—alongside our students—a world in crisis and as we work to make our teaching meaningful for all students.

References

AAUP. (2018). Data snapshot: Contingent faculty in US higher ed. *American Association of University Professors.* https://www.aaup.org/sites/default/files/10112018%20Data%20Snapshot%20Tenure.pdf

AAUP. (2020/1940). 1940 Statement of principles on academic freedom and tenure. *American Association of University Professors.* https://www.aaup.org/report/1940-statement-principles-academic-freedom-and-tenure

Adedoyin, A. C., Moore, S. E., Robinson, M. A., Clayton, D. M., Boamah, D. A., & Harmon, D. K. (2019). The dehumanization of Black males by police: Teaching social justice-Black life really does matter. *Journal of Teaching in Social Work, 39*(2), 111–131.

Alt, D., & Raichel, N. (2020). Reflective journaling and metacognitive awareness: Insights from a longitudinal study in higher education. *Reflective Practice, 21*(2), 145–158. https://doi.org/10.1080/14623943.2020.1716708

Arar, K., Haj-Yehia, K., Ross, D. B., & Kondakci, Y. (Eds.). (2019). *Higher education challenges for migrant and refugee students in a global world.* Peter Lang.

Bauman, D. (2020, October 6). The pandemic has pushed hundreds of thousands of workers out of higher education. *The Chronicle of Higher Education.* https://www.chronicle.com/article/how-the-pandemic-has-shrunk-higher-educations-work-force

Boston Review: A Political and Literary Forum. (n.d.). Thinking in a pandemic. https://bostonreview.net/project/thinking-pandemic

Chronicle of Higher Education. (n.d.). Combating coronavirus. https://www.chronicle.com

Creswell, J. W., & Creswell, J. D. (2018). *Research design: Qualitative, quantitative, and mixed methods approaches* (5th ed.). Sage.

Doe, S., & Langstraat, L. (2014). *Generation vet: Composition, student veterans, and the post-9/11 university.* Utah State University Press.

Dreyer, L. M. (2015). Reflective journaling: A tool for teacher professional development. *Africa Education Review, 12*(2), 331–344.

Dunlap, J. C. (2006). Using guided reflective journaling activities to capture students' changing perceptions. *TechTrends, 50*(6), 20–26.

El-Alayli, A., Hansen-Brown, A. A., & Ceynar, M. (2018). Dancing backwards in high heels: Female professors experience more work demands and special favor requests, particularly from academically entitled students. *Sex Roles, 79*(3–4), 136–150.

Evans, L., & Moore, W. L. (2015). Impossible burdens. White institutions, emotional labor, and micro-resistance. *Social Problems, 62*(3), 439–454.

Felder, R. M. (2016). *Teaching and learning STEM: A practical guide*. Jossey-Bass.

Felder, R. M., & Brent, R. (1996). Navigating the bumpy road to student-centered instruction. *College Teaching, 44*(2), 43–47.

Fernández, Ó., Lundell, D., & Kerrigan, S. (2019). Taking high-impact practices to scale in capstone and peer mentor programs, and revising University Studies' diversity learning goal. *The Journal of General Education (University Park, Pa.), 67*(3–4), 269–289.

Freire, P. (2003). *Pedagogy of the oppressed* (M. B. Ramos, Trans.). Continuum. (Original work published 1970.)

Fox, J. A., & Savage, J. (2009). Mass murder goes to college: An examination of changes on college campuses following Virginia Tech. *The American Behavioral Scientist, 52*(10), 1465–1485.

Giroux, H. A. (2004). *Take back higher education: Race, youth, and the crisis of democracy in the post-Civil Rights Era* (1st ed.). Palgrave Macmillan.

Glaser, B. G., & Strauss, A. L. (1967). *The discovery of grounded theory: Strategies for qualitative research*. Aldine Publishing Company.

Gramlich, J. (2019, August 16). What the data says about gun deaths in the U.S. *Pew Research Center.* https://www.pewresearch.org/fact-tank/2019/08/16/what-the-data-says-about-gun-deaths-in-the-u-s/

Hamington, M., & Ramaley, J. (2019). University Studies leadership: Vision and challenge. *The Journal of General Education (University Park, Pa.), 67*(3–4), 290–309.

Hochschild, A. R. (1983). *The managed heart: Commercialization of human feeling*. University of California Press.

Hodges, C., Moore, S., Lockee, B., Trust, T., & Bond, A. (2020, March 27). The difference between emergency remote teaching and online learning. *EDUCAUSE.* https://er.educause.edu/articles/2020/3/the-difference-between-emergency-remote-teaching-and-online-learning

Kember, D. (2008). Promoting student-centred forms of learning across an entire university. *Higher Education, 58*(1), 1–13.

Kremenitzer, J. P. (2005). The emotionally intelligent early childhood educator: Self-reflective journaling. *Early Childhood Education Journal, 33*(1), 3–9.

LaBelle, J. T., & Belknap, G. (2016). Reflective journaling: Fostering dispositional development in preservice teachers. *Reflective Practice, 17*(2), 125–142.

Lee, E., & Hannafin, M. (2016). A design framework for enhancing engagement in student-centered learning: Own it, learn it, and share it. *Education Tech Research Development, 64*(4), 707–734.

Luborsky, M. R. (1994). The identification and analysis of themes and patterns. In J. F. Gubrium & A. Sankar (Eds.), *Qualitative methods in aging research* (p. 294). Sage.

Mack, K. M. (Ed.). (2019). *Culturally responsive strategies for reforming STEM higher education: Turning the TIDES on inequity* (1st ed.). Emerald Publishing Limited.

MacNell, L., Driscoll, A., & Hunt, A. N. (2015). What's in a name: Exposing gender bias in student ratings of teaching. *Innovative Higher Education, 40*, 291–303.

Mangan, K. (2020, March 30). As Liberty University reports first Covid-19 case, students and parents grapple with conflicting information. *The Chronicle of Higher Education.* https://www.chronicle.com/article/as-liberty-university-reports-first-covid-19-case-students-and-parents-grapple-with-conflicting-information/

Masucci, M., & Langton L. (2017). Hate crime victimization, 2004–2015. *U.S. Department of Justice*. https://www.bjs.gov/content/pub/pdf/hcv0415.pdf

Mckenna, S. (2013). The dangers of student-centered learning—A caution about blind spots in the scholarship of teaching and learning. *International Journal for the Scholarship of Teaching and Learning, 7*(2).

McMurtrie, B. (2020a, March 20). Teaching in a crisis: Coronavirus pushed professors online. Can they keep up? *The Chronicle of Higher Education*. https://www.chronicle.com/article/the-coronavirus-has-pushed-courses-online-professors-are-trying-hard-to-keep-up/?cid2=gen_login_refresh&cid=gen_sign_in

McMurtrie, B. (2020b, November 5). The pandemic is dragging on. Professors are burning out. Overwhelmed and undersupported, instructors see no end in sight. *The Chronicle of Higher Education*. https://www.chronicle.com/article/the-pandemic-is-dragging-on-professors-are-burning-out

Merriam, S. B., & Tisdell, E. J. (2016). *Qualitative research: A guide to design and implementation* (4th ed.). Jossey-Bass.

Murray, T. A., Federico, P., Anderson, C., & Johnson, L. (2019). POGIL in the classroom: Using active learning strategies to re-energize post-tenured faculty. *Peer Review: Emerging Trends and Key Debates in Undergraduate Education, 21*(4), 12.

Palmer, P. J. (2007). *The courage to teach: Exploring the inner landscape of a teacher's life* (10th-anniversary ed.). Jossey-Bass.

Pettit, E. (2020, October 26). Covid-19 cuts hit contingent faculty hard. As the pandemic drags on, some question their future. *The Chronicle of Higher Education*. https://www.chronicle.com/article/covid-19-cuts-hit-contingentfaculty-hard-as-it-drags-on-some-question-their-future

Plutchik, R. (2001). The nature of emotions: Human emotions have deep evolutionary roots, a fact that may explain their complexity and provide tools for clinical practice. *American Scientist, 89*(4), 344–350.

Rendón, L. I., & Nepo, M. (2009). *Sentipensante (sensing/thinking) pedagogy: Educating for wholeness*. Stylus Publishing LLC.

Saldaña, J. (2016). *The coding manual for qualitative researchers* (2nd ed.). Sage.

Sandier, B. R. (1991). Women faculty at work in the classroom, or, why it still hurts to be a woman in labor. *Communication Education, 40*(1), 6–15.

Schön, D. A. (1983). *The reflective practitioner: How professionals think in action*. Temple Smith.

Schuessler, J. B., Wilder, B., & Byrd, L. W. (2012). Reflective journaling and development of cultural humility in students. *Nursing Education Perspectives, 33*(2), 96–99.

Seidman, I. (2019). *Interviewing as qualitative research: A guide for researchers in education and the social sciences* (5th ed.). Teachers College Press.

Smawfield, D., & Brock, C. (2012). *Education and natural disasters*. Bloomsbury Publishing Plc.

Sprague, J., & Massoni, K. (2005). Student evaluations and gendered expectations: What we can't count can hurt us. *Sex Roles, 53*, 779–793.

Stommel, J., Anonymous, Boedy, M., Chopra, T., Murch, D., Hardesty, M., & Anonymous. (2020). Reflections on faculty life in a pandemic: Faculty perspectives on the COVID-19 crisis [Special issue]. *Academe, 106*(4).

Sumerau, J. E. (2016, August 5). Cisgender me-search. *Inside Higher Ed*. https://www.insidehighered.com/advice/2016/08/05/most-research-cisgender-scholars-can-be-defined-me-search-essay

Taylor, S. J., Bogdan, R., & DeVault, M. (2015). *Introduction to qualitative research methods: A guidebook and resource.* https://ebookcentral-proquest-com.proxy.lib.pdx.edu

Thorpe, K. (2004). Reflective learning journals: From concept to practice. *Reflective Practice, 5*(3), 327–343.

Turk, J., Salazar, M. C. S., & Ramos, A. M. (2020, October 8). College and university presidents respond to COVID-19: 2020 fall term survey. *American Council on Education.* https://www.acenet.edu/Research-Insights/Pages/Senior-Leaders/College-and-University-Presidents-Respond-to-COVID-19-2020-Fall-Term.aspx

Youmans, M. K. (2020). Going remote: How teaching during a crisis is unique to other distance learning experiences. *Journal of Chemical Education, 97*(9), 3374–3380.

CHAPTER 13

Trauma-Informed Indigenous Adult Education: Developing Practices to Support and Nurture Decolonization

Hilistis Pauline Waterfall and Elodie Button

INTRODUCTION

The history of formal education for Indigenous communities throughout the world is a traumatic one. In settler colonial societies like Canada, the United States, New Zealand, and Australia, education has been used as a tool of colonization and attempted cultural erasure. In Canada, we live with the legacy of residential schools, a horrific state and church-sanctioned system of genocide in which children were violently separated from their families, forbidden to speak their languages and practice their cultures, and made to endure abhorrent human rights abuses. In addition to residential schools, Indigenous people continue to be oppressed by systemic racism in many ways. Following the leadership of many Indigenous communities, steps are being taken to address and rectify these injustices.

As adult educators working with Indigenous learners, we have lived and witnessed the sustained impacts of intergenerational trauma on the students in our classrooms and in our communities. We have worked hard to build, over time, personal and program practices which are culturally grounded and trauma-informed. Over the last six years, we have been blessed to work together in service of Indigenous adult education programs in the context of

H. P. Waterfall
Bella Bella, BC, Canada

E. Button (✉)
Victoria, BC, Canada

P. Thompson and J. Carello (eds.), *Trauma-Informed Pedagogies*,
https://doi.org/10.1007/978-3-030-92705-9_13

environmental stewardship. We have learned in the classroom, on the land, and on video calls, the positive impact of integrating trauma-informed practice into adult education. In sharing some of our personal learnings here, we hope to contribute to a stronger collective journey toward trauma-informed Indigenous adult education that reduces harm and supports healing.

It is important to acknowledge that Indigenous communities, pedagogies, and knowledges are extremely diverse. The practices we offer in this chapter may not be appropriate or relevant in every context, and the unique gifts, circumstances, and territories of each Indigenous community must be prioritized always. The extensive community-based work and academic scholarship on Indigenous adult education, on decolonizing post-secondary institutions, and on trauma-informed Indigenous services are foundational to the reflections we share in this chapter. Our intention is to offer practical, introductory concepts for educators or others who are wanting to begin to consider how trauma-informed practice can be integrated into Indigenous adult education in support of learning and in nurturance of decolonization.

SITUATING OURSELVES

We begin by situating ourselves in this work, so that you may understand where we come from and what our shared perspectives are grounded in. Our respective experiences, skills, and histories are very different; yet, the shared work that we have undertaken as educators gives relevant insight and perspectives on this decolonial journey.

My name is Hilistis Pauline Waterfall. I am a member of the Haíłzaqv Nation, born and raised in Bella Bella, British Columbia until I was sent to residential school at 12 years of age. I am a mother of three adult children, grandmother of six, and great-grandmother of two. My husband, John, arrived in Bella Bella as a member of the Royal Canadian Mounted Police in 1968. After we chose to marry, he was required to make a decision to stay in the force or leave—interracial marriages were discouraged. He made the right choice! My ancestral name, Hilistis, comes from an ancient nu'yem, story, of how our animal clan system came into being. Translated it means "starting on a journey and staying on course until returning to come full circle." After attending Day School, Residential School, College, and University, it became apparent that the circle of education for Indigenous students was rife with trauma and abuse. When I returned home to live and work as an educator in 1974, I realized that there was a great capacity-building potential among our people, so I founded Heiltsuk College. We had a very high success rate, with learners thriving in the safe and nurturing environment in which they formed college family systems and took care of each other. The successes of this work have continued in my work with the First Nations Stewardship Technicians Training Program. In this paper I will give insight into how trauma-informed adult education experiences promote healing through a decolonized model of learning.

My name is Elodie Button. I have been working in non-formal and community-based education for 20 years, and for the last five years, I have been working exclusively with Indigenous adult learners. My mother is from France, and my father is from England, and I was born and raised in unceded Algonquin Anishinaabe territories near what is currently called Ottawa, Ontario. I now reside with my partner and daughter on unceded ləkʷəŋən and W̱SÁNEĆ territories in what is currently known as Victoria, British Columbia. My life is oriented to the commitments and relationships to which I am accountable as a non-Indigenous woman living in a settler colonial state. I honor the historical and contemporary relationships Indigenous people have to the lands I have learned from, lived on, and traveled through. I am deeply passionate about the ways in which we can more effectively support social change and decolonization through the process of facilitating transformative learning grounded in trauma-informed educational practices.

Trauma-Informed Adult Education

Foundational to trauma-informed Indigenous adult education are the principles of trauma-informed care, an understanding of the impacts of trauma on the learning brain and body, and most crucially, Indigenous pedagogies, experiences, and histories. Being trauma-informed means both understanding how violence, victimization, and trauma affect individuals, families, and communities and applying that understanding in order to prevent harm and promote healing and growth (Carello et al., 2019; Harris and Fallot, 2001).

In context of Indigenous experiences, trauma-informed support is a strengths-based model that is centered on individual, family, and community approaches and experiences. In consideration of the ongoing impacts of colonialism and intergenerational trauma, it is necessary to wrap services and support around each learner based on their needs. This holistic pedagogy reinforces the inherent and traditional way of growing and learning which results in building trust and confidence. Wrap-around supports include being aware of and responsive to needs as they arise in order to support students in a respectful and sensitive way. For example, there may be hints of someone being hungry, so offering a healthy breakfast program to all students can mitigate this problem. Seeking and offering counseling support when a student is under duress or disclosing trauma is another example of wrapping services around the person.

Adult educators, program coordinators, facilitators, funders, and administrators each have a responsibility to meet adult learners where they are, including their context, their lived experience, and their learning styles. In Indigenous adult education, we also take into consideration the diverse cultural backgrounds that learners are born into. Education can contribute to community-building, personal healing, and intergenerational transformation, and it can reproduce oppressive and (re)traumatizing dynamics. Indigenous leadership must always be at the center of this work, and there are important roles for non-Indigenous people as well, including the responsibility to learn about systems of oppression and work toward their dismantling. We enact our commitments to trauma-informed adult education through our personal practice as educators and through programmatic processes.

PERSONAL PRACTICE

Creating trauma-informed adult education requires a commitment to developing a personal trauma-informed practice, for both Indigenous and non-Indigenous educators. This practice is an unfolding journey, and there are many paths to building our knowledge and skills in these areas. However, learning, unlearning, the cultivation of humility, learning to listen deeply, and taking care of ourselves are some elements of this journey that we wish to share here.

Learning

A commitment to lifelong learning and adapting is an essential aspect of an educational trauma-informed practice. In addition to devoting time to learning about the impacts of trauma on the brain and body, it is important to be dedicated to learning about the numerous systems of oppression which create and perpetuate harm to all people, but not all people equally, including racism, colonialism, white supremacy, patriarchy, transphobia, heterosexism, ableism, and capitalism. We must understand these systems and the ways we are impacted by them and/or are upholding them, so that we can understand the impacts they have on our students and so that we can dismantle them together. Learning about these systems of oppression includes learning about the ways in which we may embody different forms of power and privilege and the ways we may unintentionally use that power and privilege to reproduce harm.

> A note for readers who are just beginning their learning journey: Take the time to listen to and to read the words of diverse communities and individuals. There is an abundance of resources available, created by brilliant people. Lean on those resources—there are podcasts, books, articles, films, theatre productions, dances, lectures, and many other amazing ways that this knowledge is being shared with the world. And most importantly: be mindful of not expecting people to teach you about their experiences—this especially means not asking marginalized people to share their experiences of violence and survival, unless they are offering or inviting an exchange of this nature.

Unlearning

Unfortunately, no one is immune to these systems of oppression, and each one of us must also embark on an unlearning journey. We invite educators to be curious, to look within themselves and find the ways that stories, biases, and prejudices have become woven through their lives. As we make a commitment to unlearning the harm and untruths we have unconsciously absorbed and perpetuated, we must also extend compassion to ourselves. There will likely be times where this journey results in experiences of emotional distress, including guilt, shame, and denial. In these moments, a practice of extending grace, forgiveness, and courage is extremely supportive and needed. In the creativity and beauty of humans, there is much hope to be found. Creating room in our collective minds and hearts and bodies for new stories of possibility affirms the limitless, generative solutions being offered in every community. As we unlearn, we create a room within ourselves to be better, more compassionate, engaging, and empathetic educators.

Listening Deeply

Learning to listen deeply is an integral component of building a trauma-informed practice in education. Learning to listen to Elders and knowledge keepers, to children, to the land, to the water, and learning to listen for the teachings being shared with us, we learn what is truly important. In a trauma-informed adult education practice, we also listen to what people and communities are needing and are asking for. This is particularly important in relation to the ways in which Indigenous communities are rebuilding their systems, organizations, family units, and are engaged in other forms of healing to achieve transformation, self-reliance, and self-governance.

It is valuable to develop a deeper awareness of our own cultural and familial communication habits and tendencies. In some cultural and familial traditions, to interrupt or speak loudly over someone is commonplace and at times is understood as a way of showing a keen interest and involvement in conversation. In many Indigenous communities, interruption is considered to be deeply inconsiderate, profoundly disrespectful, and can be relationship damaging. In addition, the legacy of 150 years of oppressive experiences in Indian Residential Institutes did not permit interactive or inclusive communication; in fact, students were more often muted and punished for speaking out. As we examine and understand our communication tendencies and histories, we orient ourselves toward compassion and are better able to find ways to build bridges between differences.

Cultivating Humility

Humility is true strength. When we are grounded in our values, when we are confident that we are all learning, growing beings, our true skills as educators emerge. We understand that our contributions are meaningful and that as educators and facilitators we can center our students rather than placing ourselves at the center.

Within our programs, we have experienced great success through the process of uplifting each student as a leader, an expert, and a knowledge holder. Through the humility of our instructors, each student in our program has an opportunity both to be a beginner and a teacher, cultivating the confidence they need. These changes are fundamental to decolonizing learning, and this empowerment is so important in building confidence and trust rooted in the talents, experiences, or interests that each educator and student can contribute to enhance the whole.

A note for non-Indigenous instructors and educators: Given the multi-generational messaging about perceived hierarchy, with Indigenous societies and people at the bottom of the stratification, it is very important that non-Indigenous teachers in particular be sensitive to and aware that they may be perceived as better or more powerful than their Indigenous students—by institutions, colleagues, themselves, or their students. Teachers in residential schools reinforced this notion of superiority. It is necessary to counter this by practicing the art of humility.

Taking Care of Ourselves

Perhaps one of the hardest practices to embody as educators and people who have a commitment to making the world a more just, peaceful, and equitable place, is the practice of self-care. Rather than suggest that there is a particular recipe for self-care, we will simply offer that trauma-informed adult education is hard work, and educators are also worthy of rest, renewal, love, connection, and joy. We believe it is beneficial to release the expectation that this is a journey in which we "arrive" or "figure it all out" and advocate for remembering that we are on a collective journey in which each person, with their unique gifts, has something to contribute, but that no one person is responsible to carry it all. We assert that we learn throughout our whole lives how to care for ourselves and each other in the ways that feel most nurturing and transformative.

PROGRAM PRACTICE

Extending beyond the personal commitments of educators, trauma-informed adult education requires building and designing programs, policies, and funding agreements to be trauma-informed as well. In our work in Indigenous adult education, we have learned that there are a few key elements of program design and delivery that are very supportive for students and instructors alike.

Understanding History and Creating Opportunities to Thrive Beyond It

Trauma-informed adult education includes creating curriculum that is built in consideration of individual and collective trauma, including an understanding of the possibility of students being triggered or re-traumatized by *what* is being taught or *how* it is being taught, and an ongoing adaptation of lesson plans to that effect. Instructors are encouraged to be mindful of the ways in which content could be triggering to students. A deeper understanding of systems of oppression and the lived experiences of their students is crucial to helping instructors identify these potential triggers.

It is equally important that educators be prepared to meet and support students in their experiences of trauma should they emerge as a result of the curriculum. Significantly as Carello (2018) has found, it is not the presence or absence of trauma that is most distressing to students, but rather the ability of instructors to show up for them in support. Our experiences have confirmed that when students and faculty come together as a family, grounded in traditional approaches to learning which include relationship and reciprocity, there are greater opportunities for support, healing, and learning overall.

Educators, coordinators, funders, and administrators must develop a strong understanding of the historical and contemporary relationships that learners and participants have toward education. Education is not neutral or benign— it has been, and continues to be, used as a tool of oppression and violence in many contexts throughout the world. In the context of Indigenous education, a key first step is to learn about and acknowledge the racist and traumatic experiences of Indigenous learners over several generations. While truth and reconciliation are emerging, past negative experiences, including but not limited to residential schools, continue to impact learners including mistrust, feelings of inadequacy, and other reactive behaviors. Educators must understand that unresolved trauma continues to trigger defensive behaviors as a form of protection against previous exploitation, neglect, and pain. Institutional experiences of inflexible, rigorous, and punitive processes have negated Indigenous students' identities, brilliance, and sense of self-worth. Understanding and recognizing this allows for opportunities to foster and reinforce personal strengths, talents, and interests in contributing to the benefit of the whole. It is essential to provide students with opportunities to develop confidence throughout educational experiences, in decision-making, communication, and relationship-based learning.

Embracing every opportunity to incorporate local content or cultural context into the curriculum is equally supportive for students, especially when drawing upon the expertise of Indigenous knowledge keepers. It is important to factor this into the planning process with the team that will deliver the learning, while also keeping a keen consideration to the increased demands placed on Indigenous Elders and knowledge keepers in an era of reconciliation. And while planning is important, there may be ways to seize teachable moments that affirm Indigenous knowledge and understandings in spontaneous ways as well.

Relationship-Based Learning

Our commitment is to relationship-based education. This reinforces traditional communal relations that foster unity, problem-solving, and consensus building that have occurred over thousands of generations. In our experience, learning that happens in and through relationship is vastly more impactful and transformational than learning that unfolds in an individual or decontextualized way. Relationship-based learning is crucial to transforming adult education. Through relationship-based learning, we are better able to support a student who is re-traumatized, either by an event in their lives or an event in the classroom. In Indigenous adult education, a commitment to relationship-based learning includes creating time for checking-in and checking-out, sitting in a circle and sharing our experiences, and prioritizing supporting individuals and/or the group above curriculum at times.

Past traumatic experiences result in some learned behaviors that aren't necessarily positive. If, for example, someone has been punished for breeching punitive rules, then the person may have difficulty expressing themselves or contributing to meaningful discussion unless there is a clear indication of support, encouragement, and understanding. It's important to be attuned to and open to these situations as they arise. Relationship-based learning provides a framework of support within which traumatic past experiences can be held, witnessed, and healed.

Elders and Knowledge Keepers and Intergenerational Learning

Creating a model of shared learning that includes Elders and knowledge keepers extends and enhances educational experiences. This traditional practice models holistic learning, understanding, and growing, and provides opportunities to expand and reinforce learning in an organic and meaningful way. It strengthens cultural identity and pride which have been and continue to be purposely negated and diminished through colonization. Including Elders in a teaching situation also reinforces their traditional roles and responsibilities within Indigenous societies—they are the keepers of knowledge, but their place within family units may have been displaced because of colonial violence, familial disruptions, and displacements. Integrating and centering Indigenous knowledge, Elders, and knowledge keepers is fundamental to nurturing healing and decolonization.

Spirituality and Ceremony

The colonial policies and practices that banned, outlawed, and attempted to erase Indigenous governance and ceremonial life, including the potlatch system, must be acknowledged and every opportunity must be given to include in educational programs various ways and means of reinforcing cultural strength and identity. This may include having ceremonies within the learning setting, which can be planned in advance or may be impromptu, to help support a learner whose trauma has been unintentionally triggered. Singing and drumming are natural ways of connecting to cultural and ancestral energies which are healing medicine to traumatized souls. One practice we have adhered to is to extend an invitation to students prior to program commencement to share if they drum, sing, tell stories, and so on.

Land-Based, Hands-On Learning, Learning in Relationship to the Land and Water

Learning in relationship to the land and waters is a way in which Indigenous pedagogies are enacted and uplifted. The land is medicine, and when it is included in educational programming for Indigenous adult learners, it supports the regulation of spirit, body, mind, and heart. Historically and traditionally, Indigenous peoples have had a close kinship with their natural world. They depend upon it for livelihood, travel, food security, etc. Because children were removed from their home and communities over several generations, this relationship has been interrupted. School programs are offered that reconnect students to the land and waters with positive and lasting impacts. This is a natural relationship based on reciprocity and including this in adult learning experiences fosters reconnecting in a safe and healing way.

Language Revitalization at Every Step

In Canada, speaking Indigenous languages was against the law for 66 years in accordance with the Indian Act. To do so resulted in unspeakable corporal punishment and abuse. At every opportunity, the inclusion of Indigenous words and sentences in the context of learning must be incorporated into the classroom. For example, the word "law" which has negative connotations can be countered with the use of Indigenous words that mean the same but in a different context. Inclusion of language and culture is a rich and healing way that reinforces holistic learning.

Flexibility

Being adaptable and flexible is necessary given the revitalization of cultural ways and family units. Life experiences such as deaths, illnesses, and accidents happen, and those impacted must be accommodated to promote healing. Creating space within learning environments for absences and support during difficult times counters the violence of colonial schedules and allows for cultural healing and renewal. Practicing this and accommodating needs in these situations is another means of reinforcing traditional norms and values of sharing, caring, supporting, and giving.

Trauma Supports

Including a counselor and specific trauma support in your program, institution, or organization is extremely supportive. Include this in funding agreements and broader program structures from the beginning whenever possible. A counselor who understands the lived experience of program participants or students is highly recommended. In our experience, having access to an Indigenous counselor available to support students has been important in the well-being of all students and staff.

Ongoing Program Evaluation

Ongoing program evaluation allows educators and adult education programs to keenly assess the extent to which they are meeting their goals and objectives. Planning for formal and informal program evaluations which occur not only at the beginning and end of a program but also throughout allows for divergent knowledge and perspectives to emerge from students. Ensuring that there are opportunities for students to provide feedback in written and oral ways, in individual and group ways, and in anonymous and personal ways, will help ensure that trauma-informed program goals are met. Including students in evaluation processes encourages confidence and reinforces the validity of one's voice and input.

Accessibility

The impacts of intergenerational trauma and systemic racism in education are felt in numerous ways, including the experiences people have had in education systems. Adult learners may have learning challenges, learning exceptionalities, or invisible learning needs. Taking the time to consider whether the classroom activities or assignments are accessible for all learners is an integral part of trauma-informed teaching. It is important also to consider that adult learners with traumatic experiences in education may be less likely to disclose any learning challenges they experience. Creating accessible programming requires time, funding, and dedication. It requires an orientation to student-centered learning and relationality above and beyond a commitment to curriculum.

Ensuring Staff Safety, Support, and Sustainability

The well-being of educators is not solely their individual responsibility. To create effectively transformative and healthy programs, the well-being of staff must be centered as well. Programs, educational institutions and funders, and communities have a responsibility to ensure the safety and well-being of their staff. Ensuring long-term sustained and flexible program funding is available wherever possible supports both students and staff success. Having in place counseling supports, benefits, sick days, and creating a culture of adequate compensation (living wage), healthy relationships, and honest communication is paramount. If an educator is not well, they cannot teach or facilitate in a trauma-informed way. The well-being of every member of the learning family is important.

CONCLUSION

Grounded in an understanding of the traumatic impacts of colonization, hetero-patriarchy, ableism, racism, and white supremacy, we can draw connections between the lived experiences of learners and the contexts in which they learn. Rather than pathologizing or individualizing the solutions to these traumas and oppressions, community-based educators can commit to developing their own trauma-informed practice which seeks to integrate a holistic, radical, systems-wide approach to create change and justice.

Senator Murray Sinclair, Chair of the Truth and Reconciliation Commission of Canada, has stated that the consequence and failure of the education system were used to harm everyone (St. Francis Xavier University, 2016). He further says that education was the cause of the pain we now experience and that it is the key to reconciliation and repairing the damage. Educators can draw on the 94 Calls to Action from the Truth and Reconciliation Commission of Canada (Truth and Reconciliation Commission of Canada, 2015). They are important to incorporate into all avenues of healing and learning as we continue to work toward a more equitable and inclusive system and society that honors peoples of all colors and ways.

The journey of learning how to create safer, more equitable, decolonized, and more transformative learning spaces is ongoing. We do not arrive, as educators, in a place where we have figured it out. The reflections in this chapter are an expression of our shared journey thus far, but this journey will continue, and these ideas will evolve. We invite you to consider your own journey in the same light.

Dedication

At the time of writing, there are continued discoveries of unmarked graves of Indigenous children who died at Indian Residential "Schools." It is inconceivable to know how they died; however, the testimonies of survivors who made it home speak to the atrocities and suffering that were rendered in the name of "education." We dedicate this chapter to those innocent children, with a commitment to assure that we do everything possible to ensure the safety and well-being of today's learners. We dedicate this to the vision of transformative change in promoting and supporting a quest for mastery learning.

REFERENCES

Carello, J. (2018). Retraumatization during training: A trauma-in formed narrative approach (Doctoral dissertation). https://ubir.buffalo.edu/xmlui/handle/10477/78089

Carello, J., Butler, L. D., & Critelli, F. M. (2019). Introduction to trauma and human rights: Context and content. In L. D. Butler, F. M. Critelli, & J. Carello (Eds.), *Trauma and human rights: Integratingapproaches to address human suffering.* Palgrave Macmillan

Harris, M., & Fallot, R. D. (Eds.) (2001). *Using trauma theory to design service systems.* Jossey-Bass.

St. Francis Xavier University. (2016, November 8). *Education, respect for each other, keys toreconciliation* Senator Murray Sinclair says in powerful keynote at STFX. https://www.stfx.ca/about/news/senator-murray-sinclair-delivers-powerful-message

Truth and Reconciliation Commission of Canada. (2015).Truth and Reconciliation Commission ofCanada: Calls to action. http://trc.ca/assets/pdf/Calls_to_Action_English2.pdf

PART IV

(Re)Assessment

CHAPTER 14

Measuring Trauma Resilience in Higher Education Settings

Andrea D. Clements, L. Lauren Brown, Susan K. Steckel, Megan Quinn, Michiel A. van Zyl, Diana Morelen, and Wallace E. Dixon Jr.

Efforts have been made over the past several years to infuse trauma-informed principles in many sectors, but higher education settings have lagged behind in this movement. Though adoption efforts are occurring, the effectiveness of these interventions needs to be studied and shared so the most beneficial interventions can be used. For clarity, we will define several closely related terms. We use the term *trauma-informed care* as an umbrella term that refers to the totality of care delivery from the theoretical to policy and practice. The

A. D. Clements (✉) · D. Morelen · W. E. Dixon Jr.
Department of Psychology, East Tennessee State University, Johnson City, TN, USA
e-mail: clements@etsu.edu

D. Morelen
e-mail: morelen@etsu.edu

W. E. Dixon Jr.
e-mail: dixonw@etsu.edu

L. L. Brown
School of Medicine, Meharry Medical College, Nashville, TN, USA
e-mail: llbrown@mmc.edu

S. K. Steckel
The University of Tennessee, Knoxville, TN, USA
e-mail: ssteckel@cars-rp.org

M. Quinn
Department of Biostatistics and Epidemiology, East Tennessee State University, Johnson City, TN, USA

P. Thompson and J. Carello (eds.), *Trauma-Informed Pedagogies*,
https://doi.org/10.1007/978-3-030-92705-9_14

163

terms *trauma-informed practice* or *trauma-informed approach* refer to more focused elements of practice such as administration or teaching in the higher education setting. Finally, we use the term *trauma resilience* as we seek to evolve the language from deficit-based trauma-focused terminology to more strengths-based and resilience-focused language that addresses feedback from the field and aligns with advances in research and practice.

Research exploring the effectiveness of trauma-informed and resilience-building approaches is central to the mission of The Ballad Health/ETSU Strong BRAIN (Building Resilience through ACEs-Informed Networking) Institute (SBI), which was founded in spring 2020 at East Tennessee State University (ETSU). This institute is made up of faculty from seven of the eight academic colleges at ETSU and is guided by an advisory board comprised of community members from Tennessee and Virginia, each representing different sectors (e.g., business, criminal justice, government), who are champions in this arena. One central focus of the SBI is to build a culture of resilience and infuse trauma-informed approaches at ETSU, then share those approaches found to be effective with other higher education institutions. This culture of resilience, or *organizational trauma resilience* (OTR) (Brown et al., 2021), refers to the capacity of the organization to weather adversity, anticipate the needs of those impacted by trauma, prevent toxic stress for organization personnel, and consequently foster "the safe, stable, and nurturing environment necessary for a thriving trauma-responsive workforce" (Brown et al., 2021, pg. 4). Use of the OTR frame as a guiding principle in any setting demonstrates the importance of addressing organizational culture as the primary driver for all other aspects of trauma-informed care implementation. The SBI is working to integrate OTR into both the implicit and explicit curricula at ETSU. What follows is an example of how an institution of higher education can integrate OTR into the implicit curriculum in a single professional college (i.e., pharmacy) through strategies such as training, coaching, and data-driven continuous quality improvement.

An internal grant program at ETSU funded pilot testing of ongoing resilience-building intervention and, of most importance to this chapter, the development of a higher education-focused organizational trauma resilience measure. The *Training for Resilience Project*, funded for the 2020–2021 academic year, investigated whether organizational and cultural changes can

e-mail: QUINNM@etsu.edu

M. A. van Zyl
School of Social Work, College of Behavioral and Community Sciences at the University of South Florida, Tampa, FL, USA
e-mail: riaan@usf.edu

A. D. Clements · M. Quinn · D. Morelen · W. E. Dixon Jr.
ETSU Ballad Health Strong BRAIN Institute, East Tennessee State University, Johnson City, TN, USA

be made at ETSU through training and coaching in trauma-informed practice within the Bill Gatton College of Pharmacy (COP). In this chapter, we report on the development of a measure of organizational trauma resilience for higher education settings. Our process of developing an instrument to quantify changes in trauma resilience entailed three general phases: 1. A search for a measurement instrument aligned with both the existing training that had been adapted for higher education and the outcome goals of the funded project; 2. In the absence of such an instrument, refinement of the selected instrument (i.e., the *Organizational Trauma Resilience Assessment* (OTRA)) for use in higher education settings; and 3. Administration and validation of the modified version of the OTRA, which we titled the *Higher Education Trauma Resilience Assessment* (HETRA).

Training for Resilience Project

All administrators, faculty, staff, and first year students in the COP were invited to participate in this pilot project, which included participating in a one-time 2.5 hour training using a trauma-informed framework developed by the Substance Abuse and Mental Health Services Administration (SAMHSA, 2014). Training includes foundational information about ACEs, the impact of ACEs and trauma on development and behavior, and relational and reflective strategies to promote organizational change to foster resilience. Key principles of SAMHSA's Trauma-Informed Practices framework include organizational safety, trustworthiness, transparency, and cultural sensitivity. Further, SAMHSA's model outlines the "4 R's" of a trauma-informed approach:

1. Realizes the widespread impact of trauma and understands potential paths for recovery
2. Recognizes the signs and symptoms of trauma in clients, families, staff, and others involved with the system
3. Responds by fully integrating knowledge about trauma into policies, procedures, and practices
4. Resists re-traumatization

In addition to the training, implementation coaching was offered as a voluntary option for all COP administrators, faculty, and staff. Research has shown that implementation coaching can help promote the application of evidence-based practices and sustainability of professional development growth and changes (Hakro & Mathew, 2020; Synder et al., 2015; Walunas et al., 2021). Specifically, coaching groups were formed based on role (i.e., administrator, faculty, staff) and groups were assigned an implementation coach that worked with them across the academic year. Coaches first met with their groups following the training and then met 4–5 additional times across the year. All implementation coaches were trained by the project's PI who is a licensed psychologist with expertise in reflective supervision and practice. The coaches were given a framework to follow in the calls, but flexibility in what was discussed to meet the unique needs of their participants. In addition to their scheduled calls, all participants were informed that they could reach out to their coach, as needed, via email or a phone call for 1:1 coaching support and were given a handout that summarized the purpose and structure of implementation coaching. Students were not included in this coaching model, because students are typically only part of the organization for a limited period of time, and the goal is that coaching concepts will become ingrained as employees buy in and that students will be informally coached in resilience-building as OTR becomes a part of the culture.

Subjective and objective indicators of feasibility, acceptability, and effectiveness of implementation efforts were built into the project including completion of online surveys, including the HETRA, at two time points across the study: Pre-training and 11-month follow-up. Other objective metrics were also collected (e.g., attendance at training, attendance at coaching meetings, number of coaching consultation emails/calls received), plus multiple student success metrics the COP has been measuring since 2015. These metrics included attrition, graduation rate, behavioral issues, number of non-passing grades made on individual exams, and number of students engaging in contracted counseling services. At the time of this writing, data collection is being finalized and analyses are yet to be conducted. A central focus of these analyses will be to compare HETRA scores, as well as these other metrics as pre- and post-measures to assess intervention effects and to do the initial validation of the HETRA itself.

While multiple constructs were assessed at each time point, the central metric of interest changes in OTR. Prior to beginning this pilot study, we were unable to find any validated instruments of this construct that were tailored to a higher education setting; thus, we sought to tailor a validated instrument to fit our setting and purpose, which brings us to the focus of this chapter.

SEARCH FOR MEASURES OF TRAUMA RESILIENCE IN HIGHER EDUCATION

SBI members tasked with assessing the intervention at ETSU sought measures of OTR suitable for use in higher education settings, but none focusing on higher education settings were found. This motivated the search for instruments that could be tailored to the higher education environment. There are several existing instruments available that measure aspects of trauma-informed care, such as *Creating Trauma-Informed Care Environments Organizational Self-Assessment* (Hummer & Dollard, 2010), the *Trauma-Informed System Change Instrument* (Richardson et al., 2012) *Trauma Transformed*, n.d.), the *Trauma-Informed Climate Scale* (Hale et al., 2019), but these primarily target human service organizations. The most widely known, but also costliest, are the *Attitudes Related to Trauma-Informed Care* (ARTIC) (Baker et al., 2016) and the TICOmeter (Bassuk et al., 2017). The TICOmeter predominately focuses on the presence of client-facing practices and procedures as aligned with the TIC paradigm and does not include a direct focus on workforce culture. The ARTIC Scale has been well tested but recently was found to not capture the effects of training in a school setting (Baker et al., 2016). Two instruments were found to be closely aligned, *The Organizational Trauma Resilience Assessment* (OTRA) (Brown et al., 2021), and the Creating Cultures of Trauma-Informed Care (CCTIC) (Harris & Fallot, 2001). Although the CCTIC is thorough and specifically tied to the SAMHSA (2014) six principles of a trauma-informed approach, it is quite a long, containing six domains of open-ended questions, the first of which contains 10 subdomains. We were concerned that survey burden may reduce response rates given our intent to use it in a repeated measures design. The OTRA had been shared months prior with the founders of the SBI by Sukey Steckel of the University of Tennessee-Knoxville College of Social Work.

When we were unable to find an instrument that met the specific needs for this pilot project, we reached back out to the OTRA authors who willingly shared a copy of the assessment as a non-proprietary instrument. The SBI team agreed that it seemed to be most closely aligned with what we were seeking. We asked three of the OTRA authors (Brown, Steckel, and van Zyl), for their willingness to collaborate to refine the instrument to fit the higher education setting. All agreed that it would be advantageous to create such a version, and the OTRA refinement collaboration began among researchers from the SBI and other higher education institutions in Tennessee. Herein we describe the OTRA and its validation, the changes made to create the higher education version (i.e., HETRA), and current and future uses of the new instrument.

THE TRAUMA-INFORMED MOVEMENT AND DEVELOPMENT AND VALIDATION OF THE ORGANIZATIONAL TRAUMA RESILIENCE ASSESSMENT (OTRA)

As an empirically supported system, trauma-informed practice offers the potential to improve systems of care, but several fair criticisms have emerged about how it is currently used and the knowledge base undergirding it. Some criticisms include that it can unintentionally promote a deficit or pathology-driven focus (Leitch, 2017), in which it can lead to labeling or even being used as an excuse for unwanted behavior or poor health choices. By shifting the focus toward resilience, past trauma is acknowledged, but the focus becomes one of healing and recovery rather than the traumatic experience(s). Views of the original SAMHSA (2014) tenets of trauma-informed care are not deficit-focused, as they promote collaboration, trust, and a strengths focus; however, trauma-formed care is coupled with knowledge of adversity, and that adversity (e.g., measurement and reporting of ACE scores; categorizing *high ACE* patients or students) sometimes becomes the focus. While there is widespread interest in adopting its framework, until very recently few instruments have been tested for validity and reliability—which is a necessary step in instrument development to ensure tools consistently and accurately measure what they are intended to measure. To reduce the potential for trauma-focused interventions to create a deficit focus, there have been calls for efforts to include a stronger focus on resilience (Leitch, 2017; Brown et al., 2021) and healing (Ginwright, 2018).

The authors of the original instrument, the OTRA (Brown et al., 2021), set out to address these criticisms; developed through a community-engaged, multi-step process, the OTRA incorporates elements from both individual and organizational resilience theory with TIC principles as a tool for assessing organizational cultural alignment with resilience-focused trauma-informed care. Items of the OTRA were generated through several processes: 1. In 2017, Brown developed items based upon SAMHSA's (2014) principles found in the document, *TIP 57: Trauma-Informed Care in Behavioral Health Services* and then tested an initial instrument for validity and reliability among staff in a southern-based AIDS Service Organization (ASO); 2. In 2018, a trauma-informed care focused community group made up of human service practitioners developed a series of items as part of a multi-year grant funded trauma-informed care initiative; 3. In 2019, Brown and Steckel teamed up with the community group and merged items tested in the ASO with items from the trauma-informed care focused community group. To efficiently merge items into one instrument, a smaller trauma-informed care working group refined the items through a series of meetings; 4. These items were then subjected to a pre-assessment test for item comprehension and cultural appropriateness. Specifically, providers convened for an annual HIV meeting were asked to assess each item by providing a 1–3 rating for both clarity and appropriateness and were asked to provide suggested word changes for any items containing unclear language; 5. The smaller trauma-informed care working group then reviewed item scores, suggested word changes, and developed a final draft of items to be tested for statistical psychometric strength; 6. In 2019, the 65-item scale was administered to a national sample of human service providers to test its statistical and psychometric properties. Agencies included a metropolitan public health department, the same ASO from earlier testing, and several faith-based charity organizations focusing on housing instability, food insecurity, immigrant and refugee services, mental health and addiction, and others. After data cleaning, data from 861 cases were included in analyses from this national study. Standard test construction and validation procedures (i.e., Classical Test Theory and Item Response Theory) were employed to reduce the 65-item instrument to a 40-item instrument with 5 dimensions. Follow-up analyses confirmed the 5-dimension structure of the final OTRA.

The OTRA has strongly contributed to the trauma-informed knowledge base by defining organizational characteristics that are indicative of organizational trauma resilience. In the manuscript reporting the full development of the instrument (Brown et al., 2021), authors define *Organizational Trauma Resilience* (OTR) as "an organizational culture that fosters the safe, stable, and nurturing environment necessary for a thriving trauma-responsive workforce." The authors present OTR as a sub-type of organizational resilience, marking an important advancement of both the trauma-informed care knowledge base as well as the ability to measure this sub-type of organizational culture. Further, OTR can be understood as a critical component of trauma-informed care implementation, as it provides a framework for assessing the aspects of trauma-informed care that relate specifically to organizational culture (e.g. leadership, policies, employee perceptions of organizational practices) in addition to the presence and quality of trauma-specific or -responsive services. In practice, the instrument provides leadership with a validated tool to measure the degree to which their organization exhibits these characteristics. Finally, the OTRA quantifies the aspects of a culture that indicate that it is resilience-focused. For example, low scores on the item "Staff are confident they can communicate issues to organizational leaders without fear of retribution" may indicate staff are governed by a culture of fear rather than one of safety, openness, or trust between supervisors and staff.

Rather than just providing a global score of organizational trauma resilience, the OTRA offers more fine-grained assessment of aspects of the organization. The five dimensions of the 40-item OTRA include: 1. Training and Sustaining a Trauma-Responsive Workforce; 2. Culture of Trust and Support; 3. Practices of Inclusivity, Safety, and Wellness; 4. Collaboration and Empowerment; and 5. Trauma-Responsive Services.

The OTRA was the first instrument of its kind to be developed through a process of community engagement and then empirically validated as a measure of adherence to a *resilience-focused*, trauma-informed care paradigm. This adherence to psychometric development principles and integration of a resilience focus differentiates it from other instruments that measure organizational alignment with trauma-informed care. Once published, the OTRA will be available[1] for wide use and applicable across a variety of service-providing settings.

The Higher Education Trauma Resilience Assessment (HETRA)

To develop the *Higher Education Trauma Resilience Assessment* (HETRA) tool, we refined the 40-item OTRA to make it more suitable for higher education settings. Below, we describe these refinements to the OTRA, then describe the complete HETRA instrument in detail. The goal of our higher

[1] Contact Lauren Brown at llbrown@mmc.edu for use.

education endeavor is to create a trauma-responsive and resilience-focused culture that reaches beyond the workforce to the student body and the institution at large, thus necessitating the ability to measure such characteristics across groups. The original OTRA focuses on assessing the degree to which an organization is trauma-resilient and concentrates primarily on human service organizations that provide clinical services. Some of the most extensive changes to the measure were to expand the target audience to include students and to differentiate among employee roles. Language was refined to ensure items were relevant to everyone in a higher education setting, changing the focus and language from creating a trauma-resilient "workforce" to creating a trauma-resilient "workplace." Changes made throughout the measure include changing "workplace" or "agency" to "organization." To clarify who was being referenced in each question, the term "staff" was changed to "employee," as the staff is only one category of employee in higher education. The term "employee" in higher education encompasses administrators, faculty, and staff. Parallel questions that asked about students were added in many instances. For example, in the original OTRA, an item asks respondents to rate their agreement with the statement: "There is open and transparent communication between leadership and staff." This was expanded into the following three items:

1. There is open and transparent communication among employees.
2. There is open and transparent communication between employees and students.
3. There is open and transparent communication among students.

Similar groups of items were constructed across sections of the measure to capture the multiple relationships within a college setting. Questions assess each group's own perspective, and wording of the questions also allows for assessment of the respondent's perception of others' perspectives. For example, one question reads, "Students feel safe bringing questions to administrators." When a student responds, this gives the student's perception. However, if a staff member responds, it captures the staff's perception of the student's perspective. When attempting to measure culture and culture change, it is helpful to capture such a breadth of perceptions.

The original OTRA is divided into five dimensions, each of which provides a lens into the functioning of a specific organizational domain. The first four dimensions were retained and largely unchanged other than the language changes mentioned above. Those four dimensions are: *Training and Sustaining Trauma Responsiveness*; *Culture of Trust and Support*; *Practices of Inclusivity, Safety, and Wellness*; and *Collaboration and Empowerment*. The fifth, *Trauma-Responsive Services* in the original instrument, was changed substantially as the original instrument dimension focused on direct services. The new instrument dimension is called *Trauma-Responsive Education* and is specifically focused on measuring aspects of trauma responsiveness specific to educational settings. For example, respondents are asked if trauma-responsiveness content is included in the curriculum. This fifth instrument dimension is what clearly differentiates the HETRA from other instruments measuring trauma-informed care or trauma resilience.

After refinement, the HETRA contains 50 items (compared the OTRA's 40) and retained the 5 subscale format. The first, *Training and Sustaining Trauma-Responsiveness in the Workplace* includes 15 items focused on training, continuing education, and investment of resources into ensuring that employees and students understand what is characteristic of a trauma-informed workplace. Items assess whether the organization is thought to provide training on ACEs and traumatic stress, health correlates of traumatic stress, cultural differences in stress response, cultural sensitivity, and organizational wellness. Items also ask about whether there are investments in ongoing training on these topics as well as investments in providing a safe physical environment.

The second section, *Culture of Trust and Support*, contains 13 items that relate to trust among employees and students, openness of communication, and how conflict is handled. It also asks about whether employees feel emotionally safe while at work.

The third section, *Practices of Inclusivity, Safety, and Wellness*, contains 10 items. While in earlier sections respondents are asked about physical and emotional safety, an item in the third section asks whether there are policies and procedures in place that support employee and student safety. Further items ask about policies or procedures that align with trauma-informed principles, such as established routines, evaluations, and feedback mechanisms. This section also asks about leveling of power differentials where possible.

The fourth section, *Collaboration and Empowerment*, contains 7 items. These items focus on the presence of collaborative decision making within the organization, collaboration across units and departments, and collaboration with other organizations.

The fifth, final, and most extensively modified section, *Trauma-Responsive Education*, contains 5 items focusing specifically on whether the organization incorporates an understanding of trauma, its effects, and resilience-building resources into the curriculum and practices of the organization. These items ask whether the educational program offers resources to students to help them understand traumatic stress and pathways to personal resilience, to address how trauma may affect the student and the students' future interactions with others, how trauma responsiveness can be incorporated in the students' future professions, and whether students are provided access to support for their own trauma-related stress.

All items on the HETRA are rated on a 5-point Likert scale ranging from 0 (strongly disagree) to 4 (strongly agree) as on the OTRA. Each item has a maximum of 4 points so that the highest score achievable is 200 and the lowest score is 0. Overall, higher scores indicate the organization is operating from a place of high trauma resilience, while lower scores suggest the organization likely has low levels of trauma resilience.

On the OTRA, the five dimensions may be reported as independent sub-scales.[2] We believe because the first four dimensions of the HETRA are quite similar to the original instrument, it is acceptable to do the same for the HETRA. Further validation efforts will seek to confirm this and will determine whether the fifth dimension still functions similarly to the fifth dimension of the OTRA. Like the OTRA, the HETRA is a self-report survey; thus, it can be administered online or on paper. Online administration typically enhances privacy and facilitates scoring and further analyses (Gavin & Rodham, 2021; Marreiros et al., 2017). The COP project administered the HETRA online, and response time was less than 15 min. Higher education respondents, both students and employees, have at least a high school education, thus reading level and technical ability make online self-administration appropriate.

Current and Future Use of the HETRA

The HETRA is a new instrument and has only recently begun to be used in practice. We intend to subject the HETRA to the same validation techniques used with the OTRA as we have adequate cases to do so, which will be reported in future publications. Although the OTRA has undergone substantial validation efforts, it has not yet been used to assess organizational change up to this point. We plan to conduct similar validation studies to those conducted with the OTRA and will also investigate the validity of change scores on the HETRA as a new area of validation as we have adequate cases to do so. The COP pilot project ran from August 2020 to July 2021 and included administration of the HETRA at baseline (prior to the initial training) and follow-up (again near the end of the project). We plan to assess changes in HETRA total score, dimension-level scores, and item-level ratings; however, these analyses will be interpreted as tentative as validation of the HETRA is not yet complete.

Thus far, the HETRA has not been used outside of this initial pilot study, but we invite others to use it in exchange for sharing de-identified data that can inform our validation efforts. We ask that those who intend to use the HETRA communicate with the HETRA authors[3] at all stages of planning, data collection, and interpretation, to ensure the most current version and interpretation are utilized. Appropriate uses include calculating mean scores for each dimension and comparing means across dimensions (see HETRA and

[2] The OTRA showed strong reliability, with Cronbach's alpha coefficients ranging from .875 to 974 for sub-scales and .974 for the total scale, and strong validity with mean corrected item total correlation scores ranging from .694 to 780 for sub-scales and .682 for the total scale. The overall scale showed strong discriminant validity, indicating each of the sub-scales measured related but different constructs (Brown et al., 2021).

[3] Contact Andrea Clements at clements@etsu.edu for use.

scoring in the Trauma-Informed Teaching Toolbox section of this book). It would also be acceptable to compare mean item ratings to identify areas of strength and to target areas for improvement. Because the psychometric properties and norms for the HETRA are not yet available, we recommend it be used with caution and that any reports or publications include a statement that results are tentative until the instrument is further validated.

Acknowledgements This project was funded buy an Interdisciplinary Research Development Committee Grant at East Tennessee State University (PI: Diana Morelen).

References

Baker, C. N., Brown, S. M., Wilcox, P. D., Overstreet, S., & Arora, P. (2016). Development and psychometric evaluation of the Attitudes Related to Trauma-Informed Care (ARTIC) Scale. *School Mental Health, 8*(1), 61–76. https://doi.org/10.1007/s12310-015-9161-0

Bassuk, E. L., Unick, G. J., Paquette, K., Richard, M. K. (2017). Developing an instrument to measure organizational trauma-informed care in human services: The TICOMETER. *Psychology and Violence, 7*(1), 150–157.

Brown, L. L., Pennings, J., Steckel, S., & van Zyl, M. (2021). The organizational trauma resilience assessment: Methods and psychometric properties. *Psychological Trauma: Theory, Research, Practice, and Policy.* Advance online publication. https://doi.org/10.1037/tra0001184

Gavin, J., & Rodham, K. (2021). Ethics of online research with human participants. In P. M. W. Hackett & C. M. Hayre (Eds.), *Handbook of ethnography in healthcare research* (pp. 23–32). Routledge/Taylor & Francis Group.

Ginwright, S. (2018). The future of healing: Shifting from Trauma Informed Care to healing centered engagement. *Medium.* Retrieved from https://ginwright.medium.com/the-future-of-healing-shifting-from-trauma-informed-care-to-healing-centered-engagement-634f557ce69c

Hakro, A. N., & Mathew, P. (2020). Coaching and mentoring in higher education institutions: A case study in Oman. *International Journal of Mentoring and Coaching in Education, 9* (3), 307–322. https://doi.org/10.1108/IJMCE-05-2019-0060

Hale, T., Kusmal, N., Sundborg, S., & Nochajski, T. (2019). The Trauma-informed Climate Scale-10 (TICS-10): A reduced measure of staff perceptions of the service environment. *Human Service Organizations: Management, Leadership, & Governance, 43*(5), 443–453. https://doi.org/10.1080/23303131.2019.1671928

Harris, M. & Fallot, R. (Eds.) (2001). *Using trauma theory to design service systems. New directions for mental health services.* Jossey-Bass. Accessed July 7, 2021 from https://www.theannainstitute.org/CCTICSELFASSPP.pdf

Hummer, V. & Dollard, N. (2010). *Creating trauma-informed care environments: An organizational self-assessment. (Part of creating trauma-informed care environments curriculum)* University of South Florida. The Department of Child & Family Studies within the College of Behavioral and Community Sciences. Accessed July 7,

2021 from https://www.hca.wa.gov/assets/program/trauma-informed-care-organi zation-self-assessment-university-south-florida.pdf

Leitch L. (2017). Action steps using ACEs and trauma-informed care: A resilience model. *Health & Justice, 5*(1), 5. https://doi.org/10.1186/s40352-017-0050-5

Marreiros, H., Tonin, M., Vlassopoulos, M., & Schraefel, M. C. (2017). "Now that you mention it": A survey experiment on information, inattention and online privacy. *Journal of Economic Behavior & Organization, 140*, 1–17. https://doi.org/10.1016/j.jebo.2017.03.024

Snyder, P. A., Hemmeter, M. L., & Fox, L. (2015). Supporting implementation of evidence based practices through practice-based coaching. *Topics in Early Childhood Special Education, 35*(3), 133–143.

Substance abuse and mental health services administration. (2014). *Trauma–informed care in behavioral health services: A treatment improvement protocol.* TIP 57. Department of Health & Human Services. Center for Substance Abuse Treatment. USA.

Richardson, M. M., Coryn, C. L. S., Henry, J., Black-Pond, C., & Unrau, Y. (2012). Development and evaluation of the trauma-informed system change instrument: Factorial validity and implications for use. *Child & Adolescent Social Work Journal, 29*(3), 167–184. https://doi.org/10.1007/s10560-012-0259-z

Trauma Transformed. (n.d.) Organizational assessment grid. Page accessed July 7, 2021 from https://traumatransformed.org/resources/assessment-grid.asp

Walunas, T. L., Ye, J., Bannon, J., Wang, A., Kho, A. N., Smith, J. D., & Soulakis, N. (2021). Does coaching matter? Examining the impact of specific practice facilitation strategies on implementation of quality improvement interventions in the Healthy Hearts in the heartland study. *Implementation Science, 16*(1), 1–12

CHAPTER 15

An Educator's Scope of Practice: How Do I Know What's Mine?

Karen Costa

What a lot of people don't know about me is that I almost left higher education. I'd gotten burned out in a full-time administrative role, and in early 2012, I resigned, not only to reclaim my health, but to stay home with my 2-year old and teach online. As I was doing my work of healing and figuring out next steps, I began a daily yoga practice that ultimately led me to complete a yoga teacher training. That was my plan: I'd escape the rigid confines of higher ed and become a yoga and wellness teacher.

In April of 2017, I attended a specialized training in teaching yoga for arthritis and chronic pain. The workshop leader, Ann Swanson, held a master of science in yoga (yes, you can earn a master's degree in yoga) and was a certified yoga therapist, a level of certification that requires many hours of study and practice beyond the role of the typical yoga teacher. Yoga therapists are not only skilled in the philosophy and postures of yoga; they are also experts on anatomy and physiology and in helping people use yoga to heal from illness and injury.

Since most of my fellow workshop attendees and I were not yoga therapists, but simply yoga teachers with basic 200-hour certifications, and since we were being trained to work with folks with arthritis and chronic pain, our teacher drilled into us (a loving, gentle, yoga teacher type of drilling) to be clear about our scope of practice (SoP).

K. Costa (✉)
100 Faculty, Gardner, MA, USA

© The Author(s), under exclusive license to Springer Nature Switzerland AG 2022
P. Thompson and J. Carello (eds.), *Trauma-Informed Pedagogies*,
https://doi.org/10.1007/978-3-030-92705-9_15

An SoP, we learned, was a way to identify the confines and possibilities of our roles as yoga teachers—what was and wasn't ours. We learned, for example, that a yoga therapist is qualified to complete a needs assessment with their client to help them develop a personalized plan for using yoga to heal and thrive. It was outside of their SoP, however, to offer psychological counseling or advice on medication to their clients.

As I sat in that training room, my mind wandered back to higher education, that space in my life that I loved but that at times felt like it was ripping my soul in half. One of the reasons that I was sitting in that workshop at all was because I'd had a hard time distinguishing between what was and wasn't mine in my job as an administrator. And so had my colleagues. And so had my supervisors.

I reflected on the old joke of how the word "other" in a job description hides all manner of sins. That one word had eaten away hours of my days. What of faculty in our classrooms? I had previously worked in a community college, where our new-traditional (first-generation, parents, full-time employees, etc.) students faced immense external challenges that impacted their academic success. I was teaching as an adjunct back then too, and was desperate to help all of my students succeed. At times, I'm sorry to say, I probably veered across the line between teacher and counselor, but no one had ever taught me where that line was, and certainly, there was no clear set of guidelines to which I could refer. Scope of practice? More like a game of whack-a-mole as we tried to do our best for our students, implementing more support programs in the face of declining state support, all while ignoring our own personal needs and health.

What, I wondered, might an SoP do for higher educators? How might it benefit faculty, staff, and students? If we all knew what was and wasn't ours, could that not only make us more effective at our jobs, at the work of teaching and learning, but also decrease the chronic stress that seemed to run rampant in our field?

I didn't end up leaving higher education. Six months after that training, I got a concussion that left me unable to work in either higher education or yoga teaching. I spent several months rehabilitating. My slate was wiped clean, which is a terrible and wonderful thing. When I began to add things back in, I came back to higher ed instead of yoga teaching, but this time, I was committed to doing it differently, for myself and others. I was committed to a new vision of higher ed that would tell the truth about the complex realities of being human, and that would seek and create spaces of positive support and growth for every member of our campus communities: faculty, students, and staff.

Enter COVID-19, stage right.

Those of us who'd been working in online education for years attempted to meet the needs of the masses of newly remote educators in the spring of 2020 (and continue to do so as the pandemic surges once again, at the time of this writing, in fall of 2021), many of whom had never taught or taken an online course. One of those offerings was my first trauma-awareness workshop, offered at the Online Learning Consortium's May "Ideate" conference. I had been doing this trauma work for years informally, but in the spirit of service, I put together everything I knew about trauma that could fit into an hour-long session. Part of that presentation was one slide on a proposed SoP for higher educators. I titled it, "An Educator's Scope of Practice," because at the time, that's really all it was. It was the SoP that I'd identified for myself after years of figuring out what belonged to me inside the walls, whether brick or virtual, of the classrooms I shared with my students.

I got an email a few weeks after the presentation from a grammar-lover who told me that it should've been written in the plural possessive. I kindly explained that it wasn't ours, not yet, and maybe not ever. It was just mine. I was throwing spaghetti at the wall in that first presentation to see what would stick. How would the professors I work with react to this model? What was I missing? How could my model be improved and adapted?

The chapter that follows is an outgrowth of this story. Having shared this model with hundreds of educators over the past year, it makes sense to move forward to exploring this model in a more formal setting, in the hopes that it will continue to make people think, feel, and talk about how a set of clearly delineated professional boundaries might benefit us in what looks to be an increasingly volatile world and higher education.

I will begin by reviewing the existing SoP models from the healthcare field before sharing my educator's SoP that I've been introducing in my trauma-aware teaching work. Again, you'll notice that this chapter continues to use the singular possessive. For me to put forth an SoP model for all higher educators doesn't feel right, not yet at least, and we'll chew on this together in the final section of the chapter on future considerations and pressing questions. There, we'll learn together about possible next steps for this work, dangers and possible pitfalls, and how we might best adapt the SoP model to our work in higher education.

EXISTING SCOPE OF PRACTICE MODELS

One is most likely to find SoP models in the healthcare field. Within the nursing field, for example, a certified nursing assistant (CNA), practical nurse (PN), registered nurse (RN), and nurse practitioner (NP) each have a different SoP. "Scope of practice helps to identify procedures, actions and processes an individual is permitted to perform" (Kusler, 2012, p. 5). It's easy to see why an SoP is important in healthcare. In this example, each of these types of nurses have received specialized training and are qualified to perform certain procedures. Knowing what one is qualified and allowed to do protects both patients and nurses.

The dental care field is another example of a healthcare field that uses the SoP model. The American Dental Hygiene Association (ADHA) presents a detailed chart (American, 2020) on their website which articulates which procedures dental hygienists can perform depending on their state. For example, a dental hygienist in New Jersey can remove a patient's sutures, but only under the direct supervision of a dentist. However, in New Hampshire, the dentist does not need to be present for dental hygienists to remove sutures; the hygienists only need to have been authorized to perform the procedures by the dentist first.

For a final example, we will return to the original impetus behind this work and review the International Association of Yoga Therapists (IAYT, 2020) Scope of Practice. This six-page document clearly outlines what yoga therapists are and are not qualified to do in their work. A yoga therapist, for example, is qualified to "Foster the client's own support networks, independent practice, and self-responsibility for his/her own well-being" (p. 4), but they are not qualified to "Undertake individual or group psychological counselling, unless appropriately qualified to do so" (p. 3).

What these models have in common is that they clearly and concisely aim to describe what each of these practitioners is and is not qualified to do. Further, the aim of all of these SoP statements is to protect the needs of both practitioners and their clients. None of the SoP models suggest that their sole purpose is the protection of clients. This is a critical distinction.

AN EDUCATOR'S SCOPE OF PRACTICE

Based on what you've read so far, if I was to ask you to make a list of your personal educator's SoP, what would it include?

That was not a rhetorical question. Grab a pen and paper or the notes app on your phone and give this a shot. You might want to draw a line down the center of the paper. On the left side, jot down answers to the following: What are you qualified to do in your role in higher education? This isn't about what you like to do, what you feel you need to do, or what you think you're good at. Within your identified role, what are you qualified to do? On the right side, write down things that you've done or been asked to do that are either not part of your job description or that you're not qualified to do.

These questions might bring up some points of frustration or confusion. Good. That's exactly what this process is about. SoP statements are meant to elicit deep, intense conversations about the nature of our work. They're also meant to evolve over time as our field evolves. Notice those feelings, name them, and carry on.

Now that you've activated your own knowledge about this topic, take a look at my educator's scope of practice in Fig. 15.1 below.

This model is grounded in my work as a trauma-aware educator, work I've been doing since I first entered higher education in 2002. It was created, however, in March of 2020, after the onset of the COVID-19 pandemic. While many of the issues that we are facing now in higher education existed pre-COVID, this pandemic has stripped us of many of our safety nets, and the intensity of these issues has rapidly increased. It is important to recognize the

Mine	Not Mine
creating positive learning conditions for all learners	policing my students' attention
consistently maintaining expertise in my subject matter area	ignorance of recent updates in my subject matter area
knowledge and application of pedagogy and learning sciences	focusing only on subject matter expertise
empathy	counseling
work to dismantle racism, sexism, and oppression in all forms, apply DEI principles	ignore equity concerns
recognize the probability of trauma in my classroom	try to assess individual trauma histories
develop self-awareness	overly focused on behaviors of others
curious about impact of trauma on pedagogy	rigidity or overreliance on what worked for me as a learner
refer, refer, refer	"not my problem"

Fig. 15.1 An Educator's Scope of Practice

influence of the pandemic on this model. That said, it is my belief that any models we create when we are at our worst will do well to serve us when we are at our best.

It is also worth noting that while this model is mine, it is informed by my work with thousands of faculty, staff, and students in higher education. It speaks to spaces where I have felt the need for clearer boundaries, as well as common frustrations, concerns, and missteps I've witnessed in the field. Again, the goal of this model is to open up conversations about what personal, departmental, and institutional SoP models might look like. Further, the intention is to provide benefits and protection to both faculty and students.

Do College Faculty Need a Scope of Practice?

Some would argue that higher education has moved from an era of elite, to mass, to universal access. I am not one of those people. Poverty, racism, sexism, and the like still act as barriers to access and success for too many

Americans. That said, the higher education of today looks starkly different than it did 100 years ago. Today's college students, despite what the mainstream media might tell you, are not most typically 18-year old, affluent, white teenagers (Barrett, 2018). The reality of college demographics is what I call the new-traditional student. These students are parents, they're working (often full-time), they come from racially and ethnically diverse backgrounds, and they are the first person in their families to attend college. For the new-trad student, being a "college student" is not their primary identity, but rather, is one of many identities that they carry. These new-trad students have different needs and have long required higher education to adapt to meet those needs (Rendon & Hope, 1996). An SoP can help us best support our new-trad students and the educators who serve them.

In addition to changing demographics, we've seen profound shifts around how mental health and illness are discussed, treated, and identified. A large number of college students of all ages live with mental illness (Mistler et al, 2013), a growing concern during the COVID-19 pandemic (Anderson, 2020). Further, with increasing numbers of courses taking place in the virtual learning environment, where personal disclosures are often easier due to a sense of anonymity, known as the "online disinhibition effect," (Suler, 2004) one can expect that the college student of today is more open in sharing their challenges than ever before. Are college faculty qualified to manage those types of disclosures? An SoP can guide us in asking that question and facing some possibly uncomfortable answers.

Add in concerns about faculty workload and burnout and an increasingly contingent workforce. Those burdens fall harder on BIPOC (Black, Indigenous, People of Color) educators and have been documented as a particular concern for Black women teaching in higher education (Matthew, 2016). As a result of the COVID-19 crisis, reports of chronic stress and faculty burnout have only increased (Flaherty, 2020; McMurtrie, 2020). An SoP can provide clarity within chaos and reduce role uncertainty for college faculty.

To speak specifically to the challenges faculty have faced as a result of emergency responses to COVID-19 in higher education, in many cases, any existing workloads were ignored as the massive enterprise of shifting into a remote format was undertaken. Whether or not faculty had any online teaching experience or not, they were foisted into the role of remote professors at a rapid pace. At the time of this writing, many colleges are continuing their plans for remote learning or have implemented other complex models like the HyFlex teaching model, which requires faculty to teach both an in-person and a virtual classroom simultaneously, while also offering students asynchronous learning options. Throughout these pedagogical changes, students are of course living through this crisis too, and they are bringing their challenges into the classroom. Many college faculty have reported to me that they feel as if they are having to act as a sort of the first responder for their students' needs, and in doing so, they are feeling completely overwhelmed. It is incredibly difficult, if not impossible, to help another person manage their crisis when we're in the middle of our own.

Exposure to secondary trauma has long been a pressing problem for first responders and mental health professionals. The National Child Traumatic Stress Network defines secondary traumatic stress as "emotional duress that results when an individual hears about the firsthand trauma experiences of another" (Secondary, 2018, para. 1) Symptoms of repeated exposure can include anxiety, depression, and fatigue (Walker, 2019). While first responders are typically trained in noticing the effects of secondary trauma, and systems are put in place to help prevent it, are the same precautions being taken to protect college educators from secondary traumatic stress? One step toward furthering this conversation is to help college faculty and staff set clear boundaries in their classrooms using an SoP.

Finally, it is worth noting that there is danger on both sides of the SoP. On the one hand, an untrained educator stepping into the role of a counselor involves risks to teacher and student. On the other hand, the SoP model is not an excuse to take a "not my problem" stance in the classroom, avoiding any responsibility for student well-being. The goal of a carefully constructed SoP is to help each educator identify their qualifications and roles in order to best support both faculty/staff and students. Further, we might also have educators on our campuses who are trained counselors, and we'd do well to inquire through the SoP model about how that dual role impacts their well-being and success in the classroom.

FUTURE CONSIDERATIONS & PRESSING QUESTIONS

Are We Qualified to Teach?

Having reviewed all of the healthcare examples of SoP models, a common theme appears: they all focus on qualifications. SoPs start with the foundational question of what the provider is qualified to do. For example, if a dental hygienist has not been trained in removing a tooth, then they are not qualified to do so, and that is therefore outside of their SoP. If the same hygienist has been trained in taking x-rays of their patient's teeth, then they are qualified to do so, and it is typically within their SoP, though you will still find some variations by state. In general though, qualifications based on acquired training guide the SoP.

It has always been a given for me that most educators are not trained to provide counseling for students. But are higher educators qualified to teach? I didn't come into this writing project wondering about that, but now that I've seen it, I cannot unsee it. Instead of denying this uncomfortable question, I'll pose it again to you: Are higher educators qualified to teach? What qualifies them to do so? Is someone with a doctorate in engineering qualified to teach? A master's degree in psychology? Have they received any training in pedagogy? If so, does that training go beyond a cursory workshop? And if the answers to these questions are "no," where does that leave us? Could the SoP model move higher education to take pedagogical training and faculty development more seriously, in addition to protecting faculty, staff, and student well-being?

What qualifications are required to stand in front of a classroom behind a podium, the sage on the stage, and lecture about your area of expertise? As we increasingly recognize the ineffectiveness of the lecture model to meet the needs of new-traditional students (Freeman & Theobald, 2020), and as we continue to learn more about how the human brain learns best, through well-designed active learning experiences that give students multiple opportunities to practice new skills and deeply reflect on their learning experiences (Whitman & Kelleher, 2016), do we need to consider the idea that today's faculty should be asked to obtain the qualifications needed to teach and support today's students?

Women and BIPOC Educators

Another pressing question in need of consideration is how this model might help and harm women and BIPOC educators. Higher education has long known that women, particularly women of color, take on additional labor that is often made invisible within their institutions. Giving these educators a tool to point to when declining additional work could be empowering and lead to clearer professional boundaries. That said, mentorship of BIPOC students is often cited as an example of the invisible labor that's being performed behind the scenes. Is mentorship part of an educator's SoP? If not, who will perform that critical work for our students? If the SoP model helps educators to decline work outside of their job descriptions, would institutions step up to hire additional labor to meet this need? How can we make sure that BIPOC educators are not unfairly punished for working within their SoP, and how can we make sure that students' needs are not ignored in the process?

Implementation Levels

At what level of higher education would we implement an SoP? Would we handle this at a national, state, institutional, or departmental level? I can practically hear people's internal warning systems going off at the thought of national or even state levels of intervention, and mine are going off too. Certainly, there could be benefits in terms of consistency at larger levels of implementation. That said, there seems to be a great risk in square pegs being forced into round holes. I have said before, and often, that there is not one "higher ed." R1 institutions and community colleges often have very little in common in terms of their missions and funding models. Does the University of Alaska have the same needs as Miami Dade College? How much does Boston University really have in common with its neighbor, Bunker Hill Community College?

My initial recommendation would be for SoP models to be developed and discussed at the institutional level, with a healthy level of flexibility provided for departments to adapt to their unique needs. Just as institutions vary across higher education, departmental needs vary within institutions. A developmental education department might want to create an SoP that looks quite different from the nursing department and the English department. Start a conversation on your campus. Consider typical scenarios that educators face when working with students in this department. Walk through the hard stuff together, and discuss the costs and benefits to all involved.

What *if* There's *no* One Else?

One of the most frustrating and all-to-common concerns that I hear from faculty when I present on the SoP model is that they feel that if they don't offer some sort of informal counseling to students that no one else will be available to do so. They report extremely limited and under resourced counseling services on their campuses, or they aren't sure how they and their students can access those services. Faculty have also shared concerns about online students and students living internationally or outside of the state where their institution is operating. These students face unique challenges when trying to access mental health support.

Whatever the cause, it's safe to assume that many faculty are making a judgment call to veer toward providing informal counseling for their students, perhaps in part due to a perceived need or lack on their campus. It is beyond the scope of this chapter to consider the availability of counseling services on college campuses, though I can say that I have worked at a college with a counselor:student ratio of 1:6000. If colleges aren't going to fully fund their counseling programs, they must consider that many faculty will attempt to fill that void, whether or not they are qualified to do so. The potential for harm to both educators and students in this scenario is high.

EXPANDING A SCOPE OF PRACTICE

Many of the SoPs in the healthcare fields that I studied have expanded in recent years. To meet the needs of an aging population, and in recognition that many healthcare providers might be qualified to carry out procedures that they're currently barred from performing, a growing number of states are considering expanded SoP laws (Nine, 2020). That said, before we can expand an SoP for educators, it would seem to be important to create one in the first place. Once the model is in place, it can be evaluated for further revision.

CONCLUSION

The SoP model has the potential to improve the college learning experience for both educators and students by forcing us to consider the importance of qualifications and role clarity in our work. As we face growing levels of stress, trauma, and mental illness in our classrooms, both in our students and ourselves, reducing uncertainty and clarifying roles can help us to better manage the challenges we face. The boundaries inherent in this model will offer higher educators and our students an effective, flexible, and supportive structure in which to teach and to learn.

References

American Dental Hygienists' Association. (2020, October). Dental hygiene practice act overview: Permitted functions and supervision levels by state. https://www.adha.org/resources-docs/7511_Permitted_Services_Supervision_Levels_by_State.pdf

Anderson, G. (2020, September 11). Mental health needs rise with pandemic. *Inside Higher Ed*. https://www.insidehighered.com/news/2020/09/11/students-great-need-mental-health-support-during-pandemic

Barrett, B. (2018, May 16). By the numbers: Trends in nontraditional student enrollment. *New America*. https://www.newamerica.org/education-policy/edcentral/numbers-trends-nontraditional-student-enrollment/

Flaherty, C. (2020, November 19). Faculty pandemic stress is now chronic. *Inside Higher Ed*. https://www.insidehighered.com/news/2020/11/19/faculty-pandemic-stress-now-chronic

Freeman, S., & Theobald, E. (2020, September 2). Lecturing disadvantages under-represented minority and low-income. *Inside Higher Ed*. https://www.insidehighered.com/views/2020/09/02/lecturing-disadvantages-underrepresented-minority-and-low-income-students-opinion

International Association of Yoga Therapists. (2020, September). Scope of practice for yoga therapy. https://cdn.ymaws.com/www.iayt.org/resource/resmgr/docs_certification_all/2020_updates_scope_ethics/2020-09_sop_v2.pdf

Kusler, D., & Sims, M. (2012). The scoop on scope of practice: It's not just for nurses. *Everything Matters: In Patient Care, 25*(3), 5–8. http://www.nationwidechildrens.org/document/get/106840#:~:text=Scope%20of%20practice%20helps%20to,education%2C%20experiences%20and%20demonstrated%20competence

Matthew, P. A. (2016, November 23). What is faculty diversity worth to a university? *The Atlantic*. https://www.theatlantic.com/education/archive/2016/11/what-is-faculty-diversity-worth-to-a-university/508334/

McMurtrie, B. (2020, November 5). The pandemic is dragging on. Professors are burning out. *The Chronicle of Higher Education*. https://www.chronicle.com/article/the-pandemic-is-dragging-on-professors-are-burning-out

Mistler, B. J., Reetz, D. R., Krylowicz, B., & Barr, V. (2013, June). The association for university and college counseling center directors annual survey. http://files.cmcglobal.com/Monograph_2012_AUCCCD_Public.pdf

National Center for Education Statistics. (n.d.). Fast facts: Distance learning. Retrieved November 23, 2020, from https://nces.ed.gov/fastfacts/display.asp?id=80

National Coalition Against Domestic Violence. (n.d.). Why do victims stay? Retrieved November 24, 2020, from https://ncadv.org/why-do-victims-stay

Nine states consider expanded scope of practice. (2020, March 12). American College of Radiology. https://www.acr.org/Advocacy-and-Economics/Advocacy-News/

Advocacy-News-Issues/In-the-March-14-2020-Issue/Nine-States-Consider-Exp
anded-Scope-of-Practice

Rendon, L. I., & Hope, R. O. (1996). Preface. In L. I. Rendon & R. O. Hope (Eds.), *Educating a new majority: Transforming America's educational system for diversity* (pp. xv–xx). Jossey-Bass.

Secondary traumatic stress. (2018, October 22). The National Child Traumatic Stress Network. https://www.nctsn.org/trauma-informed-care/secondary-trauma tic-stress

Suler, J. (2004). The online disinhibition effect. *Cyberpsychology & Behavior, 7*(3), 321–326. https://doi.org/10.1089/1094931041291295

Walker, T. (2019, October 19). "I didn't know it had a name": Secondary traumatic stress and educators. National Education Association. https://www.nea.org/advoca ting-for-change/new-from-nea/i-didnt-know-it-had-name-secondary-traumatic-str ess-and

Whitman, G., & Kelleher, I. (2016). *Neuroteach: Brain science and the future of education*. Rowman & Littlefield Publishers.

CHAPTER 16

Utilizing an Ecological, Trauma-Informed, and Equity Lens to Build an Understanding of Context and Experience of Self-Care in Higher Education

Shraddha Prabhu and Janice Carello

CONTEXTUALIZING NARRATIVES ON SELF-CARE

What do you think of when you hear the term *self-care*? Getting a good night's sleep, going for a walk, meditating, journaling, winding down with a glass of wine, treating yourself to a favorite food or activity? A quick Google search on "self-care" will return results for books featuring titles such as *The Self-Care Prescription* (Gobin, 2019) and *The Burnout Cure* (Meilke, 2019); listicles extolling the benefits of self-care (e.g. Page, 2020) and explaining why individuals are failing at taking enough of "me-time" (e.g. Davis, 2018); images of women performing yoga poses, taking a bath, or wearing a beauty mask; definitions describing self-care as, "a conscious act one takes in order to promote their own physical, mental, and emotional health" (Scott, 2020). Considering the ways in which popular media—and even much of the academic literature—portrays and conceptualizes self-care, it is understandable that people often conflate self-care with self-improvement (Cassata, 2019) self-indulgence (Lawler, 2021), and consumerism (Sissenich, 2021). This cultural framing of self-care, as a tool to ensure optimum functioning so that one can continually

S. Prabhu (✉) · J. Carello
Department of Social Work, Edinboro University of Pennsylvania, Edinboro, PA, USA
e-mail: sprabhu@edinboro.edu

J. Carello
e-mail: jcarello@edinboro.edu

© The Author(s), under exclusive license to Springer Nature Switzerland AG 2022
P. Thompson and J. Carello (eds.), *Trauma-Informed Pedagogies*,
https://doi.org/10.1007/978-3-030-92705-9_16

strive to "have it all," "do it all," "be it all," is propped up by a 4.2 trillion-dollar global wellness industry, that was estimated to be growing at the rate of 6.4% annually in 2017 (Yeung & Johnston, 2018).

These individualistic, consumerist conceptualizations of self-care are closely tied to the capitalistic idea that labor derives its value primarily from its ability to create capital wealth and drive economic growth. (Shermer, 2018; Sissenich, 2021). It contrasts with the human rights and equity framework of *right to work* as one of the tools for improving the quality of life for human beings. The International Covenant on Economic, Social, and Cultural Rights identifies work as a means for improving quality of life, increasing access to opportunities; characterized by safe, healthy, and just labor conditions, including, access to time and opportunities for rest, leisure, and reasonable limitations of working hours (1966). Prioritization of the capital value and role of labor also contradicts the World Health Organization's recognition of self-care as a holistic, multi-systemic approach to promoting well-being within a given society (WHO, 2021, n.p.). The World Health Organization (WHO, 2021) defines self-care as a "broad concept which also encompasses hygiene (general and personal); nutrition (type and quality of food eaten); lifestyle (sporting activities, leisure, etc.); environmental factors (living conditions, social habits, etc.); socioeconomic factors (income level, cultural beliefs, etc.); and self-medication" (n.p.). In other words, the WHO recognizes self-care as encompassing individual, organizational, and macro-level interventions.

This paper explores self-care not as an individual responsibility to ensure optimum functioning and productivity in service of neoliberal production within institutions of higher education but as an act of honoring oneself, as a basic human right, and as resistance to reductionist individualism. We argue that individual approaches to self-care are incongruent with a trauma-informed, human rights, and equity-focused approach to education. We reflect on the importance of addressing structural barriers to access to resources for self-care. We examine the impact of intersectional positioning on the well-being of educators, and students in higher education. We call for vigilance to language, leadership styles, institutional policies, and processes that provide lip service to the importance of self-care without addressing any systemic barriers to self-care. Finally, we advocate for adopting the anti-colonial, collectivist approach to self-care and community care.

The Cost of Neo-Liberalization of Education

Any discussion on self-care for communities inhabiting the higher education landscape must be contextualized by accounting for the political, economic, and socio-cultural shifts shaping the experience of this ecosystem.

Shifts in Mandates of Higher Education

Primary, secondary, and tertiary education can play a significant role in fostering an educated and informed public as well as advancing the scientific knowledge base within a given nation state. Further, higher education is associated with fostering upward socio-economic mobility, advancing innovation in the industry, and addressing persistent and emergent social concerns. Given the essential role of formal education, the impact of the shift of education from a public good to a commodity is noteworthy (St. John et al., 2018). This shift has come in tow with the political mainstreaming of neoliberalism as an ideology and policy model. *Neoliberalism* refers to a set of ideological and economic frameworks that emphasizes the belief that sustained economic growth is necessary for human progress, emphasizes minimal state intervention in economic and social affairs, and reimagines citizens as consumers, "whose democratic choices are best exercised by buying and selling, a process that rewards merit and punishes inefficiency" (Monbiot, 2016; Smith, 2019).

In keeping with this neoliberal re-imagining of progress and well-being, since the 1970s, in the United States, there have been consequential shifts in education policy, from a focus on investment in human capital to commodification of education (St. John et al., 2018). The impacts of these shifts are multifaceted as borne out by the changes in the distribution of and enrollment at post-secondary degree-granting institutions (Cahalan et al., 2020; Hussar et al., 2020), funding (Pew Charitable Trust, 2019; U.S. Treasury Data Lab, 2019), costs of education (Cahalan et al., 2020; Hussar, et al., 2020), labor organization and protections (American Association of University Professors, 2021; Hussar, et al., 2020), and inequities in and higher cost of access to education particularly for minoritized groups (Cahalan et al., 2020).

Shifts in Public Investment in Higher Education

Federal and state governments have overlapping educational policy goals including achieving equity in access to quality post-secondary education. However, shifts in the nature and availability of funding for higher education have been characterized by limited and fragmented investment at the federal level and decreases in state investment which creates barriers to achieving the stated goals (Mitchell et al., 2018). In 2018, for example, state appropriations allocated to higher education averaged only 6 percent, (Cahalan et al., 2020) and federal spending on post-secondary education in the form of federal student aid, grants and contracts was 3.6% of the federal spending budget (U.S. Treasury Data Lab, 2019). For comparison, 10–11% of all federal spending and close to 52% of federal discretionary budget spending is on defense and national security (Congressional Budget Office, 2012).

State funding has historically been channeled to pay for the general operations and sustainability of public higher education institutions. State per student funding declined from 140% more than the federal government spending in 1990 to 12% above the federal government spending in 2015 (Pew Charitable Trust, 2019). On the surface, it appears federal funding has increased: even at 3.6%, the federal government is spending more money than ever before on higher education. In 2017, Pell Grants were 71% higher than in 2008. Meanwhile, between 2008 and 2017, federal veteran's education benefits grew 249% (Pew Charitable Trust, 2019). The face value of the increase in federal funding is, however, misleading as these shifts in funding have been accompanied by increasing privatization of higher education and passing on the significant cost of higher education to students and their families (Cahalan et al., 2020). For example, in 1975–1976, Federal Pell Grants covered 67% of the average cost of college; however, by 2018–2019, the maximum Pell Grant covered only 25% of the average college costs (Cahalan et al., 2020). Concurrently, between 1980–2018 there was a 48% increase in total cost for college borne by parents and students (Cahalan et al., 2020; Hussar et al., 2020). Furthermore, while the federal veteran's education fund, particularly the post 9/11 GI Bill, significantly increased the amount of support made available to veterans, at 63.3% a majority of the federal veteran's education funds go to private non-profit and private for-profit institutions (Pew Charitable Trust, 2019).

This decline of public investment in higher education has occurred even as the cost of education has risen exponentially. For example, between 1975–1976 to 2018–2019, there was a 152% increase in the average cost of attending a 4-year public college cost (Cahalan et al., 2020). In 2018, the average college cost was twice as high at both private non-profit and private for-profit institutions than public institutions (Cahalan et al., 2020; Hussar et al., 2020). Much of this cost is passed on to students and their families.

ACCESS TO EDUCATION AND INEQUITIES IN WEALTH CREATION

The impact of the confluence of the neo-liberalization of education and increased diversity of campus communities is manifested in persistent inequities. In 2015–2016, the cumulative loan amount borrowed, at $43,900, was highest among students completing bachelor's degree from private for-profit institutions. During the same time-period, the cumulative loan amount borrowed by students who completed bachelor's degree from private non-profit and public institutions was $33,900 and $28,620, respectively. This discrepancy in the cost of education is particularly noteworthy as between 1974 to 2018, the number of degree-granting private for-profit institutions increased by 366% compared to 8% increase in public institutions and 4% increase in private non-profit institutions (Cahalan et al., 2020). It is also telling that the average net price for undergraduate education borne by families of dependent full-time undergraduate students who were in the lowest income quartile increased from 45% in 1985 to 94% in 2016 (Cahalan et al., 2020).

The brunt of this shift away from public investment in education weighs particularly heavily on communities that have been minoritized, perpetuating historic disparities in the accumulation of intergenerational wealth (Perry et al., 2021) For example, in 2016, 69% of bachelor's degree completers borrowed funds in order to access undergraduate education; with Black (85%) and Pacific Islanders (89%) bachelor's degree completers being over-represented among those having to borrow funds in order to access post-secondary education (Cahalan et al., 2020). This combination of having to finance higher education with debt and the income disparity between Black and white workers further reinforces the racial wealth gap, where white college graduates have over seven times more wealth than Black college graduates (Perry et al., 2021). It further compounds disparities in material equity and accumulation of inter-generational assets, e.g., between 2000–2017, for people younger than 35, there was a 19% difference in homeownership rates between similarly educated Black and white college graduates (Choi & Goodman, 2020).

Inequities in Labor Compensation and Protections

The focus on relentless economic growth, the reliance on and exploitation of part-time, adjunct, and contingent faculty in the name of fiscal sustainability, and the deepening of existing socio-economic disparities, limited public investment in and rising cost of education and related student debt are the most distinctive and adverse impacts of neo-liberalization of higher education. Between 1999–2018, there was a 49% increase in faculty in higher education in the US; however, 46% of the faculty work force served part-time (Hussar et al., 2020). In 2019–2020, the average part-time faculty pay per section was $3,556 or $ 21,336 for teaching a 3–3 load, notably, below the federal poverty guideline of $25,750 for a household of four family members (Department of Health & Human Services, 2019). Further, during this time-period, 66% part-time faculty surveyed received no institutional contributions toward retirement and 64.8% received no institutional contributions toward medical benefits (American Association of University Professors, 2021). The percentage increase in the binary-gender-based salary gap between 1999–2018 is also instructive; the gap was 56% for Instructors, 47% for Assistant Professors, 38% for Full Professors, and 8% for Associate Professors. The disparities in salaries of full-time faculty based on the type of institution are also note-worthy. In 2018–2019, average salaries for full-time faculty were $97,300 at private non-profit universities, $85,100 at public universities, and $53,700 at private for-profit universities (Hussar et al., 2020).

STRUCTURAL BARRIERS TO SELF-CARE
AND WELL-BEING IN HIGHER EDUCATION INSTITUTIONS

Minority Stressors

Student and faculty representation in institutions of higher education is getting increasingly diverse. However, access to education, security of socio-economic upward mobility, and the experience of navigating institutions that have historically been created for and catered to upper class and upwardly mobile, cis-gender, able-bodied, white men compound the experiences of inequities discussed above and resultant stressors. Despite professed commitments to diversity and equity and an increasingly diverse student body, as of 2018, 40% of the full-time faculty in higher education institutions identified as White male; 35% identified as White female; and Black, Native American, and Latinx representation was 2% or less each (Hussar et al., 2020). Data regarding the representation of people with various sexual orientations, non-binary gender identities, immigration status, and disabilities in higher education institutions are hard to come by.

Given that institutions of higher education are microcosms of the societies that they are embedded in, faculty and students from marginalized communities experience significant stressors related to their intersecting social positions. Though not yet studied specifically in relation to burnout, as noted above, it is important to note that faculty and staff with marginalized racial, ethnic, and gender identities also experience discrimination and microaggressions which negatively impact their sense of well-being and belonging as well (Cho et al., 2020; Harris, 2017; Periyakoil et al., 2020; Pete, 2020; Pitcher, 2017; Tindall & McWilliams, 2012). Considering the stressors that lead to burnout, it is not surprising that Duke et al (2020) found that perceived empowerment to communicate needs, feeling like contributions to the department were valued, and department commitment to supporting faculty well-being were institutional characteristics associated with decreased experiences of burnout.

Students also face stressors related to their intersecting identities. Hong (2015), for example, found that disabled students identified physical and emotional stressors related to managing conditions or symptoms, including side effects of medications, as well as social stigma or shame associated with having a disability and needing accommodations. Adjusting to new norms and developing a sense of belonging are also stressors for first-generation and international students (Fluharty, 2020; Newton et al, 2021). Additional stressors identified by women in doctoral programs included program inflexibility, responsibility overload, and negative stereotypes cast upon professional women (Batterson, 2004). Students with marginalized racial, ethnic, gender, and religious identities also routinely cope with experiences of discrimination and microaggressions (Piña-Watson et al., 2019; Tineo et al., 2021).

Other Sources of Occupational Stress in Higher Education

A review by Sabagh et al. (2018) observed that the "massification, internationalisation and increasing demands for exceptional instructional quality and research quantity in environments that have also seen heightened competition for students, faculty and resources" have fostered academic climates that are highly demanding and that negatively impact faculty development, student learning, and institutional productivity (p. 131).

Student Stressors

In recent years, experts have started to prioritize college student mental health and well-being, as illustrated by and summarized in a recent National Academies of Sciences, Engineering, and Medicine (2021) report titled *Mental Health, Substance Use, and Well-being in Higher Education: Supporting the Whole Student.* As the report observes, increased levels of mental illness, emotional distress, and substance use have been problematic for college students in the United States for decades. Common stressors reported by college students in the U.S. and worldwide include loneliness, homesickness, interpersonal relationship conflicts, financial concerns, academic pressures, and personal health problems (Acharya et al., 2018; Hubbard et al., 2018; Musabiq & Karimah, 2020; Pitt et al., 2018; Read et al., 2012).

Students who are employed by their institutions face additional stressors as well. A recent study explored burnout among resident assistants (RAs) and, counterintuitively, found no difference in burnout scores between students who chose to return as RAs the following academic year and those who chose to leave employment (Stoner, 2017).). In other words, students who chose to return as RAs were just as emotionally exhausted as those who did not, yet they returned anyway. Possible explanations for returning despite being burned out include the need for financial, housing, and meal plan benefits, the difficulty in securing and performing another job to cover those benefits, or cultural problems that predispose RAs to having higher levels of emotional exhaustion (Stoner, 2017).

Faculty and Staff Burnout

As colleges and universities work toward becoming more trauma-informed, they must also recognize the importance of supporting the well-being of faculty and staff (Chatterjee & Wroth, 2019). As Maslach and Leiter (1997) note, "when the workplace does not recognize the human side of work, then the risk of burnout grows, carrying a high price with it" (p. 18). A recent survey on faculty quality of life found that while most faculty reported satisfaction with their quality of life, one-third of participants reported suffering from burnout, with women reporting more burnout, more exhaustion, and lower quality of life (Alves, et al., 2019). Another study found that part-time faculty experienced a moderate level of burnout and that "freeway flyers" (i.e. faculty who earn most of their income from teaching at multiple universities) experienced higher levels of exhaustion than "moonlighting" or "auxiliary" faculty whose primary source of income is from sources other than teaching (Hubbard Jackson & Boyer, 2019). Burnout among academic staff is understudied; however, preliminary research supports what many of us know from experience which is that burnout is a problem for staff as well (Curran & Prottas, 2017; Khan et al., 2019).

Factors that have been found to influence burnout in general include, heavy workload, lack of control for e.g., over priorities, schedule, workload, unclear job expectations, insufficient reward and feelings of continuously doing more for less, dysfunctional dynamics in the workplace, lack of social support or sense of teamwork, absence of fairness, trust, openness, and respect (Chatterjee & Wroth, 2019; Maslach & Leiter, 1997; Mayo Clinic, 2021) Additional factors that influence faculty burnout, in particular, include caregiving responsibilities; service responsibilities; impulse to meet students' academic, mental health, and other needs; invisible labor such as supporting students of color, contributing to the national debate on racism; teaching load and number of students; pressure to publish and secure grants; and job insecurity (Lakcritz, 2004; Kennette & Lin, 2019; McCurtie, 2020; Padilla & Thompson, 2016).

Pandemic Stressors

COVID-19 stressed already stressed individuals and systems. A 2020 survey found that faculty and staff mental health as well as student mental health were among the most pressing issues faced by college presidents during COVID-19 (McClure, 2020; Turk & Chessman, 2020). COVID exacerbated prior student stressors and created new ones including infection fears, boredom, and inadequate information and supplies (Son et al., 2020). Two-thirds of faculty surveyed in June 2020 reported feeling "very" or "extremely" stressed or fatigued (Turk & Chessman, 2020). As one college educator tweeted in August 2020: "I feel like I'm already in Week 11 of a 15-week semester. And classes haven't even started yet" (Calarco, 2020).

As we write this chapter a year later, many students, faculty, and staff are still feeling depleted. Hopefully, the worst of the COVID-19 pandemic is behind us. We will, however, continue to routinely work with students and colleagues who are experiencing various forms of adversity. We will continue to experience adversity ourselves. Many of us will likely continue to blame ourselves for the negative effects and perceived lack of productivity that may result as we attempt to cope with these stressors. And many of us will also resort to less healthy coping devices due to lack of access to resources such as preventative or emergency health care, adequate childcare, affordable housing, or savings to weather crises. The reality, though, is that no amount of exercise, bubble baths, chocolate, or wine can serve as a salve for the harm caused by oppressive systems, mitigate the toll of a pandemic, or remedy the stressors caused by trying to survive in resource constrained environs. Prescribing self-care as an antidote to systemic inequality is, however packaged, akin to victim blaming at best and to gaslighting at worst.

As Miller, Hubble, and Mathieu (2015) point out, "Put bluntly, workplace initiatives focused on individual self-care and work-life balance are not only doomed to fail but may make us worse" (p. 22). To improve student, faculty, and staff well-being effectively and ethically we must reconceptualize self-care as both a human right and an institutional duty. Additionally, as Lewis and colleagues (2016) observe: "A human rights perspective also strengthens a trauma-informed approach to service delivery because it demands that providers address the structural and institutionalized factors that make some people more vulnerable to traumatic events, perpetuate traumas among vulnerable populations, and exacerbate the consequences of traumatic events on populations differentially" (p. 190). In other words, to create trauma-informed colleges and universities, we must address not only the content of our curriculum but also the educational policies, practices, and culture that render some students and educators more vulnerable to experiences and negative effects of trauma, adversity, and stress (Bloom & Sreedhar, 2008; Frazier et al., 2009; SAMSHA, 2014).

Addressing Structural Barriers to Accessing Resources for Self-Care

Self-care is often emphasized or framed in the context of responsibility rather than a basic human right impacting the quality of life of individuals, families, communities, and the larger society. Self-care is prescribed as an antidote to systemic stressors so that one can continue to be productive, continue to give more of oneself in service of others, usually with a focus on the impact on institutional revenues and profit margins. Challenging this dominant narrative requires vigilance toward and commitment to dismantling language, leadership styles, institutional policies, and processes that provide lip service to the importance of self-care without addressing any systemic barriers to self-care. Critical to addressing this challenge is recognizing that while a majority of American institutions of higher education remain, particularly with regard to the staffing of administration and faculty, cisgender, heterosexual, able-bodied, and European-American centric, the increasing diversification of university communities requires that we examine whether these systems, its mandates, and processes are designed for inclusivity.

Addressing structural barriers to access to resources for self-care involves ensuring access to affordable health care, paid time off, labor protections, increasing the affordability of education, access to culturally competent health and well-being services, educational cultures, policies, and practices that make space for individual and group recovery from stress and dysregulation. Recognition of academia as a space that is newly accessible and historically exclusive and therefore making concerted efforts to minimize and mitigate minority stress and create truly inclusive cultures. Addressing the stressors unique to temporary staff, adjunct faculty, and student employees. Ensuring that perspectives, voices, lived experiences, and work of those who are minoritized are centered in policy development, process implementation, and reform.

Practicing Radical Self-Care

"If you're silent about your pain, they'll kill you and say you enjoyed it."
Zora Neale Hurston, Their Eyes Were Watching God.

In her seminal essay, "A Burst of Life," Audre Lorde (1988) posits that self-care is not elitist, it is necessary, particularly when we exist in resistance to defined and oppressive norms and strive for access and equity within exclusive systems. For people with intersections of marginalized identities, self-care is, as Audre Lorde has said and Angela Davis has attested, radical (AFROPUNK, 2018; Houseworth, 2021; Pate, 2014). It is anti-colonial. It is an individual action of anti-imperialism—an act of reclaiming our bodies, our minds, and souls as ours and not just existing in service of others, in service of capitalist production. Radical self-care as conceptualized by Black, queer, feminists is an act of honoring oneself, as a basic human right, as a shield against unrelenting onslaughts, and as resistance to reductionist individualism (Brooks-Brown, 2017; Cox, et al., 2012; Tatum, 2012; Tindall & McWilliams, 2012). It is not an excuse for consumerism, nor is it sullied by blame, guilt, and shame for not practicing enough of it to stay productive. Radical self-care is rooted in an understanding that we have inherent worth, not tied to acceptance, prestige, power, and productivity. It is nourished by the understanding that navigating systems that are oppressive and exclusive takes a toll on our mind, body, and spirit—and that we deserve repair and restoration (Tindall & McWilliams, 2012).

Just as neoliberalism and capitalism fosters lovelessness (Goggans, 2016), radical self-care is also organically connected to self-love and equity work (AFROPUNK, 2018). Radical self-care requires showing up for oneself as well as honoring one's connectedness to and reliance on community well-being and upliftment. Radical self-care is honoring ourselves, imbuing love in our labor and relationships, and building resilient and empowered communities. Many of us in academia are variously positioned to embody power and privilege that we can leverage to create equity. Collaborative solidarity requires that we do the internal work and align our engagements in and outside the classroom, in community and university service, and our conduct and dissemination of research to recognize and correct inequities (Goggans, 2016). We prioritize and advocate for collective, social, and economic rights. We recognize and honor that our own well-being is deeply connected to the well-being of the those that are othered. We must pay heed to the indomitable Angela Davis's wise words, "It is in collectivities that we must find reservoirs of hope and optimism" (2016).

References

Acharya, L., Jin, L., & Collins, W. (2018). College life is stressful today: Emerging stressors and depressive symptoms in college students. *Journal of American College Health, 66*(7), 655–664.

AFROPUNK. (2018, December 17). *Radical Self-Care: Angela Davis*. [Video]. Youtube. https://www.youtube.com/watch?v=Q1cHoL4vaBs

Alves, P. C., Oliveira, A. F., & Paro, H. B. M. S. (2019). Quality of life and burnout among faculty members: How much does the field of knowledge matter? *PLoS ONE, 14*(3). https://doi.org/10.1371/journal.pone.0214217

American Association of University Professors. (2021). *2020–2021 Faculty Compensation Survey: Survey report table 15*. https://www.aaup.org/2020-21-faculty-compensation-survey-results

Batterson, S. E. (2004). *Graduate women's survival in academia: Identifying specific sources of stress and valuable coping strategies for females in doctoral clinical psychology programs*. [Doctoral dissertation, Alliant International University]. ProQuest Dissertations Publishing.

Bloom, S. L., & Sreedhar, S. Y. (2008). The sanctuary model of trauma-informed organizational change. *Reclaiming Children and Youth, 17*(3), 48–53.

Brooks-Tatum. (2012, November 9). *Subversive Self-care: Centering Black Women's Wellness*. The Feminist Wire. https://thefeministwire.com/2012/11/subversive-self-care-centering-black-womens-wellness/

Brown, M. A. (2017, February 14). *Love as political resistance. Lessons from Audre Lorde and Ocavia Butler. Bitchmedia.* https://www.bitchmedia.org/article/love-time-political-resistance/transform-valentines-day-lessons-audre-lorde-and-octavia

Cahalan, Margaret W., Perna, Laura W., Addison, Marisha,Murray, Chelsea, Patel, Pooja R., & Jiang, Nathan. (2020). *Indicators of Higher Education Equity in the United States: 2020 Historical Trend Report*. The Pell Institute for the Study of Opportunity in Higher Education, Council for Opportunity in Education (COE), and Alliance for Higher Education and Democracy of the University of Pennsylvania (PennAHEAD).

Calarco, J. [@JessicaCalarco]. (2020, August 6). *I feel like I'm already in Week 11 of a 15-week semester. And classes haven't even started yet..* [Tweet]. Twitter. https://twitter.com/JessicaCalarco/status/1291468776492404737

Cassata, C. (2019, September 3). *Why you don't need a lot of time or money to make self-care a priority*. Healthline. https://www.healthline.com/health-news/self-care-is-not-just-treating-yourself

Chatterjee, R., & Wroth, C. (2019, May). WHO redefines burnout as a 'syndrome' linked to chronic stress at work. NPR Illinois. https://www.nprillinois.org/post/who-redefines-burnout-syndrome-linked-chronic-stress-work#stream/0

Cho, Andrew, & Men, Sopang "Pang". (2020). Navigating weird comments, stereotypes, and microaggressions as Southeast Asian American faculty at a predominantly

White community college. In N. D. Hartlep & D. Ball (Eds.), *Racial Battle Fatigue in Faculty* (pp. 57–69). Routledge.

Choi, J. H., & Goodman, L. (2020, February, 27). Why do Black college graduates have lower homeownership rate than white people who dropped out of high school? Urban Institute. https://www.urban.org/urban-wire/why-do-black-college-gradua tes-have-lower-homeownership-rate-white-people-who-dropped-out-high-school

Congressional Budget Office (2012). *The U.S. federal budget: A closer look at discretionary spending.* https://www.cbo.gov/sites/default/files/BS_Discretionary_print. pdf

Cox, M. A., Simmons, S.A., Lomax, A. T. (2012, November 12). *Take care: (Notes on Black (Academic) Women's Health Forum.* https://thefeministwire.com/2012/ 11/take-care-notes-on-the-black-academic-womens-health-forum/

Curran, T. M., & Prottas, D. J. (2017). Role stressors, engagement and work behaviours: A study of higher education professional staff. *Journal of Higher Education Policy and Management, 39*(6), 642–657.

Davis, A. Y. (2016). *Freedom is a constant struggle: Ferguson, Palestine, and the foundations of a movement.* Haymarket Books.

Davis, T. (2018, December 28). *Self-care: 12 ways to take better care of yourself.* Psychology Today. https://www.psychologytoday.com/us/blog/click-here-happin ess/201812/self-care-12-ways-take-better-care-yourself

Department of Health and Human Services. (2019). U.S. federal poverty guidelines used to determine financial eligibility for certain federal programs: 2019 poverty guidelines.   https://aspe.hhs.gov/topics/poverty-economic-mobility/poverty-gui delines/prior-hhs-poverty-guidelines-federal-register-references/2019-poverty-gui delines

Duke, N. N., Gross, A., Moran, A., Hodson, J., Demirel, N., Osterholm, E., Sunni, M., & Pitt, M. B. (2020). Institutional factors associated with burnout among assistant professors. *Teaching and Learning in Medicine, 32*(1), 61–70.

Fluharty, M. (2020). First-generation student sense of belonging, stress, and support. [Doctoral dissertation, Northeastern University]. http://hdl.handle.net/2047/D20 398312

Frazier, P., Anders, S., Perera, S., Tomich, P., Tennen, H., Park, C., & Tashiro, T. (2009). Traumatic events among undergraduate students: Prevalence and associated symptoms. *Journal of Counseling Psychology, 56*(3), 450–460.

Gobin, R. L. (2019). *The self-care prescription: Powerful solutions to manage stress, reduce anxiety & increase wellbeing.* Althea Press.

Goggans, A. (2016, February 15). What Black queer feminism has taught me: Intersectionality, nurturance culture and transformative relationships. *The Well Examined Life.* https://wellexaminedlife.com/2016/02/15/what-black-queer-feminism-has-taught-me-intersectionality-nurturance-culture-and-transformative-relationships/

Harris, J. C. (2017). Multiracial campus professionals' experiences with multiracial microaggressions. *Journal of College Student Development, 58*(7), 1055–1073.

Harris, M., & Fallot, R. D. (Eds.). (2001). *Using trauma theory to design service systems.* Jossey-Bass.

Hong, B. S. S. (2015). Qualitative analysis of the barriers college students with disabilities experience in higher education. *Journal of College Student Development, 56*(3), 209–226. https://doi.org/10.1353/csd.2015.0032

Houseworth, E. L. (2021, January 14) *The radical history of self-care.* Teen Vouge. https://www.teenvogue.com/story/the-radical-history-of-self-care

Hubbard Jackson, C., & Boyer, P. G. (2019). Burnout in part-time postsecondary faculty at Midwestern university. https://files.eric.ed.gov/fulltext/ED597922.pdf

Hubbard, K., Reohr, P., Tolcher, L., & Downs, A. (2018). Stress, mental health symptoms, and help-seeking in college students. *Psi Chi Journal of Psychological Research, 23*(4), 293–305.

Hurston, N. Z. (1937). *Their eyes were watching God.* First Perennial Classics.

Hussar, B., Zhang, J., Hein, S., Wang, K., Roberts, A., Cui, J., Smith, M., Bullock Mann, F., Barmer, A., and Dilig, R. (2020). *The Condition of Education 2020* (NCES 2020–144). U.S. Department of Education. National Center for Education Statistics. https://nces.ed.gov/pubsearch/pubsinfo.asp?pubid=2020144

Kennette, L. N., & Lin, P. S. (2019). Focusing on faculty stress. *Transformative Dialogues: Teaching & Learning Journal, 12*(1), 1–4.

Khan, A., Din, S. U., & Anwar, M. (2019). Sources and adverse effects of burnout among academic staff: A systematic review. *City University Research Journal, 9*(2), 350–363.

Lackritz, J. R. (2004). Exploring burnout among university faculty: Incidence, performance, and demographic issues. *Teaching and Teacher Education, 20*(7), 713–729.

Lawler, M. (2021, May 18). *What is self-care and why is it so important for your health?* Everyday Health. https://www.everydayhealth.com/self-care/

Lewis, L. A., Kusmaul, N., Elze, D., & Butler, L. D. (2016). The role of field education in a university–community partnership aimed at curriculum transformation. *Journal of Social Work Education, 52*(2), 186–197.

Lorde, A. (1988). *A burst of light: And other essays.* Courier Dover Publications.

Maslach, C., & Leiter, M. P. (1997). *The truth about burnout: How organizations cause personal stress and what to do about it.* Jossey-Bass.

Maslach, C., & Leiter, M. P. (1999). Take this job and...love it! *Psychology Today, 32*(5), 50–53.

Mayo Clinic. (2021, June 4). *Job burnout: How to spot it and take action.* https://www.mayoclinic.org/healthy-lifestyle/adult-health/in-depth/burnout/art-200 46642

McClure, K. R. (2020, August). Burnout is coming to campus: Are college leaders ready? https://www.edsurge.com/news/2020-08-14-burnout-is-coming-to-campus-are-college-leaders-ready

McCurtie, B. (2020, November). *The pandemic is dragging on: Professors are burning out.* Chronicle of Higher Education. https://www.chronicle.com/article/the-pandemic-is-dragging-on-professors-are-burning-out

Mielke, C. (2019). *The burnout cure: Learning to love teaching again.* ASCD.

Miller, S., Hubble, M., & Mathieu, F. (2015, May/June). Burnout reconsidered: What supershrinks can teach us. *Psychotherapy Neworker.* https://www.psychotherapynetworker.org/magazine/article/36/burnout-reconsidered

Mitchell, M., Leachman, M., Masterson, K., & Waxman, S. (2018). *Unkept promises: State cuts to higher education threaten access to equity.* Center on Budget and Policy Priorities. https://www.cbpp.org/research/state-budget-and-tax/unkept-promises-state-cuts-to-higher-education-threaten-access-and

Monbiot, G. (2016, April 15) Neoliberalism—The ideology at the root of all our problems. *The Guardian.* https://www.theguardian.com/books/2016/apr/15/neoliberalism-ideology-problem-george-monbiot

Musabiq, S. A., & Karimah, I. (2020). Description of stress and its impact on college student. *College Student Journal, 54*(2), 199–204.

National Academies of Sciences, Engineering, and Medicine. (2021). *Mental health, substance use, and wellbeing in higher education: Supporting the whole student.* The National Academies Press. https://doi.org/10.17226/26015

Newton, D. C., Tomyn, A. J., & LaMontagne, a. D. (2021). Exploring the challenges and opportunities for improving the health and wellbeing of international students: Perspectives of international students. *Journal of the Australian and New Zealand Student Services Association, 29*(1), 18–34.

Padilla, M. A., & Thompson, J. N. (2016). Burning out faculty at doctoral research universities. *Stress and Health, 32*, 551–558.

Page, S. (2020, March 26). *5 ideas to help you reap major self-care benefits.* TotalWellness. https://info.totalwellnesshealth.com/blog/5-ideas-self-care

Pate, S. (2014, April 30) *The radical politics of self-love and self-care.* The Feminist Wire. https://thefeministwire.com/2014/04/self-love-and-self-care/

Periyakoil, V. S., Chaudron, L., Hill, E. V., Pellegrini, V., Neri, E., & Kraemer, H. C. (2020). Common types of gender-based microaggressions in medicine. *Academic Medicine, 95*(3), 450–457.

Perry, M. A., Stienbaum, M. & Romer, C. (2021, June 23) *Student loans, racial wealth divide, and why we need full student debt cancellation.* Brookings Institute. https://www.brookings.edu/research/student-loans-the-racial-wealth-divide-and-why-we-need-full-student-debt-cancellation/

Pete, S. H., Bull, S. A., & Old. (2020). Tribal college American Indian faculty perspectives on sub-oppression, racial microaggression. In N. D. Hartlep & D. Ball (Eds.), *Racial Battle Fatigue in Faculty* (pp. 137–149). Routledge.

PEW Charitable Trust (2019, October 15). *Two decades of change in federal and state higher education funding: Recent trends across levels of government.* The PEW Charitable Trusts. https://www.pewtrusts.org/en/research-and-analysis/issue-briefs/2019/10/two-decades-of-change-in-federal-and-state-higher-education-funding

Piña-Watson, B., Romero, A. J., Navarro, R. L., & Ojeda, L. (2019). Bicultural stress, coping, and psychological functioning among Mexican-descent and White college students. *Journal of Clinical Psychology, 75*, 1249–1266.

Pitcher, E. N. (2017). 'There's stuff that comes with being an unexpected guest': Experiences of trans* academics with microaggressions. *International Journal of Qualitative Studies in Education, 30*(7), 688–703. https://doi.org/10.1080/09518398.2017.1309588

Pitt, A., Oprescu, F., Tapia, G., & Gray, M. (2018). An exploratory study of students' weekly stress levels and sources of stress during the semester. *Active Learning in Higher Education, 19*(1), 61–75.

Read, J. P., Wardell, J. D., Vermont, L. N., Colder, O., & P., & White, J. (2012). Transition and change: Prospective effects of posttraumatic stress on smoking trajectories in the first year of college. *Health Psychology, 32*(7), 757–767.

Sabagh, Z., Hall, N. C., & Saroyan, A. (2018). Antecedents, correlates and consequences of faculty burnout. *Educational Research, 60*(2), 131–156.

Scott, E. S. (2020, August 3). *5 self-care practices for every area of your life.* VeryWell Mind. https://www.verywellmind.com/self-care-strategies-overall-stress-reduction-3144729

Shermer, T, E. (2018, April 24). The right to work really means the right to work for less. *The Washington Post.* https://www.washingtonpost.com/news/made-by-his tory/wp/2018/04/24/the-right-to-work-really-means-the-right-to-work-for-less/

Sissenich, N. (2021, April 23). Consumerism is not self-care: How marketing undermined a radical concept and turned it into a multibillion-dollar industry. *The Science Survey.* https://thesciencesurvey.com/editorial/2021/04/23/consumerism-is-not-self-care/

Smith, N. (2019, June 28). *Neoliberalism.* In *Encyclopedia Britannica.* Retrieved August 1, 2021 from https://www.britannica.com/topic/neoliberalism

Son, C., Hegde, S., Smith, A., Wang, X., & Sasangohar, F. (2020). Effects of COVID-19 on college students' mental health in the United States: Interview survey study. *Journal of Medical Internet Research, 22*(9), E21279.

Stoner, J. C. (2017). Revisiting resident assistant burnout: Functions of gender, community composition, choice to continue employment, and job satisfaction. *Journal of College and University Student Housing, 44*(1), 30–46.

St. John, P. E., Daun-Barnett, N., & Moronski-Chapman, M. K. (2018). *Public Policy and Higher Education: Reframing strategies for preparation, access, and college success* (2nd ed.). Routledge.

Substance Abuse and Mental Health Services Administration. (2014). SAMHSA's concept of trauma and guidance for a trauma-informed approach. Author. https://store.samhsa.gov/system/files/sma14-4884.pdf

Tindall, T. J. N., McWilliams, S. M. (2012, November 8). *Hanging up the Cape: Practicing the ethic of self care.* The Feminist Wire. https://thefeministwire.com/2012/11/hanging-up-the-cape-practicing-the-ethic-of-self-care/

Tineo, P., Lowe, S. R., Reyes-Portillo, J. A., & Fuentes, M. A. (2021). Impact of perceived discrimination on depression and anxiety among Muslim college students: The role of acculturative stress, religious support, and Muslim identity. *American Journal of Orthopsychiatry.* Advance online publication. https://doi.org/10.1037/ort0000545

Turk, J., & Chessman, H. (2020, July). *College and university presidents respond to covid-19: July 2020 survey.* https://www.acenetedu/Research-Insights/Pages/Sen ior-Leaders/College-and-University-Presidents-Respond-to-COVID-19-July-2020.aspx

U.S. Treasury Data Lab. (2019, October) *Federal investment in higher education.* Data Lab. https://datalab.usaspending.gov/colleges-and-universities/#section-overview

World Health Organization. (2021). *What do we mean by self-care?* https://www.who.int/reproductivehealth/self-care-interventions/definitions/en/

Yeung, O. & Johnston, K. (2018, October). *Global wellness economy monitor.* Global Wellness Institute. https://globalwellnessinstitute.org/wpcontent/uploads/2018/10/Research2018_v5FINALExecutiveSummary_webREVISED.pdf

CHAPTER 17

What Are We Centering? Developing a Trauma-Informed Syllabus

Janice Carello and Phyllis Thompson

How do we as college educators describe our course syllabi: a contract, an instruction manual, a roadmap, an invitation, a collaboration, a waste of time? What do our syllabi reflect about our teaching style, our authority style, the type of relationship we hope to have with students? What do we mean when we direct students—literally and figuratively—to "Read the syllabus"? What explicit and implicit meanings do our syllabi convey? Do we secretly—or not so secretly—want students to like us, respect us, fear us, revere us, understand us, need us, pity us, remember us, leave us alone?

(Re)Assessing Our Standard Teaching Policies and Practices

Most college educators receive little or no formal instruction on how to teach and often rely upon inherited attitudes, assignments, policies, and syllabi. As Knoblauch and Brannon (1984) observe, however, teaching approaches are

J. Carello (✉)
Social Work, Edinboro University, Edinboro, PA, USA
e-mail: jcarello@edinboro.edu

P. Thompson
Women's, Gender, and Sexuality Studies, East Tennessee State University, Johnson City, TN, USA
e-mail: thompsop@etsu.edu

203

P. Thompson and J. Carello (eds.), *Trauma-Informed Pedagogies*,
https://doi.org/10.1007/978-3-030-92705-9_17

rooted in philosophical perspectives, whether teachers want to think philosophically about them or not. Further, Knoblauch and Brannon point out that our teaching methods are often at philosophical odds with each other, and they argue, therefore, that educators must "become conscious of the philosophical dimensions of their work because nothing short of that consciousness will make instruction sensible and deliberate, the result of knowledge, not folklore, and of design, not just custom or accident" (p. 2). In other words, to be effective educators we must understand why we teach what we teach.

Extending this argument, practicing what we teach as trauma-informed college educators means regularly re-assessing our policies and practices to understand not only why we teach *what* we teach but also to understand why we teach *how* we teach and to consider the impact of how we teach on ourselves and our students. One of the hallmarks of trauma is that it leaves people feeling powerless and disrupts our individual and collective sense of control, connection, and meaning (Herman, 1997). As Gunawardena and colleagues (2019) point out, "Shifting control to learners helps meet their needs and increase their investment in the experience" (p. 5). Helping ourselves and our students recover a sense of agency means asking questions about positionality, power, and privilege: How will we use our authority in our physical and virtual classrooms? How will we be used by authority? How will students develop and exercise their authority? Whose knowledge and voices will we amplify? Whose needs and what values are we centering?

Interrogating our pedagogical practices is essential. As Venet (2021) argues, "If schools focus on the impacts of trauma that they think they see and not on the inequitable conditions within schools that cause, exacerbate, or perpetuate trauma, then the promise of a trauma-informed approach has failed" (p. xviii). Likewise, if college educators focus only on the individual impacts of trauma on students and do not interrogate the ways in which our own course policies, practices, and cultures inadvertently recapitulate inequality, abusive relationship dynamics, or oppressive power dynamics, then we would argue that we are failing to fully understand what it means to be trauma-informed and that we are failing to center student learning. Adapting trauma-informed approaches to college teaching and learning invites us to re-assess our standard teaching policies and practices to help keep students engaged in our classes and to make learning accessible for all students, including those who have experienced trauma, adversity, crisis, and inequality.

CENTERING STUDENT LEARNING

College syllabi typically reflect the competing needs and values of our institutions, our disciplines and professions, our students, and our personal and professional selves. How do we develop policies and practices that address the many competing individual and institutional needs and that do not leave students or teachers feeling incapable, alone, or overwhelmed? At one extreme are the one-page syllabi that does not cover any information required by the institution and that seem to reflect only the instructor's needs and values. At another extreme are the 30 + page syllabi developed by a course lead or committee that detail every aspect of a course and that teaching faculty are not permitted to personalize in any way. Most syllabi fall in between these extremes.

Since the start of the COVID-19 pandemic, one of the common concerns college educators express is how to effectively balance rigor with flexibility. How do we hold students to high standards during individual or collective crisis, especially those who may be disproportionately impacted by systemic inequalities? How do we give a failing grade to a student who is ill, who is being abused, who lost a job, who just lost a loved one?

Also, how do we as educators stop demanding perfection from ourselves during individual or collective crisis, especially those who may be disproportionately impacted by systemic inequalities? How do we not feel guilty or fear negative evaluations for giving a failing grade to a student who is ill, who is being abused, who lost their job, who just lost a loved one? How do we not feel like we are failing in our role as educators when we have to assign failing grades?

These are complex questions to which there are no single or simple answers. Just as there is no one right way to be trauma-informed, there is no one right way to create a trauma-informed syllabus. Fortunately, there are numerous ways to respond compassionately to trauma, to operationalize trauma-informed principles, to make learning accessible, to prioritize connection over compliance, to convey hope, and to create spaces for teaching and learning. Though this chapter poses some unanswered questions for reflection, in what follows, we also share some anecdotes and examples that reflect our ongoing attempts to infuse trauma-informed values and principles and to restore a sense of control, connection, meaning for ourselves and our students. Readers will also find policy, assignment, and activity examples in the Trauma-Informed Teaching Toolbox in Appendix A of this book, some of which we reference in this chapter. Those interested can also find an annotated syllabus example on the Resources page of Janice's blog (https://traumainformedteaching.blog/resources).

Making Courses Accessible

Setting the Tone

Trauma-informed teaching is about making education accessible. One way to think about creating accessible learning environments is to think of the ways in which threat creates barriers to learning. In Chapter 3 of this book, for example, Mays Imad describes some of the ways in which traumatic experiences create neurobiological barriers to learning. So one way to think about accessibility using a trauma-informed lens is creating learning environments in which students' and teachers' threat responses can be managed so they can feel safe and connected enough to take risks, to make mistakes, and to learn. Arao and Clemens (2013) invite instructors to think about constructing ground rules for class participation, engaging in discussion, receiving ideas that are different than our own, and interacting with one another in ways that create accessible and, they describe, "brave" learning environments. Will Koehler's activity in the Trauma-Informed Teaching Toolbox brings a trauma-informed lens to "Creating Brave Spaces."

Course syllabi are often students' first encounter with us and can set the tone for the course. So the language we use in our syllabi matters. One way that we try to reduce the sense of threat and increase the sense of connection is to model nonviolent communication skills (e.g., Rosenberg, 2005) in our syllabi. For example, Janice tries to use "I" statements instead of "You" statements and makes requests rather than demands throughout the syllabus to model assertive, nonviolent communication skills and to take ownership of the personal, professional, and institutional needs and values reflected in her course policies and practices. She also provides concrete examples and states what to do instead of what not to do when possible. Language can also promote students' sense of belonging in the course. Phyllis provides a guide on inclusive language in her syllabus and models its use. For example, in the policy section of the syllabus, Phyllis uses person-first language when discussing accommodations for people with disabilities and gender-inclusive language when referring to first-year students (instead of freshman) in the course.

Language that is vague, scolding, sarcastic, or dismissive can be perceived as threatening which can result in students feeling a need to protect themselves, armor up, and put their energy into defending themselves instead of into connecting with us, their peers, and the course material. Demands such as "you must" put people in a position of having to comply or rebel and often feel very discouraging. Statements such as "you need" assume we understand the other person's needs better than they do. So instead of making statements such as, "Students must submit by the due date or receive a late penalty," we make statements such as, "To give timely feedback and assign full credit, I need the assignment submitted by the due date." Instead of "You must cite properly," we state, "I need to need to see all of the references cited correctly to assign a passing grade." Brené Brown (2018) reminds us that "clear is kind" (Blog) and that is the case for one's syllabus, too.

Integrating Universal Design

Another way to think about accessibility is in terms of Universal Design (UD). As Harrison (2006) points out:

> The UD movement has emerged from a new understanding of disability as a social construct much like those that defined women and people of color in what we now recognize as unacceptably sexist and racist ways. In this new understanding of disability, society creates the negative sense of disability as a

deficit. Disability in and of itself is not a problem, but the environment in which we ask people with disabilities to function often is. (p. 152)

Likewise, using a trauma-informed lens, we understand the learning environment in which we ask college students who have experienced trauma to learn is often problematic; therefore, we seek to change our course policies and practices rather than to change students. Universal Design principles have been applied to learning environments in the form of Universal Design for Learning which "aims to change the design of the environment rather than to change the learner" (CAST, 2018). Colleges and universities are required by law to extend accommodations to students with documented disabilities, but many disabilities are not documented or documentable. Requiring students to obtain a diagnosis to provide documentation and secure accommodations pathologizes and places the burden on individual students. By contrast, integrating components of Universal Design or Universal Design for Learning (UDL) acknowledges diverse abilities and benefits all students.

For example, as Tobin and Belling (2018) point out, many college students are busy adult learners who are juggling work and family responsibilities and who regularly use their mobile devices to access course content and complete course requirements. So in addition to striving to create a welcoming course environment and providing information about the office which students can contact to apply for formal accommodations, we also endeavor to make our course syllabi and other course materials accessible to diverse learners and technologies. For example, we follow accessibility guidelines (e.g., Portland Community College, 2015) for making documents accessible to screen readers and ensuring closed captioning is available for all videos. In the Trauma-Informed Teaching Toolbox, Christine Rine provides some best practices for online course design that are designed to enhance accessibility and engagement. We have also found that making sure our syllabus and our courses are logically and consistently organized reduces the number of questions from students who cannot find things which in turn reduces stress for us as well as for our students.

Providing Course Information

Most colleges require the name of the college, the title of the course, and the semester and year at the top of the syllabus. If not, it is a good idea to include this information and to remind students to keep a copy of all of their syllabi. In addition to needing a copy during the semester, students may also be asked to produce syllabi at a later date for a variety of reasons, including course substitution, transfer credit, graduate program application, or education verification for professional licensure. Reminding students in advance to keep syllabi helps minimize disappointment in both the short and long term.

Additionally, most colleges require instructors to include information about the course such as the course catalog description and course objectives. Even if your college does not require it, including information about the course format and structure can help enhance trustworthiness and transparency by letting students know what to expect. Though it may seem obvious to instructors, often it is not clear to students whether they have signed up for a seated, online, or hybrid course or when and where they are supposed to attend class physically or virtually. It also helps to provide this and all information about the course in plain language, since students often do not understand what terms like *synchronous* or *asynchronous* mean.

In addition to course expectations, students also need clarity around course supports, particularly those available outside of class and class time. For instance, most departments require faculty to schedule weekly office hours that are reserved for students. While most faculty list office hours in a prominent place on their syllabi, providing additional information about who and what office hours are for, where they are held, and how to find that location, whether on-ground or online, increases not only our course's transparency but also its equity and accessibility by ensuring that all students have an understanding of "the ropes."

COURSE COMMUNICATION

Names and Pronouns

In addition to listing our contact information on syllabi, we also let students know how we would like them to refer to us, including our pronouns. For example, Janice lets students know that her pronouns are she/her and asks them to call her by her first name or by Professor or Dr. Carello if they are uncomfortable calling a professor by their first name. Phyllis also models sharing her pronouns, which are she/her, and, like Janice, invites but does not demand that students call her by her first name or share their pronouns. Though we also provide this information on the first day for seated or synchronous courses and in video or discussion board introductions for asynchronous online courses, we find it can be helpful for students to have this information in writing for quick reference, especially at the beginning of a semester when they are getting to know several new instructors.

Student's names do not always match the names listed on the course roster, so in our syllabi we also provide information to students on how to go about changing the way their name appears in the course management system and on-screen during online synchronous class meetings. Although a lengthier process that requires submitting a Name Change Request Form, we also provide information to students on how to change the way their name appears on university email, all course rosters, grade and attendance reports, and their student ID card. Lars Stoltzfus also describes a helpful first day of class activity in the Trauma-Informed Teaching Toolbox. In their discussion of the activity, Stoltzfus explains why names and pronouns are a safety and a confidentiality issue for many transgender students who could be inadvertently outed by the professor's use of the course roster in a seated class or the name that appears on email or discussion board in an online course. Empowering students to change the appearance of their names creates safety and builds trust.

Response Time

One of the most common complaints we get from students in our roles as program directors is that instructors do not reply in a timely manner or that they do not reply at all. So in addition to contact details, names, and pronouns, we also let students know the best way to reach us (e.g., email, phone, during office hours) as well as how long they can expect to wait to get a response from us. We also let students know what to do if they do not get a response within the normal time frame, as some get very anxious about sending more than one email which may result in avoiding us or in going around us and not really getting the help they need.

Most of us are buried in email. Unless required by our institutions, we need not have identical response times. We encourage faculty (a) to develop response times that promote their own health and safety, (b) to respond in a timely manner to demonstrate care and respect for students and enhance their sense of safety, (c) to be consistent with response times to enhance predictability which enhances trustworthiness, and (d) before hitting "send," to give the email a quick emotional proofread to augment the mutuality fostered through timely and consistent response times. People heal in relationships. In our experience, it has been very powerful for students to know they can depend on us to respond to them predictably, especially when they ask for help. Often students are not seeking a solution so much as they are seeking connection. Knowing they can come to us with small concerns increases the likelihood they come to us with larger concerns, which also increases the likelihood we can refer them to strategies and resources that will help them successfully complete our course.

Question Forums

It is considered a best practice in online courses to have a separate discussion forum where students can ask and get answers to course-related questions. We have found this type of forum is also helpful for use with seated courses. Typically, several students have similar questions, so responding to them in this type of forum saves us and students from repetitive emails. Often there is a feature that allows participants to subscribe to the forum and be notified by email when new posts are made. Students can be encouraged to post answers to questions when they know them to enhance empowerment and collaboration. There is often also a feature that allows students to post anonymously which can help reduce stress for students who may find it difficult to ask for help. In seated courses, the use of a parking lot is another option for asking questions anonymously. Students can write their questions on sticky notes and post them at any time during the class or as they walk out the door at the end of class. The other perk of the parking lot is its immediacy; students can "post" their questions as soon as they occur to them and the professor can collect and answer questions before the end of that class or at the beginning of the next class. This practice promotes question asking and builds trust.

Additionally, we find it helpful to remind students in the syllabus as well as in the forum of the type of questions and information to include and not include in this type of forum. For example, we remind students that this is a public forum, so they should ask general questions about course content, assignments, policies, and such. If they have personal questions and concerns such as grades or assignment feedback, we remind them to contact us by email or to set up a time to chat individually about those kinds of questions and concerns.

Check-Ins

Informal check-ins with students serve two main purposes. First, they provide timely and specific feedback that helps inform course delivery. If several students are struggling with a concept, skill, or assignment, for example, we can use the feedback to provide additional instruction or make adjustments. Second, they provide an opportunity for students to communicate individually, privately, and regularly with us so we can help them track their progress, individualize their learning, and ensure their success in the course. There are numerous ways to check in with students in seated, online, and hybrid courses.

At the beginning of the semester, for example, Phyllis creates a survey using Microsoft Forms that asks students how they are doing; if they have access to reliable internet, a computer, course material; what concerns they have related to the course; and what could the instructor do that would make them feel supported this semester? The survey is short, ten questions only. Once everyone has answered, Phyllis creates word clouds on a few of the questions to amplify not only the range of answers but also that many of us are feeling the same way and having the same concerns and to open up class discussion, particularly around what students need to feel supported and what support looks like to them. A second survey is administered at mid-term to follow-up and check in with students.

In online courses, Janice invites students to submit bi-weekly check-ins that ask about students' experiences in the course so far and inquire about progress on specific assignments. In seated courses, Janice uses index cards at the beginning and end of class cards on which students are invited to ask and to respond to questions related to course content and processes.

Social Forums

Many instructors also create a social forum to foster a sense of community in their online and seated courses. This type of forum provides a space where faculty and students can socialize, share news and events, and chat informally. Some instructors encourage students to use this type of forum to find peers to form study groups or to share information about campus and community events and resources which exemplifies the trauma-informed principle of support.

Like some of our colleagues, we sometimes designate weekly themes for social forums such as "Pet Week," "Hobby Week," or "Favorite Song Week" where students post pictures of their pets, pastimes, and pleasures. Other instructors share weekly puzzles, inspirational quotes, or mindfulness activities. These types of social activities and rituals help humanize students and instructors and help class members develop a sense of community and connection.

COURSE MATERIALS

In order for students to provide informed consent to take the course, it is necessary to spell out in the syllabus what will be done by whom, by when, where, how, and at what cost. It also helps to explain why (i.e., how the material or assignment ties to the course objectives). Courses are sometimes offered only during specific semesters, or taught only by certain instructors, and by choosing not to take a course at a particular time students can incur negative consequences such as delayed graduation. Applying the trauma-informed principle of empowerment, voice, and choice helps prevent students from feeling trapped or like they face a double-bind: negative consequences if they do, negative consequences if they don't.

CONTENT

Information about required texts and technology is required by most institutions. Even when it is not, we provide information about required and recommended texts and technology. We also try to integrate low-cost or free course materials and, when that is not possible, make texts readily available to borrow from multiple locations. Additionally, we provide cues about required and recommended materials and try to help students prioritize content. If everything is important, nothing is important. What may take us only a couple of hours to read or skim may take students who are less familiar with the content and course objectives considerably longer.

Making learning environments accessible and inclusive for all students also means integrating course materials and modalities that reflect diverse identities, perspectives, and ways of knowing. This means integrating texts and media created by authors, researchers, and artists with diverse racial and ethnic backgrounds, gender identities, and sexual orientations. In social work courses that Janice teaches, this also means integrating materials that depict non-white individuals in the role of the helping professional rather than only as clients who need help. In the gender-based violence courses that Phyllis teaches, this means adapting the power and control wheel so it represents how violence may affect the LGBTQ or other historically marginalized populations differently than cisgender, heterosexual populations, and in her YA Literature courses, it means constructing a multi-cultural reading list that highlights authors from across intersections of race, ethnicity, gender, sexuality, neurodiversity, and ability/disability and works across genres and formats. Belongingness is a key factor in creating learning environments that are accessible and inclusive for all and is realized when students feel seen, validated, and respected (Strayhorn, 2018). An anti-oppressive, equity approach provides a framework for asking questions that will decolonize course planning and syllabus construction. For more information about decolonizing syllabi see Resources in Appendix C.

CONTENT WARNINGS

Even if we don't explicitly teach about trauma in our courses, there are other reasons students may experience an intense stress response while participating. For us, content warnings—or "trigger warnings" as they are commonly called—are signals that we are going to engage with difficult material. In our experience, content warnings help students engage with the material rather than avoid it. For example, in one of Janice's courses, a student privately shared a concern with her about needing to leave the room when military sexual trauma was discussed. Janice replied that she appreciated the student letting her know and that she trusted the student would do what they needed to take good care of themself. The student may have left the classroom once for a few minutes but came back and was able to stay present during the class discussions. One important message that content warnings convey is that students are not trapped. Another important message is that we are on the students' side and collaborating with them toward the mutual goal of learning and succeeding in the course.

In our syllabi and on course schedules, we let students know in advance that some of the material presented in the course—and some of the ways in which is presented—may be upsetting or temporarily overwhelming at times. We also encourage students to pay attention to how the course material— and the way the material is delivered and discussed—is affecting them so they can take steps to minimize and bounce back from any distress. We model pausing to take note of how we are showing up to our classes, our level of distress or discomfort, or need to regulate. We practice checking in, resetting, and replenishing (Tikasz, 2020). We also encourage students to speak with us about any concerns about content they find distressing or offensive and remind them of campus and community resources that are available to them. For a specific trigger warning wording example, see also Molly Wolf's submission in the Trauma-Informed Teaching Toolbox. And in face-to-face courses, we provide tools to help students re-regulate, such as "The Basket" that Phyllis describes in the Trauma-Informed Teaching Toolbox.

Course Assignments

We also use a variety of assignment types: individual, collaborative, experiential, quizzes and exams, short and long papers, analytic, creative, written, oral presentation. On course syllabi, we provide detailed instructions for assignments as well as information about the purpose of the assignment, how to complete it, and how it will be graded. We find that scaffolding assignments help students build on prior learning and high-impact practices help students understand the relationship between concepts and implementation. Breaking down assignments into smaller pieces also helps prevent overwhelm for us as well as our students and generally results in higher quality assignment submissions (and therefore higher grades). We also find that having big projects due about two-thirds of the way through a course rather than the very end of the course typically results in less stress for all and higher quality submissions. Additionally, letting students know about how long it takes you to grade assignments can cut down on stress and emails. In this chapter, we do not include details about any specific assignments or assignment types. However, readers may be interested in learning more about Danielle Peloquin's "Panels and Pain: Teaching with Comics during Times of Trauma" or Kim Hardner's "Partner Exams" in the Trauma-Informed Teaching Toolbox.

Course Policies

K-12 education differs from college education in many ways. One major difference is that K-12 is mandatory and there is an effort to leave no child behind, while college is competitive and there is often a culture of trying to weed out students who are perceived or classified as "weak." How many of us have had the instructor literally or figuratively direct us on the first day to look to our left and to our right and take note that many of us wouldn't survive the semester?

Another difference is the financial costs of failing: students don't come out of K-12 school in financial debt. Failing a course, however, can literally cost students hundreds or thousands of dollars. Failing out of college can cost tens of thousands of dollars. Inflexible policies that center obedience rather than learning or aim to weed out students can inadvertently burden students with debilitating, lifelong debt. Trauma-informed, equity-centered course policies are designed to reduce barriers to learning and to promote retention, not to weed out.

Below are suggestions for a few common course policies. There are numerous university-wide or departmental-level policies that educators may also need to include in course syllabi, such as academic integrity, grade appeals, or privacy policies related to the Family Educational Rights and Privacy Act (FERPA) or the Health Insurance Portability and Accountability Act (HIPAA). Even if not required, we recommend including information about Title IX reporting requirements at your college as well as confidential reporting options so that students are aware of the resources available to them and informed about what will happen if they share with you that they have experienced sexual harassment or assault. Transparency about these processes can help build and maintain trust.

Attendance

Most colleges require instructors to keep attendance records since attendance affects financial aid eligibility. Many educators who have strict attendance policies have good intentions. We know that students are more engaged and learn more when they attend classes regularly. Class culture and learning dynamics are also affected if there are numerous students who are absent. To help motivate students to attend, educators sometimes create strict policies that reduce the final grade by a certain percentage for each "unexcused" absence or that automatically fail students after a certain number of absences regardless of their current course grade. Despite their good intentions, however, inflexible policies such as these center obedience and punishment, which we would argue are not congruent with a trauma-informed approach. What might attendance policies look like that focus on connection rather than correction or punishment?

First, we encourage instructors to begin with what to do and what we do value rather than what not to do or what we don't value. Attendance builds relationships, promotes connections, amplifies thoughts and opinions, and increases opportunities for feedback as well as the quality of one's work.

There are times when absences are necessary. We encourage that instructors not require a doctor's note for absences. Acquiring a doctor's note costs time and money, and the most common forms of illness or chronic conditions that lead to non-attendance do not necessitate a doctor's visit and would not be covered by insurance. Requiring a doctor's note is also intrusive: students should not be required to share private health information with us for any reason, including to avoid a grade penalty. Students might also come to class while sick or contagious to avoid the penalty. As we have seen with the COVID-19 pandemic, coming to class while sick puts all class members at risk, and sometimes these risks can be fatal.

Similarly, we also encourage instructors to not require any other forms of documentation to "excuse" absences such as obituaries or court notifications. In addition to privacy issues, requiring such documentation risks positioning students and educators as adversaries rather than allies. It also sends a message that we as educators know more about our individual adult students' needs than they do. Classifying absences as "excused" versus "unexcused" perpetuates a dynamic whereby instructors get to judge whether a student needs to miss class or not; this dynamic can lead to unnecessary power struggles. On a humorous note, not requiring excuses may also reduce the large number of grandparent deaths reported each semester.

What are trauma-informed alternatives? One option is to create an attendance policy that requires students to meet with the instructor if they miss more than a specific number of classes. Another option is to have students complete an alternate assignment for each class they miss. Instead of requiring students to produce documentation to excuse the absence, instructors might require students to show evidence that they engaged with the learning materials assigned for that class or that they consulted with peers about what they missed. And yet another option might be to collaborate with individual students or with the class to develop strategies for dealing with absences. In the opening to her feminist theories course, Phyllis suggests that attendance builds the kind of "good company" that Sara Ahmed (2016) describes one might find valuable to include in their feminist killjoy survival kits, described in the first reading selection of the semester. The first writing assignment of the semester is to agree or disagree, empowering students to critically think and write through the attendance section of the syllabus for this class. The goal with this or any alternative is to enhance collaboration and mutuality with students and to empower them to connect to us, their peers, and the course content in order to support learning and development.

Grading

Just as we scaffold learning and promote feedback early and often, grading strategies that come in multiple formats, are regular and consistent, and have different purposes will serve our students well to augment and complement learning rather than just function as compensation for it. In other words, how are grades relational, not transactional? How is grading trauma-informed and learning-centered, not punitive?

What does the grade reflect? Oftentimes, the grade is a reflection of the student's investment in the materials and readiness to move to the next stage. For instance, in Phyllis' online feminist theories course, after watching the video lecture, students participate in an interactive learning activity to check knowledge of new course concepts covered in that module. Knowledge checks and retrieval practice help students retain information over time and promote learning (not memorizing) by offering students the opportunity to test their skill levels (Lang, 2016). Students are empowered to "test" themselves, a challenge by choice model until they score 100% or may stop at any time along the way. With course concepts checked, students can proceed to the application activity that gives them the opportunity to employ the new concepts learned. When students are empowered to choose how far they will go with a learning activity or what kind of assignments they will take on, grading not only reflects skill levels but also students' choices about their education, how they learn, and what is important to them to learn. Grades become more meaningful and carry more information in this way.

Grades, however, are not the same as feedback. Just as there are multiple assignment types, there are multiple ways to employ feedback. Rubrics, contract grading, self-evaluation, reflection, and conversation with students build on this collaborative strategy between teacher-learners and learner-teachers to foster empowerment, voice, and choice around grading as part of the process of learning. We also ask ourselves to what extent has the student learned to evaluate themselves on their mastery of the course content and skills? How much did the student learn if they cannot identify and articulate how much and what they learned? In professional courses, such as the social work courses Janice currently teaches, students are evaluated on demonstration of professional competencies and must learn how to effectively self-reflect on and engage in regular supervision of their professional practice.

Course objectives help us scaffold learning across the whole of the curriculum not just one course and give students a sense of when and at what point they will learn different skills. In this way, scaffolding promotes retention and ensures success because students gain the skills today that they will need to be successful tomorrow. Objectives are not about obedience to course rules or regurgitation of course content but a map for course mastery. Course objectives are scaffolded skills one will be able to demonstrate at the end of the course; course questions are the big questions one should be able to entertain at the conclusion of the course.

Late Work

We encourage instructors to encourage students to turn work in on time without punishing them for turning work in late. We recommend that instructors extend the same grace others give us as adults/professionals. Simple policies eliminate conflict with students. Janice's "No Questions Asked Late Days" policy and Elizabeth Kleinfeld's "Revise and Resubmit" activity in the Trauma-Informed Teaching Toolbox provide examples of extending this kind of authenticity and professional courtesy to students.

WRITING EXPECTATIONS

On the one hand, we want to teach students how to communicate effectively in their personal and professional lives which in the United States typically means mastering the basics of standard English as well as academic research writing conventions. On the other hand, we recognize that standard English is only the standard because it is the dialect spoken by those in positions of power. Most students do not continue in academic professions; even when they do, it is important for students to have opportunities to speak and make meaning in non-standard dialects. As Elizabeth Kleinfeld points out in the "Revise and Resubmit" policy in the Trauma-Informed Teaching Toolbox, as academics we are often asked to revise and resubmit when there are developmental problems with our manuscripts. Publishers will ask us to correct grammar, punctuation, spelling, and documentation errors, and sometimes will just fix them for us.

HELP SEEKING RESOURCES

Increasing clarity and equity around "the ropes" of college, as mentioned prior, can be also extended to providing brief descriptions of available supports in order to normalize their use and reduce stigma. For instance, including an Honors student's praise of the Writing Center—along with its location, hours, and how-to on scheduling—may help reduce stigma around use of this support. Drawing on an equity framework, we understand that "support" may look different across population groups. We ask ourselves what sort of information does our syllabus offer around housing or food insecurities, healing resources, and resources that meet the needs of international students.

In addition to providing contact information and links to campus resources in our syllabi, we also provide information about community resources. Campus resources are often limited, or students may feel more comfortable seeking help in the larger community for various reasons, especially commuter or online students. Examples of such resources can be found in Appendix C.

CONCLUSION

In addition to getting some new ideas, we hope that you recognize ways in which what you are already doing is congruent with a trauma-informed approach. We hope that you recognize that creating a trauma-informed syllabus means understanding the ways in which faculty and students are impacted by traumatic experiences and developing policies and practices that demonstrate compassion for ourselves as well as our students.

While students may still need to be reminded to read the syllabus, when they do we can be confident that instead of—or in addition to—checklists of Dos and Don'ts, students feel welcomed, like they belong, and are able to discern the caring human who is eager to learn with them.

The syllabus is one's first impression, sets the tone for the course, and can also be viewed as an invitation into a relationship with the instructor, community (classmates), and course materials/concepts. It creates a frame for how those relationships will work, sets the stage for learning, acknowledges belonging, and invites participation. A trauma-informed syllabus disrupts received wisdom about who can learn and what is worth learning. A trauma-informed syllabus models the values that as instructors we aspire to live in and provides a road map for the transformative spaces we aspire to create.

REFERENCES

Ahmed, S. (2016). *Living a feminist life*. Duke University Press.

Arao, B., & Clemens, K. (2013). From safe spaces to brave spaces: A new way to frame dialogue around diversity and social justice. *The Art of Effective Facilitation: Reflections from Social Justice Educators*. Ed. By L. M. Landreman. Stylus, pp. 135–150.

Brown, B. (2018, October 15). Clear is kind. Unclear is unkind. https://brenebrown.com/blog/2018/10/15/clear-is-kind-unclear-is-unkind/

CAST. (2018). Universal design for learning guidelines version 2.2. http://udlguidelines.cast.org

Gunawardena, C. N., Frechette, C., & Layne, L., et al. (2019). Designing for culture, learning, and community. In C. N. Gunawardena (Ed.), *Culturally inclusive instructional design* (pp. 1–13). Routledge.

Harrison, E. G. (2006). Working with faculty toward universally designed instruction: The process of dynamic course design. *Journal of Postsecondary Education and Disability, 19*(2), 152–162.

Herman, J. (1997). *Trauma and recovery: The aftermath of violence—from domestic abuse to political terror.* Basic Books.

Knoblach, C. H., & Brannon, L. (1984). *Rhetorical traditions and the teaching of writing.* Boynton-Cook.

Lang, J. (2016). *Small teaching: Everyday lessons from the science of learning.* Jossey-Bass.

Portland Community College. (2015). *Accessibility handbooks.* https://www.pcc.edu/instructional-support/accessibility/handbook/

Roberts, M. T., The Syllabus: A tool that shapes students' academic experiences. Center for Urban Education. http://cue-equitytools.usc.edu/

Rosenberg, M. B. (2005). *Nonviolent communication: A language of life.* Puddle Dancer Press.

Strayhorn, T. (2018). *College students' sense of belonging: A key to educational success for all students.* Routledge.

Tobin, T. J., & Behling, K. T. (2018). *Reach everyone, teach everyone: Universal design for learning in higher education.* West Virginia University Press.

Tikasz, D. (2020). *The PRN Framework.* Hamilton Health Sciences.

Venet, A. S. (2021). *Equity-centered trauma-informed education.* Norton.

Appendix A: Trauma-Informed Teaching Toolbox

A1 Equity-Centered Trauma-Informed Wheel of Practice

Phyllis Thompson and Heidi Marsh

Description: Re-envisioning trauma-informed principles as a wheel (See below) highlights three significant aspects of our practice: (1) that the principles are relational, not separate and discrete, (2) that equity is the lens that informs our understanding of each of the principles and has impact on our implementation of them, and (3) that healing happens in relationship.

Goals or Hopes: The graphic representation of Safety; Trustworthiness and Transparency; Peer Support; Collaboration and Mutuality; and Empowerment, Voice, and Choice as wheel, being held in place by Cultural, Historical, and Gender Issues as hub, provides a new framework for thinking through practice that acknowledges the critical value of an intersectional approach and reflects anti-oppressive practice at the heart of trauma-informed care. Our hope is that faculty, students, and staff might use this tool to collaborate to interrogate their own practice, to engage in discussion about the ways in which they center equity in their trauma-informed work, and to explore how, when using principle six as the lens for understanding the other principles, our practice changes as we cross population groups and intersecting identities. For instance, this wheel can be used at a departmental team-building retreat where break-out groups can think through the questions and raise their own in discussion (e.g. what does peer support look like between two full-time staff members versus between a staff member and student worker?). Alternatively, in a class on gender-based violence, faculty might examine the syllabus to ensure the listed resources are broad, recognizing that safety looks different as we cross populations groups and people need different resources (e.g. not putting the police or University Compliance office as the only avenues for reporting options).

Trauma-Informed Principles Exemplified: Safety; Trustworthiness and Transparency; Peer Support; Collaboration and Mutuality; Empowerment, Voice, and Choice; and Cultural, Historical, and Gender Issues

Additional Information: The shift from line to wheel emphasizes the way the principles interact, build on, and fortify one another. The wheel not only models this relational nature of the principles but also what we know about trauma response and recovery as a nonlinear process. What one remembers, for instance, from a traumatic event may not present in chronological order or may contain gaps and missing pieces. While healing from trauma is possible, it is a misconception to believe that trauma happens and then is over. Like a circle that does not have a perceptible end point, neither does trauma response. And just as our trauma responses are ever-evolving, so should the ways we tend to and build relationships with our students and colleagues higher education settings. Understanding that an event that occurred in the past can have ongoing damaging physical and mental effects on someone in the present is critical to understanding the needs of those we work with. Lastly, the design of the wheel reminds us that healing happens in relationship. Re-positioning principle six from the end of the list to the inner circle is significant because it places Cultural, Historical, and Gender Issues, or intersectionality, not only at the center of the wheel but also of practice. Chapter 2 provides more details about an equity-centered trauma-informed approach, but we hope this visual representation provides you with practical information for moving from concepts, principles, and theory to your practice of them.

A2 *Higher Education Trauma Resilience Assessment*

Andrea D. Clements, L. Lauren Brown, Susan K. Steckel, Megan Quinn, Michiel A. van Zyl, Diana Morelen, and Wallace E. Dixon, Jr.

Instrument Description: The HETRA was created from the Organizational Trauma Resilience Assessment (OTRA), a rigorously validated measure,[1] through a collaborative process. The HETRA allows for individuals in all roles in higher education (e.g., students, faculty, staff, administrators) to express their perspectives and allows for assessment of strengths and weaknesses of the overall organizational culture with regard to the Substance Abuse and Mental Health Services Administration's (SAMHSA) trauma-informed and resilience-informed practices. See HETRA document below.

Goals or Hopes: The goal of the HETRA was to create a survey instrument to assess the degree to which a higher education institution is trauma-resilient as measured through the perception of students and employees (faculty, staff, etc.). Further, we are currently validating the HETRA in an effort to offer it as the survey of choice for higher education institutions. We hope that the HETRA will serve as a validated instrument for use among higher education institutions globally to measure organizational resilience.

Trauma-Informed Principles Exemplified: In addition to exemplifying all six SAMHSA TIC principles, the HETRA emphasizes resilience.

Additional Information: The HETRA is a new instrument that has only recently begun to be used in practice. We invite others to use it in exchange for sharing de-identified data that can inform our validation efforts. We ask that those who intend to use the HETRA communicate with the HETRA corresponding author[2] at all stages of planning, data collection, and interpretation, to ensure the most current version and interpretation are utilized. Because the psychometric properties and norms for the HETRA are not yet available, we recommend it be used with caution and that any reports or publications include a statement that results are tentative until the instrument is further validated.

---

[1] Brown et al. (in press).

[2] Email Andrea D Clements, PhD, for use at clements@etsu.edu.

Higher Education Trauma Resilience Assessment (HETRA)

The purpose of this instrument is to assess your organization's resilience—the degree to which your organization is a safe, stable, and nurturing environment. Please think of (insert institution name) as you answer these questions. You will be asked about employee (faculty, staff, etc.) and student perceptions. Please rate your perception of what you believe to be true even if the question is not asking specifically about you.

Rate each question using the following:

Strongly Disagree
Disagree
Unsure
Agree
Strongly Agree
Prefer not to Answer

Scoring of the HETRA: There are 50 items on the HETRA. All items are rated on a 5-point Likert scale ranging from 0 (strongly disagree) to 4 (strongly agree).

Subscale scores: Each item has a possible value from 0 to 4. To calculate subscale scores, total the ratings given on questions within that subscale. Divide that total by the number of items responded to on that subscale. This will yield a score from 0-4. Higher scores would indicate greater trauma resilience. This method of calculation will allow all subscales to be scored on the same scale so they can be compared to one another. If fewer than 80% of items are completed for any subscale, the subscale should not be used.

Total score: To calculate the total score, sum the subscale scores, which will yield a score from 0-20. Higher scores would indicate greater trauma resilience.

Higher Education Trauma Resilience Assessment

	Dimension 1: Training and Sustaining Trauma-responsiveness in the Workplace
1	There is ongoing training on how traumatic stress affects the brain and the body.
2	There is ongoing training on the relationship between past or current traumatic events and mental illness, substance abuse, and/or homelessness.
3	There is ongoing training on cultural differences in how people understand and respond to traumatic events.
4	There is ongoing training on how employees may be impacted by working with people who have experienced traumatic events.
5	Our organization provides tools and opportunities for employees to reflect on how personal experiences might influence their professional life.
6	There is ongoing training on crisis prevention techniques including de-escalation strategies.
7	There is ongoing training on how to establish and maintain healthy professional boundaries.
8	Continuing education is provided on ways to work competently with people who have experienced traumatic events.
9	Continuing education and support are provided to promote cultural sensitivity.
10	All employees are trained on the principles of trauma informed practices including the impact of toxic stress on the workforce.
11	Our organization demonstrates **commitment** to providing ongoing training for employees on trauma/toxic stress
12	Our organization demonstrates **commitment** to providing ongoing training for employees on organizational wellness/resiliency
13	Materials about trauma/toxic stress (what it is, how it impacts people, available treatment) are visible throughout the organization.
14	Our organization ensures there is **funding** to support ongoing training on trauma/toxic stress
15	Our organization ensures there is **funding** to support ongoing training on organizational wellness
16	Our organization ensures there is **funding** to maintain a safe physical environment.

Dimension 2: Culture of Trust and Support

17	Employees feel safe bringing questions to people in leadership.
18	Students feel safe bringing questions to faculty
19	Students feel safe bringing questions to administrators
20	Employees feel supported by supervisors.
21	Students feel supported by organization employees.
22	There is open and transparent communication between leadership and employees.
23	There is open and transparent communication among employees.
24	There is open and transparent communication between employees and students.
25	There is open and transparent communication among students.
26	People in leadership positions listen to concerns respectfully, even if they disagree.
27	Employees are confident they can communicate issues to people in leadership positions without fear of retribution.
28	When conflict arises in the organization it is addressed effectively.
29	Employees feel emotionally safe while at work.

Dimension 3: Practices of Inclusivity, Safety, and Wellness

30	Our organization has **written policies and procedures** that address physical, mental, and emotional safety for **students**.
31	Our organization has **written policies and procedures** that address physical, mental, and emotional safety for **employees**.
32	There are routines, rituals, or traditions within our organization to help all people feel included.
33	Our organization regularly **evaluates** if **students feel safe and valued** in the organization.
34	Our organization regularly **evaluates** if **employees feel safe and valued** in the organization.

35	Our organization regularly **evaluates** if our practices **promote wellness**.
36	Our organization regularly integrates employee feedback into policies, practices, and procedures.
37	Our organization regularly integrates student feedback into policies, practices, and procedures.
38	Our organization promotes collaborative decision-making to reduce power differentials in employee to employee relationships whenever possible.
39	Our organization promotes the reduction of power differentials in faculty to student relationships whenever possible.

Dimension 4: Collaboration and Empowerment

40	Employees have a voice in organizational decision-making.
	Not included
41	Our organization promotes collaboration between departments or units.
42	Our organization collaborates with outside organizations to give employees the benefit of shared expertise.
43	Our organization collaborates with outside organizations to give students the benefit of shared expertise.
44	Supervisors and employees work together to create shared expectations for job performance outcomes.
45	Employees use collaborative problem solving to address issues when they arise.

Dimension 5: Trauma-responsive Education

46	Understanding how trauma may affect students is incorporated into this educational program.
47	Understanding how trauma may affect students' future interactions with others is incorporated into this educational program.
48	This organization offers resources to help students learn about traumatic stress and pathways to personal resilience.
49	This organization offers trauma-responsive resources for students to use in their future profession.
50	This organization provides students access to support for trauma related stress if needed.

A3 Self-Assessment Tools for Creating Trauma-Informed Learning and Work Environments

Janice Carello

Description: *Creating Trauma-Informed Learning Environments: Self-Assessment Questions for Educators* (see below) is designed for use by educators to help create more trauma-informed physical and virtual class environments. *Creating Trauma-Informed Work Environments for Faculty and Staff: Questions to Facilitate Self-Assessment* (see below) is a tool designed to facilitate assessment of non-classroom work environments within educational settings such as offices, programs, and departments. The trauma-informed principles presented in the tools have been adapted from the Substance Abuse and Mental Health Services Administration's (2014) *SAMHSA's Concept of Trauma and Guidance for a Trauma-Informed Approach*. The questions in the tools have been adapted from Harris and Fallot's (2011) CCTIC Self-Assessment and Planning Protocol. Those interested could also use numeric ratings in addition to or instead of verbal responses to help identify specific areas of strength and areas for improvement. Additionally, numeric ratings could be used for comparison purposes from year to year. Alternative rating systems could be used as well such as letter grades or Likert scale ratings. The assessments provide a limited number of questions and examples to help operationalize each principle. Questions can and should be added that help operationalize these trauma-informed principles in specific educational settings.

Goals or Hopes: These tools are meant to help those using them understand ways in which their individual and collective actions, behaviors, and values are already aligned with trauma-informed principles—in other words, what they are already doing that is trauma-informed. The tools are also meant to help facilitate self-reflection on and dialogue about ways in which faculty, staff, and students can work together to further the development of a trauma-informed climate in their learning and work environments. Since the emphasis is on strengths and growth, the workplace and classroom specific questions provide positive examples to help us catch ourselves and each other doing well instead of doing something "wrong."

Trauma-Informed Principles Exemplified: Safety; Trustworthiness & Transparency; Support & Connection; Collaboration & Mutuality; Empowerment, Voice, & Choice; Cultural, Historical, & Gender Issues; Resilience, Growth & Change.

Additional Information: When I first started developing these tools in 2016, I emailed Roger Fallot to seek permission to adapt the CCTIC Self-Assessment and Planning Protocol that he developed with Maxine Harris. Dr. Fallot kindly provided encouragement and feedback. At that time, I had only shared a class-room version of the adaptation, so he also shared his concern that I had neglected a very important aspect of trauma-informed care: that the setting must be responsive to the needs of staff as clients—or in this setting, educators and students. As he pointed out, since the focus of being trauma-informed is to change culture, it is important to pay equal attention to the needs of those who provide services so they do not feel burdened by the trauma-informed change process or like they are being unfairly tasked with completing the bulk of the work. I thanked him for his generous feedback and his blessing and reas-sured him that I was also working on adapting an assessment geared toward creating trauma-informed environments for faculty and staff. I have revised the tools many times since then, and will likely revise many times more. With each iteration, I keep in mind Dr. Fallot's feedback.

References

Fallot, R. D., & Harris, M. (2011). *Creating Cultures of Trauma-Informed Care (CCTIC): A self-assessment and planning protocol.* https://www.res earchgate.net/publication/272167009_Creating_Cultures_of_Trauma-Inf ormed_Care_A_Self-Assessment_and_Planning_Protocol

Substance Abuse and Mental Health Services Administration. (2014). *SAMHSA's concept of trauma and guidance for a trauma-informed approach.* https://store.samhsa.gov/system/files/sma14-4884.pdf

Creating Trauma-Informed Learning Environments: Self-Assessment Questions for Educators

---

PHYSICAL, EMOTIONAL, SOCIAL, AND ACADEMIC SAFETY

Key Question: To what extent do physical and virtual work settings help students feel safe, accepted, and respected, including feeling safe to make and learn from mistakes?

Classroom Specific Questions: To what extent

- Is the physical or virtual course environment accessible, comfortable, inviting, and easy to navigate?
- Do students feel safe in individual and group settings?
- Do you communicate using assertive, nonviolent communication methods?
- Are you attentive to signs of student distress?
- Do you understand signs of student distress in a trauma-informed way?
- Do students feel comfortable brining their course-related concerns, vulnerabilities, and emotional responses to you?
- Do you respond promptly and professionally to emails and questions posted in online forums?
- Do you refer to people by their correct name and pronouns?
- Are students provided low stakes opportunities to make and learn from mistakes prior to being evaluated?

TRUSTWORTHINESS & TRANSPARENCY

Key Question: To what extent do course policies and practices maximize trustworthiness and transparency by making expectations clear, ensuring consistency in practice, maintaining appropriate boundaries, and minimizing disappointment?

Classroom Specific Questions: To what extent

- Does the syllabus provide clear information about what will be done, by whom, by when, under what circumstances, at what cost, and for what purpose?
- Are professional boundaries maintained in physical and virtual course settings?
- Are dilemmas effectively handled between role clarity and accomplishing multiple tasks (e.g., navigating working on a research project with a student or serving as both advisor and course instructor)?
- Are clear expectations communicated regarding the completion, submission, and evaluation of course activities and assignments?
- Are course expectations reasonable?
- Is unnecessary disappointment avoided?

SUPPORT & CONNECTION

Key Question: To what extent are students linked with appropriate peer and professional resources to help them succeed academically, personally, and professionally?

Classroom Specific Questions:
- Do you integrate regular individual check-ins with students?
- Do you post or have on hand referral information for campus, community, peer, and professional resources, such as counseling, health, and tutoring services or providers?
- Are you available to provide support during office hours, before/after class, or through some other means?
- Do you facilitate peer activities that help students connect with their peers and provide mutual support?
- Do you provide information on relevant campus or community groups and organizations?

COLLABORATION & MUTUALITY

Key Question: To what extent do educators and students act as allies rather than as adversaries and make opportunities to share power and decision-making?

Classroom Specific Questions: To what extent
- Do you and your students perceive each other as allies?
- Is student accountability handled in a way that conveys "What's happened to the student?" versus "What's wrong with the student?"
- Do students provide input on course content?
- Do students have a role in evaluating their learning?
- Are student learning preferences and needs given substantial weight?
- Do learning experiences cultivate a model of doing "with" rather than "to" or "for" students?
- Do you prioritize learning outcomes over rule obedience?

EMPOWERMENT, VOICE, & CHOICE

Key Question: To what extent are students encouraged to make choices, to speak up, and to develop confidence and competence in their knowledge and skills?

Classroom Specific Questions: To what extent
- Do students get clear, consistent, and appropriate messages about their rights and responsibilities?
- Do student have choices about course content, activities, and assignments?
- Do you communicate a conviction that students are the ultimate expert on their learning?
- Do you provide multiple modes and opportunities for students to speak?
- Do you remove or reduce negative consequences for exercising particular choices? (e.g., by implementing flexible attendance and late work policies)
- Do students have opportunity to negotiate an alternative assignment that meets the course objectives?

CULTURAL, HISTORICAL, & GENDER ISSUES

Key Question: To what extent are policies and practices responsive to issues of privilege and oppression and support a diverse, equitable, and inclusive community?

Classroom Specific Questions: To what extent

- Do you integrate course content that has been created by and that represents people with diverse identities and perspectives?
- Are course policies and practices responsive to and respectful of students' diverse experiences and identities (e.g., using progressive stacking during discussion, employing alternative grading methods)? To which experiences and identities are they responsive?
- Do you address stereotypes and biases in the learning environment (e.g., using correct pronouns, addressing microaggressions)? Which stereotypes and biases are addressed?
- Are you aware of personal and disciplinary biases and how they may impact learning (e.g., privileging or disparaging particular dialects, writing styles, research methods, or ways of knowing)?
- Do opportunities exist to for students to communicate using non-academic dialects and writing conventions?
- Are course spaces, materials, and activities accessible?

RESILIENCE, GROWTH, & CHANGE

Key Question: To what extent do policies and practices emphasize strengths and facilitate resilience, growth, and change?

Classroom Specific Questions: To what extent

- Do you recognize each student's strengths and resilience?
- Do you build in opportunities for students to demonstrate improvement?
- Do learning and feedback emphasize student growth more than student deficits?
- Do you communicate a sense of realistic optimism about students' capacity to reach their goals?
- Are students helped to understand and reflect upon their own and others' growth and change processes?

Creating Trauma-Informed Work Environments for Faculty and Staff: Questions to Facilitate Self-Assessment

PHYSICAL, EMOTIONAL, SOCIAL, AND ACADEMIC SAFETY

Key Question: To what extent do physical and virtual work settings help faculty and staff feel safe, accepted, and respected, including feeling safe to make and learn from mistakes?

Workplace Specific Questions: To what extent

- Is the physical or virtual work environment safe and welcoming (e.g., accessible restrooms, clear signage, sufficient space, adequate privacy, inviting décor)?
- Do faculty and staff feel safe in individual and group settings?
- Are faculty and staff given clear information and instructions about tasks, policies, and procedures?
- Do faculty and staff respond promptly and professionally to email and other forms of communication?
- Do you refer to people by their correct name and pronouns?
- Do faculty and staff feel safe to make and learn from mistakes?
- Do faculty and staff feel comfortable bringing their work-related concerns, vulnerabilities, and emotional responses to meetings or to a supervisor or mentor?
- Do faculty and staff model assertive, non-violent communication?

TRUSTWORTHINESS & TRANSPARENCY

Key Question: To what extent do policies and practices maximize trustworthiness and transparency by making expectations clear, ensuring consistency in practice, maintaining appropriate boundaries, and minimizing disappointment?

Workplace Specific Questions: To what extent

- Do faculty and staff have a clear understanding of one another's work and role?
- Do faculty and staff make their expectations of one another clear?
- Are expectations consistent and fair for all faculty and staff?
- Can faculty and staff count on each other to follow through with responsibilities?
- Do faculty and staff maintain effective boundaries?
- Do leaders and supervisors make rationales for policy and practice changes clear?
- Are changed plans announced, explained, and consistently followed through?
- Is unnecessary disappointment avoided?
- Can leaders and supervisors be trusted to listen respectfully to supervisees' concerns— even if they do not agree with some of the possible implications?

SUPPORT & CONNECTION

Key Question: To what extent are faculty and staff linked with appropriate peer and professional resources to help them succeed academically, personally, and professionally?

Workplace Specific Questions: To what extent
- Do faculty and staff have on hand referral information for campus, community, peer, and professional resources?
- Are wellness resources available (e.g., though health care benefits or employee assistance programs)?
- Are leaders and supervisors available to provide support during office hours or through some other means?
- Is self-care encouraged and supported with policy, practice, and resources?
- Is professional development encouraged and supported with policy, practice, and resources?
- Is formal or informal mentoring made available?

COLLABORATION & MUTUALITY

Key Question: To what extent do faculty and staff act as allies rather than as adversaries and make opportunities to share power and decision-making?

Workplace Specific Questions: To what extent
- Do faculty and staff perceive themselves as allies?
- Do faculty and staff understand the role that they play, the importance of this role, and the impact they have in this role?
- Is there appropriate attention to accountability and shared responsibility?
- Do work experiences cultivate a model of doing "with" rather than doing "to" or "for" others?
- Are faculty and staff accountability handled in a way that conveys "What's happened to you?" rather than "What's wrong with you?"
- Are faculty and staff encouraged to provide suggestions, feedback, and ideas?
- Do leaders and supervisors communicate that all opinions are valued even if they are not always implemented?

EMPOWERMENT, VOICE, & CHOICE

Key Question: To what extent are faculty and staff encouraged to make choices, to speak up, and to develop confidence and competence in their knowledge and skills?

Workplace Specific Questions: To what extent
- Do faculty and staff get a clear and appropriate message about their rights and responsibilities?
- Is there a balance of autonomy and clear guidelines in performing job duties?
- Can faculty and staff can make choices about how they meet job requirements?
- Are faculty and staff given the opportunity to have meaningful input into factors affecting their work (e.g., office décor, schedule, flex time, pedagogical or methodological approaches)?
- Do all faculty and staff receive training related to trauma, including the impact of workplace stressors?

CULTURAL, HISTORICAL, & GENDER ISSUES

Key Question: To what extent are policies and practices responsive to issues of privilege and oppression and support a diverse, equitable, and inclusive community?

Workplace Specific Questions: To what extent

- Are efforts made to recruit and retain diverse teams, diverse leadership, and a diverse workforce?
- Is pay equity promoted?
- Are stereotypes and biases addressed in the work environment (e.g., using correct pronouns, addressing microaggressions)? Which stereotypes and biases are addressed?
- Are policies and practices responsive to and respectful of faculty and staff's diverse experiences and identities? To which experiences and identities are they responsive?
- Are faculty and staff aware of personal, disciplinary, or cultural biases and how they may impact the work environment (e.g., privileging or disparaging particular dialects, writing styles, or research methods)?
- Are holidays of all cultures acknowledged?
- Are efforts made to ensure work spaces, materials, and activities are accessible?

RESILIENCE, GROWTH, & CHANGE

Key Question: To what extent do policies and practices emphasize strengths and facilitate resilience, growth, and change?

Workplace Specific Questions: To what extent

- Are each faculty and staff member's strengths and resilience recognized?
- Does performance feedback emphasize growth more than deficits?
- Are faculty and staff helped to understand and reflect upon their own and others' growth and change processes?
- Are faculty and staff offered development, training, or other opportunities to build skills and abilities and to pursue career goals?
- Is a sense of realistic optimism conveyed about each faculty and staff member's capacity to reach their goals?

A4 *Creating Brave Space*

William J. Koehler

Activity Description: Students are assigned three readings prior to class: "Integration Idea – Trust II: BRAVING" (Brown, 2019), "Creating Brave Spaces within and through Student-Faculty Pedagogical Partnerships" (Cook-Sather, 2016), and "From Safe Spaces to Brave Spaces a New Way to Frame Dialogue Around Diversity and Social Justice" (Arao & Clemens, 2013). Readings are reviewed and discussed in class.

In class, the instructor first asks students to generate a word list associated with"safe discussion" (e.g., boring, comfortable, unthreatened) and then with-"unsafe discussion" (e.g., dangerous, disrespectful, offensive). With students' assistance, the instructor places each word in both lists along a continuum from safe to dangerous.

The instructor then prompts students to consider where a "brave space" would be along this continuum. More words are generated associated with-"brave space" (e.g., uncomfortable but safe, not boring, engaging, etc.). Guidelines for "brave space" are developed using collaboration.

Students are then placed into groups. Each group is arbitrarily assigned to represent a position on a controversial topic (e.g., Does reverse racism exist? Is euthanasia humane?) without revealing their personal opinion on the matter. The instructor facilitates a debate-style discussion utilizing the guidelines for "brave space" (Brown, 2019)

Goals or Hopes: A goal of this teaching tool is to establish student trust and confidence in the student-faculty pedagogical process of meaningful dialog. Another goal is to assist students with differentiating between what is uncomfortable in a growth-producing way versus what is unproductive. The third goal of this activity is to allow students to practice articulating their thoughts in an environment that is scaffolding them to success. The hope is that students feel empowered to engage in thoughtful interaction with concepts presented in the course.

Trauma-informed Principles Exemplified: Trustworthiness, Collaboration, Empowerment

Additional Information: So far, I've used Creating Brave Space in a face-to-face undergraduate BSW Human Diversity course and in a face-to-face graduate MSW Psychopathology course. The BSW course was small—12 students from a broad range of intersections of diversity including age, SES, race, ethnicity, sexual orientation and gender. The MSW course was slightly larger—17 students with less diverse representation across gender, age, SES, race, and ethnicity. The BSW class was more easily engaged in the activity but required more guidance as far as interpretation and application of the reading material. The MSW class demonstrated more mastery of the material but seemed to struggle to stay within the "brave space" interaction style. Where the BSW students seemed to feel safe and emboldened to speak within the structure, the MSW students became preoccupied with how to stay within the"rules." Both classes provided positive feedback regarding the exercise, however, and stated they felt it was translatable to other parts of their lives where difficult conversations arose.

References

Arao, B., & Clemens, K. (2013). From safe spaces to brave spaces: A new way to frame dialogue around diversity and social justice. In L. M. Landreman (Ed.), *The art of effective facilitation: Reflections from social justice educators.* Stylus Publishing.

Brown, B. (2019). *Classroom integration ideas—Trust II: BRAVING.* https://brenebrown.com/classroom-integration-ideas/

Cook-Sather, A. (2016). Creating brave spaces within and through student-faculty pedagogical partnerships. *Teaching and Learning Together in Higher Education, 1*(18), 1.

A5 First Day of Class Introductions: Trans Inclusion in Teaching

Lars Stoltzfus

Activity Description: For students and faculty alike, the first session of a given class is charged with excitement, anxiety, Zoom difficulties, or fear in the first few minutes as the instructor settles in to see how their roster aligns with the students actually in attendance. In place of the traditional roll call method of introductions—where an instructor calls out names and makes real-time adjustments based on student feedback—this trauma-informed way of doing introductions prevents instances of outing a transgender student due to a discrepancy in their legal name and their actual name. It also avoids placing a student in the uncomfortable position of correcting the person in power—the instructor—when misgendered, outed, or called by the wrong name.

This activity requires passing out index cards to students (if in person) or creating a quiz or short essay assignment in one's virtual course management system (if online). Ask students to answer the following questions:

- What is the name you go by, and how do you pronounce it?
- What is your student ID?
- What are your pronouns?
- What are your reasons for taking this course?
- Is there anything else you would like me to know as we begin our semester (e.g., you work a 40-h week, you don't like correcting someone if they misgender you, you hate chemistry, etc.)?

With the student ID, an instructor can compare a student's actual name with their name on the roster or in the course management system, make adjustments, and practice pronunciation. The instructor can easily access these index cards or quiz results in subsequent class meetings to see student information. This short survey also creates an opportunity for students to disclose additional information—like their pronouns or concerns regarding a course—without feeling forced into sharing via a class discussion. This style of doing introductions does take a bit more time on the instructor's part. However, the co-constitution of a course environment valuing respect and self-determination has positive ripple effects throughout the semester.

After turning in their surveys, introductions can be verbalized in several ways depending on class size and subject. Shuffling the cards and asking each student to read a small section of the syllabus or asking students to share something they hope to learn during the semester, for instance, allows instructors and students alike to connect names with faces. These simple introductions can be used in an online class as well. Virtual courses may have the additional affordance of students being able to input their own names (and perhaps pronouns) on a video call or the drawback of needing an IT Department to change one's name within a course management system. Providing information about navigating these systems *before* the semester begins encourages students to submit an introductory comment in a thread or speak up on Zoom because they know the name that will be displayed is the name they actually use.

Goals or Hopes: The goal here is to create a classroom environment where students do not have to contend with hypervigilance accompanying the trauma of being outed, deadnamed, and/or misgendered during roll call introductions. The unease of knowing one's classmates suddenly know information they would *never* otherwise know may create an environment of distrust in one's classmates and instructors. Doing introductions via this short survey hopefully creates a more inclusive and thoughtful course environment. By respecting student identities and providing confidentiality through this discreet survey, students will feel respected and safe. This, in turn, generates a feeling of trust and increased engagement as students implicitly and explicitly understand that the course instructor values student autonomy and self-presentation.

Trauma-Informed Principles Exemplified: Transgender students routinely experience being outed as transgender through traditional methods of classroom introductions as their legal name—and, sometimes, the assumed gender accompanying such a name—is what is on the roster, and thus what they must answer to in order to be counted. By handling introductions differently, students will not experience the jarring dissonance of being forcibly outed to a group of peers they do not know in an already stressful situation. This activity creates a sense of safety and trust as students know the instructor will respect them. It also creates a sense of empowerment as students have control over their own bodily narrative in a classroom.

Additional information: I initially began doing this to protect the confidentiality and bodily integrity of my transgender students. It soon became apparent, though, that this activity benefits cisgender students as well: international students who are weary (and wary) of instructors mangling their names know they will not have to provide an "American" name in order to feel a sense of belonging in the course, students who go by a nickname or middle name can clearly state how they should be addressed, and students who may have other concerns can let me know on the very first day of class without fear of judgment or guilt. It has resulted in better holistic environments as I learn more about my students right away, and they learn that their identities will be respected and protected.

A6 The Basket: Setting the Stage for Learning

Phyllis Thompson

Activity Description: We know that students are sometimes triggered by the day's reading assignment, lecture, or video clip. When this occurs, students spend all their available energy and mental resources managing the stressor rather than participating in the learning happening in the room. The student may have difficulty focusing, be unable to concentrate, lose the ability to form and articulate ideas, or experience physical ailments such as headache, dizziness, or stomachache. This is dysregulation, and it compromises learning. The basket provides a bridge from the dysregulation the student is experiencing back to regulation, empowering them to pause, re-regulate, and re-set the stage for learning.

My basket is lavender, located just inside the entrance to the class, and filled with individual activities students can pick up as they walk in the door, such as crayons and coloring pages, pipe cleaners, yarn, string, beads, glitter, glue sticks, shaping dough, rubbing stones, lavender and other essential oils. The practice of coloring, creating shapes with colorful pipe cleaners, or shaping dough is calming and invites us to be mindful of how we are feeling, to recognize when we are tense or anxious, to acknowledge how these feelings affect our thinking, how long they last, and that they are not constant but probably come and go.

Goals and Hopes: My goal in positioning the basket prominently at the entrance to the classroom is to welcome students as they are, to center rather than conceal how we are showing up to our lives, and to promote mindfulness practices that help us self-regulate. My hope is that the activities in the basket invite students to pause long enough to take stock, be mindful, breathe, and re-regulate.

Trauma-Informed Principles Exemplified: Safety, Trustworthiness, Peer support, Empowerment, Choice

Additional Information: I introduce the basket on the first day of class with an activity. Sometimes, I use the teacup activity that invites students to reflect on whether their proverbial teacup is overflowing with warm tea and honey or a toxic liquid. We talk about what "tea and honey" means for each of us and use this as a warm-up activity for creating a list of comfort agreements that will guide classroom our practice for the semester and list of supports students need from me as instructor. As a reminder of what it means to each of us to fill our cups with tea and honey, I provide teacup coloring pages in the basket, and the basket is thereafter available every class period of the semester. I have found that my lavender basket helps me create safety by acknowledging that there is pain in the room. Because the basket becomes a daily part of our self-care practice in the course, is part of our collective narrative, is consistent, and is not a discrete learning activity in one unit that we then neglect or forget for the remainder of the semester, it helps build trust. Because it normalizes the practice of pausing, it becomes part of our peer support system, empowers us, and gives us concrete tools we can use to re-set and re-regulate. For the student who learns best when they fidget the most, it provides activities. For the student who needs to keep hands busy to keep mind focused, it provides options. For the student who wants to hold space for how they are feeling in their body, emotions, or mind about the conversation taking place, it provides some tools to slow down for that reflection while also staying present for the class. Setting the stage for learning means being intentional about fostering comfort and care while being willing to allow crisis in the door. During crisis, it is critical to cultivate a classroom environment that holds space for uncertainty, fear, pain, and anxiety while also introducing mindfulness practices that invite and guide us back to self-regulation.

A7 *Moment of Action*

Kelly Smith and Hans Bernier

Activity Description: Each class session begins with a Moment of Action that serves a broader positive social impact to encourage student participation with a trauma-informed lens. These actions are optional, with attempts to develop opportunities related to the course curriculum and the school or students' geographical location, while often drawing connections to recent events. The instructor introduces the Moment of Action and the rationale for sharing it by making connections to current affairs, disciplinary Codes of Ethics, and the course materials.

This practice provides an easy and predictable access point at the beginning of every class. Time is built in for reflection, creating opportunities for students to share their perspectives on the Moment of Action before transitioning into the coursework. Constructing connections with students through the Moment of Action is viable in a traditional setting and is especially meaningful when developing community in a virtual environment.

Goals or Hopes: The goal for the Moment of Action as an opening activity is to build student resilience and collaboration during uncertain times. The Moment of Action welcomes students into class and establishes a platform for empowerment during destabilizing circumstances, such as those caused by the COVID-19 pandemic and necessary resurgence of civil unrest due to anti-Black racism. This activity acknowledges some of the many ways to collaborate within education to share our collective voice on important and relevant issues. Students may also bring a Moment of Action to the class community by sharing resources with the instructor before class.

Trauma-Informed Principles Exemplified: The Moment of Action enacts many trauma-informed principles. The Moment of Action is a trauma-informed practice that increases student resilience with its flexibility to meet specific student needs while also offering a sense of predictability at the start of each class session. The Moment of Action creates openings that acknowledge and recognize individual strengths and experiences while centering on collaboration and mutuality. The Moment of Action generates opportunities for problem-solving and inclusion in decision-making, thereby leveling power differences between the instructors and students. The collaborative nature of these activities and the chance to suggest Moments of Action further help students trust their perspectives matter to the class community. Peer support is also present in the Moment of Action, initiating space for students to build healing relationships with one another based on social work's principles and values. Finally, students are empowered to choose whether or not to engage with each Moment of Action.

Additional Information: We used Moments of Action to open each class session in the virtual summer intensive course we taught for master's level students at Columbia University's School of Social Work. Students positively reviewed the Moment of Action practice throughout formal and informal course feedback. Some Moment of Action examples we utilized included connections to voter information and registration, shared opportunities to sign online petitions for various social justice campaigns, and review proper capitalization practices for writing names of racial and cultural groups. We also used hashtags and social media to thank and support public figures facing racist and misogynistic attacks and shared documentary clips hoping students might view the films later.

These actions culminated in our final Moment of Action of the course. Students wrote emails to themselves sharing congratulations and recognition of accomplishments, reminding themselves why they began their MSW degrees, listing a goal they hope to achieve soon, including a piece of advice for their future selves. Students were encouraged to draft these emails and "schedule send" the messages to themselves for arrival during their graduation week.

A8 No Questions Asked Late Days Policy

Janice Carello

Policy Description and Wording: This no questions asked late day policy has been the most popular policy change I have made. I have used several versions of the policy which is adapted from a policy in a graduate course I took from Dr. Ariel M. Aloe (2012) who extended students seven late days. Example 1 below is a version that extends unlimited late days. I currently use this version in my graduate-level courses where the emphasis is on professional communication. Example 2 below is a version that limits the number of late days. This example specifies five; more or fewer could be extended depending on the type and length of the course. I have used several versions of this second example in the past and find it works well in courses with students or assignments that benefit from firmer deadlines, for example in undergraduate courses or with assignments with time-sensitive deadlines. No matter which version I use, I also find that most students still submit their work on time.

Example 1: Each student has unlimited late days that may be used without any consequence to the assignment grade. To use late days: notify me by email at least 30 min before the assignment is due. Late days start immediately after the due date and run for 24 h. If you do not notify me in advance (or as soon as possible if circumstances did not permit prior notification) the assignment will be graded as late. Late assignments cannot earn a grade higher than B.

Example 2: Each student has a total of 5 late days that may be used on major assignments without any consequence to the assignment grade. Late days cannot be used on Check-Ins or Forums. To use late days: notify me by email at least 30 min before the assignment is due. Late days start immediately after the due date and run for 24 h. If more than 5 late days are accumulated, or if you do not notify me in advance, the assignment will be graded as late. Late assignments cannot receive a grade higher than B.

Goals or Hopes: A late days policy acknowledges that life happens and that all of us need an extended deadline occasionally. With this policy, there are no questions asked: students are empowered to assert their right to these days without explanation. Some instructors and students prefer limiting the number of late days helps provide needed structure and accountability. For me, the emphasis is on encouraging students to contact me rather than avoid me when they need extra time. Since implementing late days policies over the past decade, I have literally eliminated conflict with students over deadlines and late work grades. I have also eliminated my stress in dealing with late work.

Trauma-Informed Principles Exemplified: Safety, Trustworthiness, Collaboration, Resilience

Additional Information: Sometimes students do choose to share the reason they are using late days, and the reason is not always crisis or illness. During a summer session I was teaching, for example, one student shared that the late days policy helped them engage in self-care and spend some much-needed time with their child. They explained it had been such a beautiful summer evening, and they had been so busy with responsibilities, that they chose to stay outside and enjoy the time with their child that evening for as long as they could instead of coming inside early and rushing to finish their homework. They wanted me to know that the late days policy afforded them space to make that choice that without fear of guilt or penalty. The assignment was completed thoughtfully and thoroughly and submitted the next day.

Reference

Aloe, A. M. (2012, Fall). *CEP 524 Experimental design in educational research* [Course Syllabus]. University at Buffalo.

A9 *The Revise and Resubmit*

Elizabeth Kleinfeld

Policy Wording: If you turn in work that is complete but is not of passing quality, you will receive a revise and resubmit request (R&R). A R&R request includes detailed comments from me about the kinds of revisions that need to be made to bring a piece to passing quality and a suggested deadline for submission of the revision. If the resubmitted work is of passing quality, you will get full credit for the assignment; if the resubmitted work is not of passing quality, you will receive another R&R. If you choose not to resubmit it, you will get no credit for the assignment. You can (and should) consult me and/or a Writing Center consultant during your revision process. You can also negotiate a different deadline if the one I've suggested isn't feasible for you.

Goals or Hopes: This policy allows me to intervene and support any student who is sincerely attempting to do the work but isn't able to achieve all of the outcomes of the assignment in the timeframe indicated in the syllabus. Often students need more time because of stress, work, neurodiversity, or any number of other factors. The timelines I construct for assignments are based on my estimation of what is reasonable; the policy acknowledges that there is a lot happening in students' lives that I am unaware of and so did not account for in my timelines. The policy also allows students to submit work that is not of passing quality without fear of judgment because I share that I receive revise and resubmit requests on almost all the article manuscripts I send out, so R&R is a normal part of the writing process.

Trauma-Informed Principles Exemplified: safety, trustworthiness, attention to gender/race/other issues

Additional Information: This policy normalizes failure as part of any learning process and allows me to position myself as a supportive coach rather than a penalizing judge. The policy is an example of labor-based grading that incorporates equity practices into the writing classroom. This means that there is no option for partial credit; students who do work of passing quality earn full credit regardless of how many R&Rs they get on a particular assignment.

A10 Trigger Warning

Molly Wolf

Policy Wording: *Trigger Warning *Please Note:* In this course you are learning about very difficult topics. In some instances, the course material may be sensitive or emotionally provocative, and may trigger a response that you weren't expecting or that becomes overwhelming.

- **In Class:** This material is emotionally difficult. It may trigger memories or feelings for you. Remember that you are not trapped in our classroom. If you need to, it's totally okay to just get up and leave the room. I promise you, no one is paying attention to you, and if they are, they will just think you need to pee. (But please come back when you are feeling up to it, so I don't worry.)
- **At Home: Try to do the readings and homework assignments during the day** whenever possible, and leave yourself enough time to wind down before bed without having this on your mind.
- **At Home: Take your time with the assignments**. When you need to stop because it is getting too emotionally difficult, allow yourself the opportunity to stop. Honor the messages your mind and body are giving you by listening to them.
- **At Home:** Should this course material be problematic, students are encouraged to reach out to campus resources or their personal therapist as they may be helpful in dealing with such concerns.
- **Please Know:** that while we are reading about issues (such as trauma), the larger truth is that **survivors of trauma can and do heal** from trauma. They go on to lead beautiful, meaningful lives. They get married, they have children, they have great jobs, etc. **The trauma is just a chapter in their story, and with great social workers like you, it is not the end of their story. Their story's not over yet, and neither is yours.**

Goals or Hopes: This policy acknowledges that the material taught in this class is emotionally difficult and may elicit strong emotions, feelings, or memories. As such, this material may 'trigger' a response from students that could a) make them feel disempowered (such as when they are surprised by triggering material), or b) flood them with emotion to the point that learning cannot occur. Using a trigger warning normalizes the fact that triggers occur for everyone and that feelings about material and triggers are okay/valid, the disruption to learning can be minimized, and the student's emotional and mental health can be safeguarded.

Trauma-Informed Principles Exemplified: Safety, Trustworthiness, Choice, Empowerment, Resilience

Additional Information: When I am teaching emotionally difficult material, which often happens in classes that deal with trauma, I always give a speech in the very beginning of seated classes that acknowledges triggering material. I remind the class participants that it is okay to get up and leave the class whenever they need to. We discuss the policy at the beginning of class as well. This policy uses compassion (by acknowledging the students' feelings, and the emotional difficulty of the material) as well as humor (by advising that it is okay to leave the room when things get hard, because we will just think they need to use the restroom).

When I am teaching courses online (asynchronously), I have the students sign this policy to acknowledge that they have read it. For both online and seated courses, I have the students write down three concrete ways they will handle "triggers" during completion of homework assignments (such as by walking away, reading a book, talking to a friend, etc.), and ask them to use that written "cheat sheet" of coping mechanisms whenever they are feeling triggered by the material. This entire 'trigger warning' policy has been very popular with students. Some have mentioned they have asked other professors to use trigger warnings in their classes as well. Students have also posted on social media about how grateful they are to have taken a class with a professor who puts this much effort into caring about students' emotional states during the learning of potentially traumatic material.

All Panels and Pain: Teaching with Comics During Times of Trauma

Danielle Peloquin

Assignment Description: Comics are more than just entertainment; they are primary sources that document the social issues, events, and trauma from the period in which they were created. Based upon your understanding of comic authors and artists as witnesses, create a character sketch that has personally experienced or witnessed the experience of a traumatic social event (COVID-19, Black Lives Matter protests, school shootings, reaction to political elections, etc.). The character sketch could represent your understanding and response to the event or be in contrast to your own experience. Character sketches might include:

1. Physical description including:

   a. Clothes
   b. Mannerisms
   c. Physical features
   d. Language
   e. Associated colors

2. Experience with and response to the social event including:

   a. Perspective of the event
   b. Interpretation of the event
   c. Immediate and lasting impact of event on the character
   d. .esponse to the event

3. Relationship and interactions with other people/characters:

   a. Relationship with "hero" in comic
   b. Growth in comparison to static characters
   c. Emotional connection to hero, friends, and enemies
   d. Extent to which relationships and interactions have changed since event

4. Dynamic character arc including:

   a. Socio-economic background
   b. Inciting incident
   c. Motivation
   d. Challenges
   e. Climax
   f. Where they are now (physically, emotionally, and socially)

Goals or Hopes: Since their birth in the 1960s, underground comixs resisted resistance. Fortunately, recent comics and graphic novels in the mainstream have drawn on this truth-telling legacy to focus on emotionally fraught social issues. These texts provide educators a way not only to engage students but also establish courageous conversations about community, health, wellness and their intersections with race, class, and sexual identity. By teaching comics and graphic novels that are grounded in these social topics, educators can foster higher-level thinking while maintaining an academic atmosphere that is nurturing and inclusive. Additionally, the creativity of comics and graphic novels lends itself to expressive projects and assignments that generate space for students to safely process their grief and anger.

Trauma-informed Principles Exemplified: Safety, Trustworthiness, Collaboration, Resilience

Additional Information: Besides being posed as electives, comics have always skirted the academic arena as literary outcasts that were unworthy of being granted admittance into academia. One of the reasons for this neglect is that comics and graphic novels have been the voice of the marginalized and disenfranchised for decades. Representations of the personal and cultural casualties brought on by oppressive and institutionalized racism, classism, anti-Semitism, nationalism, xenophobia, and homophobia have long been included within the paneled pages of comics and graphic novels. While these issues are front of mind for students and these stories the ones that frame their experience, prescriptive classroom discussions and rigid instructional strategies often keep such "matters" and possibly deep learning at arm's length.

Historically, educators have believed the stigma that follows comics and graphic novels as being academically inadequate. This is due in part to the fact that comics were perceived to be low culture and, literally and figuratively, disposible. For decades, scholars discounted comics as escapism created by Jewish authors and artists during the height of twentieth century antisemitism. Currently, academics use the popularity and widespread consumption of comics as evidence of its utilitarian purpose which is deemed to be at odds with scholarly texts. Subsequently, most educators do not feel comfortable teaching with this medium because they are unfamiliar with its construction, history, and literary or social merit. Due to the current social and academic upheaval, this is the quintessential time to start investigating creative instructional strategies that combine academic acumen with emotional intelligence. Comics and graphic novels provide educators an opportunity for deep learning and critical thinking practices while engaging students in the issues that are front and center in their lives.

A12 Partner Exams

Kimberly L. Hardner, DSW, LSW

Activity Description: Partner exams can be a useful trauma-informed tool to implement in the classroom, both in the face-to-face setting and online. Partner exams provide students with the option of taking exams either individually or with a partner and can be used with any type of exam questions including multiple choice, matching, short-answer, and essay questions. Students can select their own partner or can ask the instructor to assign them a partner for the exam. In order to take the exam with a partner, students should notify the instructor of their intention to take the partner exam and identify their partner one week prior to the exam so that the instructor can match other students who are interested. Exams are graded individually, so each student submits their own exam and their answers/responses do not need to match those of their partner.

Goals or Hopes: When traditional exams are given, students are expected not to talk and to keep their eyes on their own papers. These rules are then enforced by a watchful instructor to ensure no one cheats, yet for some students this setting might be a trauma trigger. Providing the option to take exams with a partner can serve as a means to enhance physical and emotional safety so that students can focus on the task at hand, demonstrating their level of understanding of course concepts. Being transparent about the ways in which partner exams demonstrate the principles of trauma-informed care in the classroom setting can serve as a way to enhance trustworthiness between students and the instructor. Partner exams promote peer support and collaboration by allowing students to talk through scenarios and engage in problem-solving and deductive reasoning with a peer, modeling the recognition in trauma-informed care that one is not alone and that shared decision-making can be empowering. Further empowerment occurs by offering students choices and opportunities to use their voice.

Trauma-Informed Principles Exemplified: Safety, Trustworthiness, Peer Support, Collaboration, and Empowerment, Choice and Voice

Additional Information: Practical considerations for the use of partner exams include finding an appropriate physical setting for face-to-face students to take the exam, being flexible with the number of partners, and being more lenient with the time of the exam for online students. The first time I utilized the practice of partner exams, 28 out of my 30 students selected the partner option. I was able to use our regularly-scheduled classroom for the 28 students and found a quiet space just across the hall for the two students who chose to take the exam individually so that I could still be available if they had any questions during the exam. In another class, I had 15 of out of 22 students select the partner exam option, so that required one group of 3 students who took the exam together since there was an odd number. For this exam, I scheduled space in the library where there was an area for students who chose to take the exam individually right next to small study rooms where the partners took their exam.

One helpful tip for the implementation of partner exams in online classes is to give students leniency as to when the exam needs to be taken, enhancing student choice. Although the online classes I taught during the pandemic were synchronous, I provided students with a 24-h period to take the exam. Once the students began the exam, they had 1 h and 15 min to complete it, just as they would in the face-to-face classroom. Students who chose the partner exam utilized Zoom to take the exam synchronously with their partner.

Feedback on partner exams from students demonstrated how helpful this practice is in promoting student choice and the importance of peer support and collaboration. Students shared that having a partner reduced stress and anxiety about the exam and allowed them to talk through differences they came across in their responses, to further explore content and topics within the exam, and to enhance their understanding and application of course content. This feedback verified my belief in the importance of providing student with choices, opportunities to collaborate, and a safe space when it comes to exams.

Reviewing exams during the subsequent class time, I also observed students to be more engaged in the large group discussion than they had been in the past. Though test scores between students who chose the partner exam versus those who chose to take the exam individually are similar, overall test scores were on average 2–3 percentage points higher than before I started providing the option of partner exams.

A13 Best Practices for Online Content Design

Christine M. Rine

Description: Course structure guidelines for online content that incorporate components of Universal Design for Learning and Trauma-Informed teaching practices are exemplified in Quality Matters (QM) standards (QM, n.d.). I have found these standards helpful as they suggest that learners are provided with:

1. A clear starting point and expectations.
2. Clarity between objectives, content, and assignments.
3. Multiple, varied, and sequenced assignments with criteria and rubrics.
4. A variety of current instructional materials that are cited and clearly connected to objectives.
5. Clear requirements for learner-learner and learner-instructor communication and assignments that promote active learning and interaction.
6. Technology tools that support objectives, engagement, and active learning with information on data privacy and protections.
7. Clear information, instructions, and access for technology support and accessibility policies and services.
8. Easy to navigate online course components that facilitate readability and accessible text, images, files, documents, websites, and multimedia items accompanied by accessibility statements.

Using the first standard as an example, we can delineate a clear course starting point and expectations by alerting learners to

1. Where and how to start our course.
2. How to access course components.
3. The purpose and structure of our course.
4. Communication expectations.
5. Policies they are expected to follow.
6. Requisite computer/digital literacy skills.
7. Prerequisite knowledge/skills to be successful.

To illustrate what these might look like in practice, I can use 'Where and how to start our course' as an example. To ensure that students clearly understand where and how to start, I make their landing page upon log-in a personalized announcement with 'Welcome' and 'Start Here' in large font and in a color that stands out from other LMS content. This message can be personalized by student name reading "Welcome Jane Doe" as an option in our LMS, thus adding to a sense of engagement and individuation.

The content that follows under 'Start Here' is clearly presented in numbered organization where I list what to know and do in the first week of the course followed by pertinent information such as an overview of the course website and how to access various course components (i.e. content by week; course resources; syllabus; materials that support assignment completion; where to submit assignments; how to communicate with me and their course colleagues; and, how to view grades and assignment feedback). I also highlight first week of class attendance expectations by asking students to complete a self-introduction video in reply to my instructor introduction video. This gives online students an opportunity to virtually meet and reply to their course colleagues and me and promotes engagement through learner-learner and instructor-learner communication.

This approach to starting our course acclimates students to the course design and expectations while establishing a positive tone; all of which goes a long way to put students at ease from the very first day of class. I believe that using these best practices for online content design not only benefits our students but also advances my professional development and ability to foster supportive learning environments as an instructor. Frankly, the better organized my course is from the beginning, the fewer student questions, concerns, and issues arise throughout. Additionally, managing as much course content as possible in the online LMS platform keeps me on track with the overall progression of the class as well as smaller elements such as grading, feedback, common areas of student confusion, and alerts me to students who need individual attention to succeed.

Goals: Best practices for structuring online content is an important consideration for those of us teaching with any distance learning components. This ranges from completely asynchronous online courses to in-person courses augmented by online content such as that contained in Learning Management Systems (LMS). I have found that students can easily become overwhelmed, stressed, and anxious when online content is confusing, difficult to navigate, and poorly organized. These initial impressions can set a persistent negative tone that can lead to poor engagement and learner outcomes. The aim of these practices is to enhance teaching and learning through student-centered design, content, and support that is both useful and suitable for learners with diverse strengths and abilities.

Trauma-Informed Principles Exemplified: Safety; Trustworthiness & Transparency; Support & Connection; Collaboration & Mutuality; Empowerment, Voice, & Choice; Resilience, Growth, & Change.

Additional Information: QM is a nationally recognized program for training and certification to assure quality courses across educational levels and delivery modalities. More information about what they offer, along with specific strategies to adapt courses to these standards, can be accessed at https://www.qualitymatters.org/.

Reference

Quality Matters. (n.d.). *Helping you deliver on your online promise.* https://www.qualitymatters.org/

Appendix B: Questions for Reflection and Discussion

Finally, we close the book with questions that provide readers an opportunity to reflect on their own lived experience as they engage with each of the chapters or discuss insights and ideas with others. We anticipate these questions could be used as a guide for writing one's own personal narrative, for classroom use, or book club discussions.

Narrative Questions for Personal Reflection

Telling our story is the first step to healing from trauma. The questions below are designed for personal reflection to elicit a narrative about your experiences during crisis and guide you on the path to telling your own story, to healing.

- How has the recent crisis affected your teaching and learning? What adjustments have you had to make?
- How have your relationships with your students and colleagues been affected by this crisis?
- What has been the most distressing or challenging part of teaching and learning during crisis?
- What policies and practices did not work very well during the crisis, and what did you learn from these disappointments?
- What policies and practices did work well, and what did you learn from these successes?
- What policies and practices that you put in place might you keep in the future?
- Looking back, what do you think and feel about your teaching and learning experiences during crisis?
- What losses, if any, are you still grieving?
- What accomplishments, if any, are you celebrating?

© The Editor(s) (if applicable) and The Author(s), under exclusive license to Springer Nature Switzerland AG, part of Springer Nature 2022
P. Thompson and J. Carello (eds.), *Trauma-Informed Pedagogies*, https://doi.org/10.1007/978-3-030-92705-9

- What questions do you still have about teaching and learning in times of crisis?
- What have you learned about yourself as a person and as an educator?
- What things might you do differently in your courses in coming semesters? What help might you need to do this?
- Are there things you would like to see others do differently in coming semesters? What help might they need to do this?
- What else might you want others to know about teaching and learning in times of crisis?

Questions for Discussion

The questions below are designed for group discussion to promote reflection, foster conversation, and build community and could be used in classroom or book club discussions.

- How do we support our students (colleagues) without coddling them or acting like their therapist?
- How do we decrease the workload and build in more flexibility without decreasing rigor?
- What are ways to support students and colleagues who are having difficulty and perhaps not showing up or responding?
- In what values work can we engage to mitigate stereotype threat, stigma, and shaming; affirm students' and colleagues' own stories, and increase student resilience in the face of crisis and inequality?
- In what ways are our current policies and practices congruent with a trauma-informed and equity-centered approach to teaching and learning? How might we bolster these?
- In what ways are our current policies and practices *incongruent* with a trauma-informed and equity-centered approach to teaching and learning? How might we realign these without shaming ourselves or others?
- What experiences have instructors brought with them to the classroom and what do we have in place for them to address their own stress/trauma so that they are emotionally and intellectually ready and available to work with students and colleagues?
- What supports outside of the classroom do we have in place for our students so that they are emotionally and intellectually ready and available when they walk into the classroom?
- How do we recognize and affirm our own, our students', and our colleagues' resilience and strengths?
- What does self-care mean to us? What is our process for healing and recovery as educators?

Appendix C: Resources

Books

Lessons from the Pandemic: Trauma-Informed Approaches to Crisis, College, Change
Janice Carello & Phyllis Thompson (Eds.)

Incorporating Diversity and Inclusion into Trauma-Informed Social Work
Laura Quiros

Equity-Centered Trauma-Informed Education
Alex Shevrin Venet

Bandwidth Recovery
Cia Verschelden

Transformative Approaches to Social Justice Education: Equity and Access in the College Classroom
Nana Osei-Kofi, Bradley Boovy, and Kali Furman

Race, Equity, and the Learning Environment: The Global Relevance of Critical and Inclusive Pedagogies in Higher Education
Frank Tuitt, Chayla Haynes, & Saran Stewart (Eds.)

What Happened to You?: Conversations on Trauma, Resilience, and Healing
Oprah Winfrey & Bruce Perry

Helping Skills for working with College Students: Applying Counseling Theory to Student Affairs Practice
Monica Galloway Burke, Jill Duba Sauerheber, Aaraon W. Hughey, and Karl Laves

Indigenous and Decolonizing Studies in Education: Mapping the Long View
Linda Tuhiwai Smith, Eve Tuck, K. Wayne Yang (Eds.)

Trauma and Human Rights: Integrating Approaches to Addressing Human Suffering
Lisa D. Butler, Filomena M. Critelli, and Janice Carello

Web Resources

Colleges and Universities for Resilience (CURE) Listserv
cure@listserv.etsu.edu
To join the CURE listserv, contact Dr. Wallace E. Dixon at dixonw@mail.etsu.edu

University at Buffalo School of Social Work Self-Care Starter Kit
http://socialwork.buffalo.edu/resources/self-care-starter-kit.html

Trauma-Informed Oregon's Trauma-Informed Resources Page
https://traumainformedoregon.org/resources/

Janice Carello's Trauma-Informed Teaching & Learning Blog
https://traumainformedteaching.blog/

Organizations

ETSU Ballad Health Strong BRAIN Institute
https://www.etsu.edu/institute/strong-brain/

Campaign for Trauma-Informed Policy and Practice (CTIPP)
https://www.ctipp.org/

National Trauma Campaign
https://traumacampaign.org/

The Institute for Trauma, Adversity, and Resilience in Higher Education
https://www.massbay.edu/trauma

FSU Student Resilience Project
https://strong.fsu.edu/

Academic Resilience Consortium
https://academicresilience.org/

Institute on Trauma and Trauma-Informed Care
http://socialwork.buffalo.edu/social-research/institutes-centers/instit
ute-on-trauma-and-trauma-informed-care.html

PACEs in Higher Education
https://www.pacesconnection.com/g/aces-in-higher-education

Community Services

Call 211 to get referrals for local community services or visit the 211 website (211.org) for more info.

Networks such as Psychology Today, Good Therapy, and Therapy Tribe provide assistance for finding therapists, teletherapy, treatment centers, and support groups nationwide.

Crisis Services

National Hope Line
Call or text 877–235-4525
https://www.hopeline-nc.org/

Crisis Text Line
Text HOME to 741,741
https://www.crisistextline.org/

Samaritans
Call or text 877–870-4889
https://samaritanshope.org/our-services/24-7-helpline/

Lifeline Chat
Call 800–273-8255 or use chat services on website
https://suicidepreventionlifeline.org/chat/

IMAlive
Click on Chat Now button on website
https://www.imalive.org/

Trans Lifeline Hotline
Call 877–565-8860
https://translifeline.org/

The Trevor Project
Call 866–488-7386, text START to 678–678, or use chat services on website
https://www.thetrevorproject.org/get-help/

Veterans Crisis Line
Call 800–273-8255 (press 1) or Text 838,255
https://www.veteranscrisisline.net/

NAMI HelpLine
Call 800–950-NAMI (6264), text NAMI to 741–741, or use chat services on website
https://www.nami.org/help

SAMHSA's National Helpline
Call 800–662-4357 (HELP)
https://www.samhsa.gov/find-help/national-helpline

Disaster Distress Helpline
Call or text 800–985-5990
https://www.samhsa.gov/find-help/disaster-distress-helpline

INDEX

A
Ableism, 86, 143, 152, 159
Academic resilience, 8, 118, 120–122
Accessibility, 78, 113, 205–208, 248
Adichie, C., 21
Adverse Childhood Experiences (ACEs), 19, 165, 171
Amygdala, 38, 66, 84
Anti-oppressive, 4–6, 16, 18, 20, 212, 219
Anti-racist, 89, 95
Antisemitism, 246
Anzaldúa, G., 19, 20, 28
Asian, 99, 105
Asian-Americans, 97, 99, 100
Assessment, 7, 9, 43, 53, 55, 89, 167–170, 176, 221, 226, 227

B
Barriers, 5, 19, 21, 22, 50, 96, 125, 127, 128, 179, 188, 189, 195, 205, 213
Bisexual, 101
Black, 2, 65, 66, 71, 88, 105, 135, 136, 180, 191, 192, 196, 244
Black, Indigenous, People of Color (BIPOC), 63, 68, 94–97, 99–101, 139, 180, 182
Bloom, S., 1, 16, 87, 121, 195
Boundaries, 5, 25, 126, 132, 177, 179, 181, 182, 184

Brave space, 58, 234, 235
Brown, B., 23, 24, 30, 206, 234, 235
Burnout, 3, 180, 192–194

C
Capitalism, 85, 152, 196
Carello, J., 3, 4, 15, 50, 59, 64, 69, 95, 151, 155
Check-in, 56, 137, 210, 241
Choral educators, 64, 72
Classroom power dynamics, 138
Coalition, 21, 27–29
College, 2, 3, 9, 77, 79, 106–108, 113–115, 117–120, 128–130, 133, 136, 142, 150, 164, 167, 180, 181, 183, 190, 191, 193–195, 203–205, 207, 208, 213, 214, 217
Comfort agreements, 23, 238
Community agreements, 51, 59
Community college, 42, 113–115, 118, 120, 176, 182, 207
Complex hope, 101–103
Complex trauma, 108
Contingent faculty, 133–136, 138, 140–145, 191
COVID-19, 2, 4, 6, 18, 49, 52, 55, 56, 58, 79, 82, 83, 85–88, 94–98, 102, 106–110, 133–137, 139, 144, 176, 178, 180, 194, 205, 214, 239, 244
Crisis, 2, 3, 6–9, 18, 20, 24, 31, 39, 57, 94, 96, 97, 101–103, 116, 120,

CPSIA information can be obtained
at www.ICGtesting.com
Printed in the USA
BVHW011435110822
644372BV00008B/135

9 783030 927042